INCLUSIVE PHYSICAL ACTIVITY

A Lifetime of Opportunities

SUSAN L. KASSER, PhD

University of Vermont

REBECCA K. LYTLE, PhD

California State University, Chico

Human Kinetics

Library of Congress Cataloging-in-Publication Data

Kasser, Susan L.
    Inclusive physical activity : a lifetime of opportunities / Susan L. Kasser and Rebecca
K. Lytle.
        p. cm.
    Includes bibliographical references and index.
    ISBN 0-7360-3684-9 (hard cover)
    1. Physical education for children.   2. Physical fitness for children.   3. Physical
education for children with disabilities.   4. Inclusive education.   I. Lytle, Rebecca K.,
1961-   II. Title.
    GV443.K36 2005
    371.9'04486--dc22

                                    2004017863

ISBN: 0-7360-3684-9

Acquisitions Editor: Judy Patterson Wright, PhD
Developmental Editor: Melissa Feld
Assistant Editor: Kathleen D. Bernard
Copyeditor: John Wentworth
Proofreader: Pam Johnson
Indexer: Dan Connolly
Permission Manager: Dalene Reeder
Graphic Designer: Fred Starbird
Graphic Artist: Kathleen Boudreau-Fuoss
Photo Manager: Kareema McLendon
Cover Designer: Keith Blomberg
Photographer (cover): Left and right photos © Human Kinetics and center photo courtesy of David Punia
Photos (interior): © Human Kinetics, unless otherwise noted here. Photos on pages 21, 25, 78, 99, 142, 152, 155, 169 © Paralyzed Veterans of America, by permission of Sports 'N Spokes; 9, 15, 40, 137, 168, 175, 213 by L. Lieberman, courtesy of Camp Abilities; 3, 26, 29, 135, 194 by T. Bolduc, courtesy of S. Kasser; 32, 193, 197, 201 by T. Bolduc, courtesy of I.D.E.A.L.; 73, 101, 199 by S. Kasser, courtesy of I.D.E.A.L.; 24, 171, 191 courtesy of David Punia; 33 (left), 212 courtesy of Randall Anderson/Rossmiller Photography; 129 courtesy of R. Lytle; 207 courtesy of René Dallaire; 33, 103, 177 © Bongarts/Sportschrome; 7, 47 © Sport the Library; 92, 94 © Getty Images; 211, 215 © Mary E. Messenger; 88 © Digitalvision/Getty; 107 © Photodisc; 121 © Associated Press
Art Manager: Kelly Hendren
Illustrators: Tara Welsch and Argosy (cartoons)
Printer: Edwards Brothers

Printed in the United States of America   10 9 8 7 6 5 4 3 2 1

Human Kinetics
Web site: www.HumanKinetics.com

United States: Human Kinetics
P.O. Box 5076, Champaign, IL 61825-5076
800-747-4457
e-mail: humank@hkusa.com

Canada: Human Kinetics
475 Devonshire Road Unit 100
Windsor, ON N8Y 2L5
800-465-7301 (in Canada only)
e-mail: orders@hkcanada.com

Europe: Human Kinetics
107 Bradford Road, Stanningley
Leeds LS28 6AT, United Kingdom
+44 (0) 113 255 5665
e-mail: hk@hkeurope.com

Australia: Human Kinetics
57A Price Avenue, Lower Mitcham
South Australia 5062
08 8277 1555
e-mail: liaw@hkaustralia.com

New Zealand: Human Kinetics
Division of Sports Distributors NZ Ltd.
P.O. Box 300 226 Albany
North Shore City, Auckland
0064 9 448 1207
e-mail: blairc@hknewz.com

Contents

Preface

As physical activity practitioners, we are committed to providing individuals within our programs well-designed and appropriate physical activity—activity believed to be invaluable to their physical, social, and emotional well-being. Yet, this commitment can sometimes be tested by the challenge of effectively programming for individuals with widely differing abilities. Regardless of the setting, physical activity professionals should remain devoted to promoting the health and wellness of all individuals—whether these participants have differences in skill, coordination, and fitness or significantly different levels of concept understanding, varying attention spans, or possibly disruptive behavior.

Although it may be challenging to accomplish, including individuals with varied ability levels, experiences, and knowledge benefits all involved. The value of this shared experience has been widely recognized and accepted. This book deals with changing perspectives and practices regarding inclusive physical activity. It presents a philosophy that supports optimal programming for all individuals, regardless of ability level. But to include individuals of diverse abilities in physical activity and to ensure optimal programming, practitioners must become critical thinkers and proficient problem solvers. They must be able to observe, assess, and implement many strategies to meet the unique needs of individuals within many contexts.

This text is designed primarily for students preparing to work with diverse populations in a physical activity capacity. It is intended to develop the knowledge and skills necessary to provide meaningful and all-inclusive physical activity. This text is also meant to be a resource for practitioners committed to offering optimal and meaningful physical activity programming for their participants. Throughout the text, the term *physical activity practitioner* is used rather than *physical educator* or *personal trainer* or *coach*. We believe the broad term of *practitioner* is more encompassing of all professionals who work in physical activity settings (such as schools, exercise facilities, community recreation groups, and sport programs) and will encourage each of them to develop more inclusive practices. The text also takes a lifespan approach to physical activity participation. Considerations and programming strategies are applied to infants and toddlers, school-age children in physical education and recreation programs, and adults within sports or community-based exercise programs. The book's most outstanding feature is its unique approach to instructional and activity modification. The FAMME (Functional Approach to Modifying Movement Experiences) model provides readers with a conceptual framework and four-step process for accommodating all individuals within physical activity. The model is designed to encourage practitioners to consider individuals within programs by connecting modifications directly to capability differences in order to provide optimal challenges and successful experiences for every participant. Each skill component (e.g., eye–hand coordination, strength, attention span) is presented in chart form with information on influencing factors and effective adaptations to accommodate varied skill levels. Throughout the text, content progresses from understanding the profession and professional responsibilities to practical strategies for programming. Strategies and techniques are offered to increase awareness of ability differences, foster more positive attitudes of peers, and increase advocacy efforts aimed at inclusive physical activity. The practitioner can readily use practical hands-on ideas any time throughout the year to help achieve a truly inclusive physical activity program.

Several important features of the book promote reflection and critical thinking. Among these are opening scenarios ("Including All Individuals") in each chapter that place readers in a particular context. The scenarios are followed by several "Think Back" questions that appear throughout the chapters to encourage readers to connect specific content to each scenario in a thoughtful and insightful way. Each chapter ends with "What Do You Think" questions and "What Would You Do?" case examples that further encourage reflective thinking and problem solving.

The book is organized into three parts. Part I, Foundations for Inclusive Physical Activity, focuses on historical and sociological aspects of inclusive physical activity and the changing perspectives as they relate to individuals with differences in ability. Strategies to overcome barriers associated with inclusive programming are also discussed within this section. Part II, Inclusive Physical Activity Program Planning and Implementation, deals with the how, when, and why practitioners make modifications in instructional settings. This section offers insight into effective collaborative partnerships, determination of programming focus and related assessment, and individualized program planning. Much of this part of the text focuses on modification strategies and provides a continuum of modifications for various skill-related abilities. Part III, Application of Inclusive Practices, illustrates inclusive practices as they relate to commonly implemented physical activities. Chapters are devoted to adapting instruction and providing activity alternatives in four major content areas: movement skills; sports and games design; health-related fitness; and adventure and outdoor recreation.

Although some practitioners support a categorical or disability-based approach and others a non-categorical or ability-based approach, a balance of these two might be best, as long as program emphasis remains on performance and skill components rather than on labels and general disability guidelines. Although the book is non-categorical in nature, there are specific points about particular person-related factors that practitioners must know before effective programming can take place. With this in mind, we have included a "disability" reference section as appendix A. This appendix includes summaries of related terminology, causes, and selected facts about common person-related conditions. More important, general considerations and contraindications, especially as they relate to physical activity participation, are presented. Eligibility criteria for infants and toddlers is included in appendix B. Related resource materials and information sources are also offered in appendix C. Appendix D describes important legislation related to "disability" rights. A variety of assessment tools appropriate for inclusive physical activity programs are included in appendix E, and appendix F includes a sample medical history and referral form.

This text is founded on a philosophy and belief that all individuals, with all their distinctive abilities and interests, can and should benefit from participation in physical activity. This involvement should be lifelong; it should be empowering; and it should be inclusive of the range of possible programs, settings, and activities available to everyone. We as practitioners are in the unique position to make this reality rather than merely possibility. This text is the first step toward the awareness and knowledge necessary for all physical activity programs to be truly inclusive.

Acknowledgments

Throughout the journey of writing this book, there have been many people who have inspired us, encouraged us, and even challenged us. We would like to thank all our mentors who brought us to this point in time both professionally and philosophically. This includes our best teachers—all the children, adults, and families we have worked with over the years; the OSU crew with whom we have shared ideas; and especially Dr. Jeff McCubbin whose commitment and support throughout our development as doctoral students and professionals in the field have been invaluable. It was during our doctoral work together several years ago that the idea for this text surfaced.

We would also like to thank those of you who helped shape this book by sharing your expertise and ideas. Thank you Dr. Lauren Lieberman, Dr. Cindy Piletic, and Dr. Elaine McHugh for your honest feedback and contribution to specific chapters. We would like to also thank Dr. Susan Nye for cowriting chapter 7, Dr. Don Lytle for cowriting chapter 8, and Dr. Reid Cross for developing and writing chapter 10.

I would also like to thank my family for their support throughout the development and writing of this book. To my husband, Don, for his eternal patience, intellect, and assistance throughout the writing process. To my children, for sharing of their mother's time and for the wonderful spirit and joy they bring to each day. And finally to my colleague, Susan Kasser, for her commitment to this project—you are truly a joy to work with.

Rebecca Lytle

Thank you to my family for your encouragement during the many years of school and professional "moves." To Kathy, I especially want to say thank you. Your unconditional support motivated me through many long days of writing and calmed me during those crazy and stressful times. And without a doubt, my thanks go to you, Rebecca—it has definitely been an enjoyable and interesting adventure and one that I am fortunate to have had with you. I share in this accomplishment with you.

Sue Kasser

Foundations for Inclusive Physical Activity

Understanding the philosophical basis for and sociocultural context of inclusive physical activity is an important prerequisite to offering physical activity programs that include all individuals regardless of age, ability, or experience. Part I includes two chapters that establish the foundation for including all individuals into physical activity programs. Chapter 1 sets the stage for inclusive physical activity programs by providing a historical perspective on inclusive practices and the changing paradigms defining ability and disability. The chapter then provides a stronger foundation by defining inclusive physical activity and detailing the benefits for participants, peers, and practitioners. An inclusive model of ability in physical activity is presented as an alternative to traditional views of disability and individualized programming; this model integrates important concepts related to capability, movement potential, and professional practice.

With the philosophical and pragmatic basis for inclusive programming set, chapter 2 provides insight into the challenges and barriers precluding the participation of all individuals in physical activity. The chapter offers contextual, individual, and task-related obstacles as well as important strategies for overcoming such hurdles to ensure that all individuals have access to and consideration in physical activity opportunities.

Redefining Ability and Inclusive Physical Activity

Learning Outcomes

After completing this chapter, you should be able to

» define inclusive physical activity;

» provide a rationale for involving all individuals in inclusive physical activity;

» examine how capability relates to person, task, and contextual factors;

» discuss the essential components of inclusive physical activity programs; and

» describe three strategies useful in facilitating an inclusive model of physical activity.

INCLUDING ALL INDIVIDUALS

The beginning-of-the-year department meeting for the physical education faculty at the city middle school had just ended. In the meeting, Teresa, the program coordinator, shared with department staff her ideas and goals for the coming year. One of the major topics of discussion involved educational programming for students who in the past had not been included in physical education classes because of their low level of skills and capabilities. Teresa informed the faculty that this year, through a coordinated and collaborative effort, *all* students would receive physical education and be included in general class activities as much as possible.

Some of the experienced teachers suggested that separate classes be offered for low-skilled students; in their view, instructors should not be expected to teach students with low skills or behavior differences in the same classes as the high-skilled students. Other teachers expressed approval of the change, saying that including students with significantly different abilities together in the same classes could have beneficial consequences. Nancy, a teacher new to the school, left the meeting with many questions. She knew that Nick Powell was on her roster for the upcoming year. She had been told that Nick had some coordination and balance difficulties as well as some cognitive processing delays. How would his presence affect the other students' learning and her plans for the class? Would problems arise that she couldn't yet envision? Could this be why some of the experienced teachers were reluctant to include all students in their classes? Nancy had thought she was set to go for the new year, but now felt a new concern about her ability to give each of her students the best possible physical education experience.

The teachers at Nancy's new school clearly had contrasting perspectives on including children with diverse movement capabilities in the same physical education class. If you were Nancy, how would you feel? Would you consider Nick "disabled"? Would you want to include him with the other students in your physical activity class? Why or why not?

As practitioners responsible for the experiences of participants within our physical activity programs, we each need to examine our perceptions and definitions of "ability" and "disability." Our views and beliefs not only influence our attitudes toward and interactions with others but also direct our professional practice when implementing physical activity programs.

The extent to which individuals with diverse abilities are included in physical activities and other segments of our society has been and continues to be influenced by society's perceptions and attitudes toward these individuals. The concept of "disability" has been and continues to be defined by the culture or times in which these individuals live. While these definitions have changed over the years, an important step toward further progress in including all individuals into physical activity is to focus on ability not on disability. Doing so should help us examine how assumptions and attitudes about ability differences influence professional practice.

In this chapter we present a philosophy of inclusive physical activity and a contemporary approach to include all individuals, regardless of ability, in physical activity programs. Although a single chapter in a book can't provide the full depth of understanding of what it means for an individual to be meaningfully included in physical activity, examining the existing views about "disability" and how aspects of these views can come together to allow for inclusive programming may promote greater awareness and appreciation.

▶ THE ROAD TOWARD INCLUSION

Many people previously shut out from educational and community programs have benefited from the social movement toward inclusion. However, this movement has taken many different paths over the past 50 years, and the road has sometimes been challenging.

Until the 1950s, individuals with disabilities were generally viewed as deviants and "undesirables" who needed to be taken care of and, in a sense, controlled rather than educated, segregated rather than integrated. Throughout the first half of the 1900s, residential institutions and special schools were the norm. Although public common schools began to surface during this time, the prevailing attitude of the early to mid-1900s reinforced the devaluing of individuals with disabilities and the practice of segregation. Soon, public schools routinely began to track students by academic ability, and special classes were the preferred education system for individuals with disabilities when allowed access. Not until the civil rights movement of the 1950s and '60s were attitudes about racial segregation and the notion of "separate but equal" challenged. For the first time in history, segregated institutions, programs, and classes were perceived as problematic for individuals with disabilities. Court cases and legislation followed, and by the 1970s individuals with disabilities were granted new rights in employment and education environments. This meant that, whenever possible, programs were established in which students with disabilities were educated in the least restrictive environment participating (alongside their same-age peers) with the support necessary for them to succeed. By the late 1970s and early '80s many more individuals with disabilities had entered the workplace, and students with disabilities began to be mainstreamed into regular education classes. This push to mainstream resulted in great numbers of students with disabilities being placed in regular education classes, usually without the support and preparation they needed. As such, "mainstreaming" became synonymous with the unsuccessful dumping of students into classes in which they were typically regarded as visitors rather than actual members of the class. Consequently, fewer and fewer students with disabilities were given access to the same classes as their peers, and the tide began shifting back toward segregated programs.

As tides shifted, so did the inclusion movement in the next decade. The late 1980s and early '90s gave rise to the "full inclusion" concept in which many professionals argued for a total merger of special and regular education. The philosophy was that all students should be educated together, with services and support provided as necessary, within one educational system. This same philosophy of inclusion was also generalized to recreational, sport, and exercise programs outside the schools. Unfortunately, this call for a unified approach to programming has not yet been realized. Many "full inclusionists" have backed off from their initial stance due to resistance from school administrators and practitioners concerned about resources, maximum learning opportunity, and curricular appropriateness. As a result, the concept of least restrictive environments and alternative physical activity settings continues today. Unfortunately, in many communities few physical activity opportunities exist for individuals with differing abilities. As perceptions have changed over time, so has the process of including individuals with disabilities into activity programs, including physical education programs. The terminology related to these practices, shown in figure 1.1, reflects evolving attitudes and beliefs.

Evolution of Terminology

Mainstreaming—the process of placing individuals with disabilities into the general education or community environment. The term is now not recommended because of its association with the perceived "dumping" of students into general educational classes without the support they need (Grosse, 1991).

Integration—describes a setting in which individuals with and without disabilities are educated or served together.

Inclusion—a philosophy that asserts all individuals, regardless of ability, should participate within the same environment with necessary support and individualized attention. Inclusion is more than simply placing individuals together—it's a belief that all individuals belong and are valued.

Figure 1.1 The evolution of terminology used in physical education.

Did You Know?

Did you know that the word "handicap" is derived from people with disabilities holding out their caps to beg for money? In such situations, the *cap* was *handy* to use. Today, use of the word "handicapped" is discouraged. Instead the term "disability" is used, and person-first language (e.g., "John has low vision") is encouraged.

▶ INCLUSIVE PHYSICAL ACTIVITY

If we're to achieve our goal of moving successfully in the direction of inclusive programming, we need to establish a common understanding of the definition, philosophy, and rationale of inclusive physical activity. We need to then examine our own belief systems and rethink how our professional practice can encompass and value inclusive practices.

Definition of Inclusive Physical Activity

Inclusive physical activity is the philosophy and practice of ensuring that all individuals, regardless of ability or age, have equal opportunity in physical activity. This opportunity should include options and decision making and create meaningful participation and success that empower all participants. In other words, inclusive physical activity is defined as *accessible physical activity programs provided to all individuals across the life span in diverse settings*. Truly inclusive physical activity thus includes all of the following:

- Infant and toddler movement experiences
- School-based physical education programs
- Community-based recreation and leisure activities
- Exercise and fitness programs
- Multilevel sport opportunities

Whether we're speaking of children learning a wide range of movement skills through games or adults improving their physical fitness and health through exercise programs, individuals of all ages can and should be able to derive the joy and benefits of inclusive physical activity (figure 1.2).

The term "inclusive physical activity" is used instead of other physical activity program–related terms to denote a shift from participation based on a disability label toward creating success for *all* interested participants. For example, "adapted physical activity" is commonly regarded as activity in which adaptations are made primarily for individuals with identifiable disabilities and provided most often within traditional school-based and postsecondary settings (DePauw & Doll-Tepper, 2000; Sherrill, 1998). Inclusive physical activity, on the other hand, attempts to ensure that all individuals have the chance to benefit from inclusive and accommodating programming, regardless of age or ability level. The concept includes not only individuals identified with disabilities but also those without disability labels who might differ in capability because of age, experience, skill, or fitness level. From this philosophical and pragmatic standpoint, accommodations are made within programs to ensure that both highly skilled and lesser-skilled participants receive the benefits of tailored instruction and optimal programming.

Inclusive physical activity is based on the concepts of opportunity and choice. All individuals should have the opportunity to participate in age-appropriate and ability-appropriate activity. As such, a range of meaningful and tailored programs must exist so that individuals with differences in ability are not automatically relegated to certain programs for the sake

Figure 1.2 People of all ages and abilities should have opportunities for meaningful physical activity participation.

of administrative or programmatic ease. Instead, all participants have options from which they may choose. Inclusive physical activity is not based on a particular setting but rather on participation in meaningful activity selected from a range of options. For this to happen, all practitioners need to be able to plan and modify activities to meet diverse needs and abilities so that all participants are offered choice and opportunity that's equitable for everyone. Physical educators should have the attitude and skills they need to allow all children to succeed, both in their general physical education classes or within smaller groups of students with and without differences in abilities. Fitness practitioners in health clubs must also become accepting and versatile enough to want to invite adults with differences in ability into their facilities and be able to design meaningful and individualized fitness programs for them. Only when practitioners across all settings and types of physical activity programs can effectively accommodate the range of differing abilities among participants will inclusive physical activity programs truly become a reality.

Philosophy of Inclusive Physical Activity

Those who work in physical activity settings are uniquely positioned to influence the health and well-being of all individuals. The concept of inclusive physical activity involves much more than simply integrating individuals with diverse abilities into physical activity. Placing or integrating children with cognitive or behavioral differences into general physical education classes or adults with movement and balance difficulties into community exercise programs doesn't mean they'll be accepted by others, improve on their performance, or find satisfaction through participation. Inclusive physical activity goes beyond providing access to programs and making accommodations to support participation. Inclusive physical activity is a philosophy that embraces the belief in "experiential equity" in which there exists a balance of opportunity, consideration,

Beliefs About Participants

- Each person is unique with differing physical, cognitive, emotional, and social capabilities and needs.
- Everyone has a right to and can benefit from inclusive physical activity opportunities.
- The abilities of an individual are always changing and are a result of relations among the individual, the context, and the particular task or activity.
- Participants have a right to personal choice and decision-making.
- Each individual in an inclusive physical activity setting benefits from the experiences of others.

Beliefs About Practitioners and Programs

- Practitioners value the diversity and range of participants within their programs.
- Practitioners consider individual interests and needs and demonstrate equitable practice in attending to these considerations.
- Physical activity experiences are enjoyable, empowering, and personally meaningful.
- Inclusive physical activity programs value, accept, support, and respect each person for what he or she brings to the situation.
- Inclusive physical activity programs involve individuals with a range of differing abilities.
- Inclusive physical activity programs allow equal access to environments and equipment and include shared activities with individual outcomes.

Figure 1.3 Beliefs underlying an inclusive physical activity philosophy.

and effort given to all participants. This philosophy recognizes the value of participant choice and decision making as well as the importance of practitioner responsibility in helping learners achieve a meaningful experience. Inclusive physical activity involves a transformation in the way we view individuals and in the way we educate and teach. Practitioners committed to the concept of inclusive physical activity are keenly aware of the significant systematic changes required in the typical teaching method to ensure that programs are fair and equitable. They appreciate and value the uniqueness of the individuals with whom they work and strive to create an environment that is accepting, empowering, and accommodating for all people to succeed (figure 1.3).

◁■ THINK BACK

Think back to why you chose to be a physical activity practitioner. With whom did you imagine working? What beliefs did you have about the participants with whom you would work? What kinds of programs did you foresee offering?

Rationale for Inclusive Physical Activity

Different people have different views about exactly what inclusion involves and how beneficial it is. Support of inclusive physical activity often varies across contexts and participant groups. Some practitioners oppose inclusive physical activity programs in educational settings but support them in recreational and leisure venues. Other people support inclusive physical activity in recreational or educational settings but promote nonintegrated sport opportunities, such as the Paralympics. Also, some parents of children with less significant ability differences might support inclusive physical education for their child but oppose it for other children. For many people, opinions on inclusive practices vary according to the abilities of the individuals participating and the particular contexts and circumstances existing.

For the most part, inclusive environments have been supported in physical education (Block, 2000) and other physical activity and sport programs (DePauw & Doll-Trepper, 2000). A rationale for adopting an inclusive physical activity philosophy has its roots in both special education (Stainback, Stainback, & Bunch 1989) and physical education (Block, 2000) and includes the following essential points:

1. *Resource redundancy.* There are two primary concerns regarding the resource redundancy issue. First, offering separate physical activity programs means requiring additional resources, including personnel, financial support, and facilities. This overlap or duplication increases resource requirements. Second, when resources are allocated to traditional programs that are not inclusive, some participants may not be provided the opportunities they otherwise could be. Inclusive physical activity programming reduces resource redundancy and extends the breadth of physical activity experiences to everyone desiring such opportunities.

2. *Instructional individualization.* The concept of instructional individualization is based on the practice that only individuals with disabilities are given individualized instruction and instructional support, whereas those without disability labels are typically grouped together and considered homogeneous in ability. In fact, no two learners function at exactly the same level. For example, within a given class of third-graders, one child might excel in math and another in reading. The same is true in physical activity. One person might have great flexibility and another excellent eye–hand coordination. An inclusive physical activity philosophy supports all individuals receiving the necessary support and accommodations to achieve personal participation goals, regardless of label or setting (figure 1.4).

3. *Breadth of benefits.* The benefits of inclusive physical activity are far-reaching—whether for young children in school-based physical education programs or for children and adults in programs conducted outside the school setting (e.g., community-based exercise or activity programs, leisure and recreational experiences, and sport arenas). For all involved, the benefits include a greater respect for individual differences and for the unique experiences each participant brings to the program (figure 1.5).

Figure 1.4 Peers routinely offer assistance to other students learning new skills during physical education classes.

Participant Benefits

- Increased respect for individual abilities and differences
- Enhanced awareness and insight into one's own strengths and nonstrengths
- Increased breadth of opportunity and experience
- Experience of a more motivating environment
- Expanded support system with less isolation for participants and significant others
- Increased sense of community and acceptance
- Increased sense of contribution to activity, program, and community goals and outcomes
- Enhanced sense of value and self-esteem

Practitioner Benefits

- Increased awareness and insight of participant differences
- Changed perspective on professional practice
- Increased breadth of strategies useful for many others
- Increased knowledge of variations of tasks and skills
- Enhanced value of diverse abilities

Figure 1.5 Benefits of inclusive physical activity.

THINK BACK

Think about how you might reframe or redefine your answers to the questions posed at the beginning of the chapter. Do you think Nancy should include students of very different abilities, including Nick Powell, in her physical education classes? Why? How do you think this would benefit her and her students?

▶ EVOLUTION TOWARD AN INCLUSIVE PHYSICAL ACTIVITY FRAMEWORK

The inclusion of individuals with varying abilities into today's society and, more specifically, physical activity programs developed from a social consciousness and regard for all individuals as valued members of their communities. The nature of this inclusion, however, has taken many forms throughout history and has mainly centered on how individuals with significant differences in ability have been viewed. To move toward more equitable and inclusive physical activity programming, we must first become clear on how individuals considered "not able" or "disabled" have been and continue to be differentiated from those with "ability." We must then rethink our definition of "ability" if inclusive programming is to be realized.

Individuals with disabilities are receiving increasingly more attention and consideration now than in the past, but comparatively little is understood about what it means to be "disabled" and how an individual's life is affected by disability (Asch & Fine, 1988; Atkinson & Hackett, 1995). Even today, individuals with disabilities are regularly considered as being more different from than similar to those without disabilities (Scheer, 1994). Then how is "disability" defined? Who forms these definitions? What consequences result from such descriptions? In all societies, "disability" is defined in relation to beliefs about "ability" and usually by those without "disabilities." The term "disability" attains meaning through various frameworks or models used to convey attitudes and perceptions. These models are based on assumptions and expectations of those with disabilities. These beliefs provide the basis not only for understanding "disability" but also for influencing interactions, providing services, and directing programs. In an attempt to internalize and understand ability differences, four prevailing frameworks exist.

Medical Model

The medical model (also known as the functional limitations model) is the oldest of the dominant views of disability, yet this model still influences teaching and professional practice today. Within this model, disability is perceived as a limitation of the individual. The model assumes the individual's deficiency is caused by a physiological or biological defect (Hahn, 1991). Typically, individuals are grouped by their shared disabling condition or by category with a primary focus on symptoms and characteristics. The medical model focuses solely on the limitation, disregarding environments that might intensify or adversely affect a person's functional abilities. This concept implies that the "problem" resides within the individual and that it is the individual who needs to change or be fixed, not the conditions of the environment (Hahn, 1988). Thus, programs and services are provided to diagnose, prescribe, and rehabilitate the individual rather than alter the environment.

Social Minority Model

Increased insight into the stigma of disability gave rise to the social minority model. The basic belief of this model is that individuals with disabilities are different from the majority and thus share a similar experience to those in other minority groups (Atkinson & Hackett, 1995; Hahn, 1991). Unlike in the medical model, the focus here is not on a medical or physiological cause but on the social consequences of having minority status—such as prejudice, discrimination, and alienation. While this broader perspective acknowledges the role of society and its practices in shaping "disability," it also assumes that all people with disability share a common experience of being disabled. In fact, however, individuals with disabilities encounter a wide range of disabling conditions and an array of experiences. The social minority model discounts individual identity and negates individual challenges, joys, successes, and other life experiences shared by all individuals with and without disabilities. Identification as a minority group also exposes individuals with disabilities to the low expectations of others and the belief that all individuals with disabilities need support or help to get by (Hahn, 1988). This view continues to emphasize disability rather than ability and perpetuate segregation rather than inclusion.

Social Construction of Disability

To view disability as a medical condition or group experience offers only a superficial understanding of disability. The most recent framework focuses on the social construction of disability in which disability is perceived as the creation of differences between able and not able (Jones, 1996). These differences are not natural or necessary but rather routinely created through social interactions and by the daily practices of an "able-bodied" society (figure 1.6). For instance, routinely building staircases instead of ramps and cutting 24-inch door openings instead of 32-inch openings create barriers that highlight differences in ability. Norms associated with ability are thus constructed by those without disabilities. Once differences have been created by the "able-bodied" population, they are then used to reinforce the status quo or "reality" of disability. It is these socially formed and established views of disability that serve to maintain beliefs and expectations about inability and need. According to this perspective, the concept of "disability" can't be appreciably understood and interpreted outside of the contexts, interactions, or personal situations that give it meaning (Asch & Fine, 1988; Scheer, 1994). Attention

Figure 1.6 Disability and the accompanying values and beliefs are often created by the norm or by those perceived as able-bodied.

© John Callahan. Reprinted by permission from John Callahan/Levin Represents.

is focused on deconstructing past beliefs and stereotypes in order to liberate, empower, and foster personal development and achievement of all individuals. Such rethinking broadens services and programs and leads to greater inclusive practices.

Did You Know?

"...the 'problem' is not the person with disabilities; the problem is the way that normalcy is constructed to create the 'problem' of the disabled person... . The word 'normal' as 'constituting, conforming to, not deviating or different from, the common type or standard, regular, usual' only entered into the English language around 1840." (Davis, 1997, pp. 9-10).

World Health Organization Model

The World Health Organization (WHO) offers a model of disablement that bridges the medical and social models (figure 1.7). The current International Class of Functioning, Disability and Health (ICF) stems from the changing perspective of disability worldwide and is based on a neutral stand with regard to causes, consequences, and determinants of functional ability. The revised model is not a minority model geared only to the disabled but instead includes everyone on the continuum of health and functioning. In addition, the model includes context as well as medical and social influences, recognizing that the extent and level of participation in activities are not solely attributed to an individual's functional ability but also to environmental

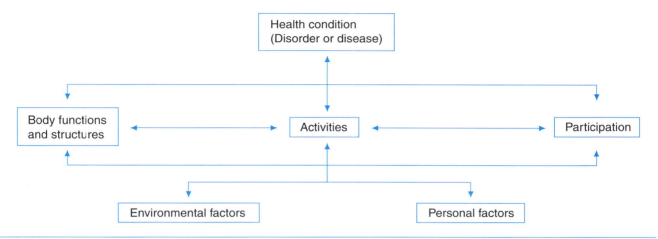

Figure 1.7 The World Health Organization (WHO) International Classification of Functioning, Disability and Health (ICF) offers a framework for interrelations between functioning and disability. It describes health and health-related domains from body, individual, and societal perspectives.

Reprinted, by permission, from World Health Organization, 2001, *The international classification of functioning, disability and health—ICF* (Geneva: Switzerland), 18.

factors. One of the critical goals of the WHO model is to create a barrier-free world. This new model asks the questions: How does this person function in the current environment? How might he or she function in a barrier-free environment? Answers to these questions help effect change in individual function and health by providing insight into more diverse strategies and practices.

THINK BACK

Think back to your thoughts about Nick Powell at the beginning of the chapter. Did you believe he had a disability? How did you come to define "disability" in that way? What was your previous experience? Which "lens" do you look through as it relates to disability based on the models presented? How do you think you developed this framework for your thinking? What contributed to your ideas and beliefs?

MOVING TOWARD AN INCLUSIVE MODEL OF ABILITY IN PHYSICAL ACTIVITY

Inclusive physical activity requires a merging of the disability frameworks with a more contemporary approach to movement potential. Achieving an inclusive physical activity program requires a change in how individuals with differing abilities are viewed, the ways in which programs are developed, and the instructional practices employed by practitioners. It necessitates an eclectic approach that considers not only how "disability" is redefined but also how movement skills and capability are achieved. The Inclusive Model of Ability in Physical Activity (IMAPA) emphasizes ability and constructing contexts for maximizing success. The model is based on an integration of elements from the models previously described. Table 1.1 lists the elements integrated from each model to create this ability-based model.

The IMAPA has its roots in the social construction model in that it is person-centered but considers both psychosocial and medical factors. This new framework, which blends all four

Table 1.1 Elements of the Inclusive Model of Ability in Physical Activity

Focus	Origin	Physical activity implications
Person centered	Medical model	Contraindications of activity
		Recommendations for activity (medical risks)
	Social minority	Labels removed
		Equity for all individuals
		Empowerment versus learned helplessness
	Social construction	Context centered
		Personal development and achievement
Context centered	World Health Organization	Contextual barriers removed
		Environmental modifications
		Task demands considered

previous models, integrates the important components relating to implications for physical activity participation. First, from the medical model perspective, information regarding medical facts or concerns is significant in terms of activities that might or might not be recommended for the individual. Next, from the social minority model, labels are removed and individuals are valued, respected, and given equality. How individuals are valued and the psychosocial consequences of these views must be considered because they relate to acceptance by others and self-determining behavior of participants. Individuals perceived and treated as disabled may feel less valued, may learn to believe they need help even when they don't, and may lack enough confidence to participate. From the social construction model, the IMAPA focuses on how individuals may become empowered and advocate for what they need. The model focuses on personal development and achievement, and it considers and plans an environment and social context that can positively influence the involvement of all individuals in physical activity. Finally, from the WHO model, the IMAPA doesn't focus on individuals with identifiable labels but rather includes all individuals within any given program. The focus is on meeting the needs of all individuals by striving to create barrier-free programs and enhancing functioning and independence.

Underlying Concepts

As we've mentioned, the IMAPA integrates aspects from the current views of disability. It also includes two distinct components that differentiate it from previous disability-based models. The first relates to the dynamic interplay of the person, task, and environment. The second focuses on capability differences, also known as "capability shifting." Both components include all individuals, regardless of capability.

Individual Capability

Many of the decisions regarding physical activity participation by individuals with differing abilities have their roots in the belief that disability is primarily a function of the individual. In other words, the disability and resulting capabilities are solely functions of the individual without regard for the task the individual is to perform and the context in which that task is executed. An underlying assumption is that the "disability" follows the individual across tasks and contexts. On the surface, this seems as if it would be true. After all, if a person has multiple sclerosis, doesn't she have it wherever she goes? Consider, though, that capabilities are not based on a label an individual has and aren't solely a function of the abilities and skills of the individual. Performance is based on individual capabilities *and* where the individual is

Figure 1.8 Ability is based on the person, the context, and the task.

performing, under what circumstances, and what the nature of the task or movement skill is. For example, an adult with limited strength caused by multiple sclerosis might have lost the ability to walk across a room. However, change the environmental context to a swimming pool, and he or she can walk quite proficiently from the increased buoyancy offered by the water. It would then be inaccurate to say this individual is "disabled" in this context. In other words, performance and success are also context-dependent.

Contemporary views are that an individual's capability, and his or her ultimate achievement, is directly connected to the task and the environment in which he or she is performing. Two recent perspectives, the ecological and dynamic approaches to movement, emphasize the interaction of the person and the environment during everyday functional tasks or movement skills. Rather than being attributed simply to individual impairments, both the capabilities of the person and what the environment supports or inhibits (Holt, 1993; Kugler, Kelso, & Turvey, 1980) contribute to skill performance and success. In other words, the individual *and* the nature of the task *and* the context in which the activity is performed all contribute to the movement outcome (figure 1.8).

Capability Shifting

The second important component of the IMAPA relates to the concept of capability shifting. From this perspective, an individual's capability for a given task can be altered by changing any one of the three factors involved in performance: the person's skill level, the context, or the task itself (figure 1.9). This ecological paradigm provides a greater opportunity for inclusion and success by allowing for strategies that focus on the task and environment rather than just on the individual. Practice shifts from being based on the concept of disability to being based on ability. For instance, a child with balance problems might have difficulty catching a ball with two hands while standing. An observer might conclude that the child has poor eye–hand coordination and isn't very capable of catching a ball. However, if we place

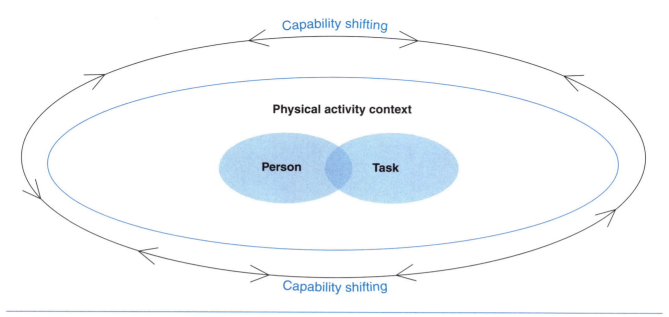

Capability shifting

Physical activity context

Person   **Task**

Capability shifting

Figure 1.9   The integrated model of ability in physical activity (IMAPA) emphasizes the dynamic interaction of the person, context, and task in terms of functioning and capability. Changes in any of these factors can increase or decrease the individual's capability or performance.

THINK BACK

Think back to Nancy's situation regarding Nick Powell. What could she do to increase Nick's capabilities in physical education?

Figure 1.10   Changing task requirements can alter performance success.

this same child in a chair, he or she might catch a ball very effectively from the same distance (figure 1.10). Without the element of balance required for standing, the child can complete the task at a much higher level of capability. Changing the task requirement from standing to sitting in a chair changed the demands of the task and thus the child's performance. Figure 1.9 illustrates an individual's capabilities and how they might shift within the dynamic of the person, task, and environment.

Putting It Into Practice

The IMAPA offers valuable insight into how ability is viewed and influenced, but practitioner strategies and skills are also essential to achieve the goal of inclusive physical activity programming. Three main concepts promote the implementation of the model and the translating of theory into practice.

Role Extension

The first strategy relates to role extension, which involves breaking through boundaries of job expectations and professional territory and extending the commitment and responsibility of physical activity by all and for all. The idea is to prepare all practitioners to be comfortable and adept working with all participants, regardless of ability. Collaboration and consultation among professionals and participants is needed to achieve this end (figure 1.11). This doesn't mean the responsibility for all planning and implementation falls on one person but that professionals who work with participants of diverse abilities

Figure 1.11   Inclusive physical activity is best realized when practitioners share knowledge and work together as a team to develop and implement programs.

work as a team, sharing roles and responsibilities to create successful learning environments. We'll discuss this collaborative approach more in chapter 3.

Reflective Practitioners

For programming to include all ability levels and succeed in improving capability, practitioners must become critical thinkers and problem solvers. Their practice must reflect their willingness to accept all participants into their programs and also to continually self-assess and adapt their instruction and style as circumstances warrant. The three Rs of inclusive reflective practice—ready, rethink, retry—are key to being an effective practitioner (figure 1.12). The first "R" emphasizes the need for practitioners to ready themselves and their programs for all participants. This requires them to work collaboratively and gather information that helps them understand the differing capabilities and needs of their participants and develop the most meaningful and effective physical activity program for each individual. The second "R" relates to reflection about the program and its participants, the goal being to continually improve on their practice and the program's effectiveness. They must rethink instructional or activity plans based on what they observe and be open to new ideas and to changing already developed programs. The third "R" encourages practitioners to retry revised plans that incorporate different strategies or modifications for increased participant involvement and success. It's important to note that this reflective process is not linear but rather cyclical in nature. Only with ongoing preparation, reflection, and revision can physical activity programs be truly inclusive. This reflective process is discussed more fully in chapter 5.

Restructuring

Along with the idea of reflective practice comes the concept of restructuring. For individuals with differing capabilities, needs, interests, and experiences to be included in physical activity programs, a restructuring of traditional curriculums and program implementation must occur. Strategies that encompass multiuse of space, multiactivity, and multilevel programs must replace strategies in which all participants are involved in similar activities at the same time and in the same way. In chapter 6 we go into more depth about varied strategies effective in broadening physical activity programs and present a functional approach to modifying

Ready	Rethink	Retry

Figure 1.12 Reflective practitioners must continually practice the cycle of "ready, rethink, and retry" to have physical activity programs be truly inclusive.

movement experiences (FAMME) model. The FAMME model is a sequence of four steps that connects modifications directly to capability differences to provide meaningful and successful participation for all participants, regardless of skill level. The model guides practitioners to consider all factors that contribute to a movement skill or task outcome—what the person can do, how the setting should be constructed, and the nature of the goal or task the individual is attempting to accomplish. This approach, coupled with role extension and reflection, allows physical educators to program more effectively for the diverse participants within their programs and assist them by offering truly inclusive physical activity experiences.

▶ SUMMARY

If the notion of disability is socially constructed, then it can be reconstructed. By reshaping, rethinking, and reforming the ways in which we offer physical activity programs, all individuals can have meaningful and rewarding physical activity involvement. Inclusive physical activity is a philosophy that goes beyond mere access to programs. It embraces the idea of accommodating and valuing all participants and includes revamping the way we structure and implement programs. An inclusive physical activity philosophy challenges practitioners to examine their own assumptions regarding ability, reflect on their instructional practice as it relates to the success of their participants, and think outside the traditional "box" that narrows choices and stifles creativity in physical activity opportunities.

What Do You Think?

1. Do you believe that the integrated model of ability in physical activity (IMAPA) extends previously existing models of disability? Is there anything you would change about the model?

2. How does an inclusive physical activity philosophy differ from previous beliefs about physical activity and ability?

3. What is your current philosophy about inclusive physical activity practices? Where did this philosophy come from?

What Would You Do?

Scenario 1.1

Joan recently graduated from college with a degree in exercise physiology and prephysical therapy and was just hired as a program specialist for a brand new sport facility in a large metropolitan area. She's very excited about putting her training to work. In addition to her bachelor's degree, she also has special certifications in aerobics and aquatics. She worked extensively at a local club during college and feels confident about her skills in working with people. During the first week of her new job she learns more about her responsibilities, which include scheduling of all classes and facilities, staff training, and serving as a personal trainer. The owner of the facility has explained to Joan that she needs to meet the needs of every individual in the community. She also learns more about the clientele at this facility.

The club by her university was filled with healthy young college students, whereas the population of this facility is much more diverse. Individuals range in age from birth to seniors. Her new facility expects to offer parent–infant classes, programs for seniors, a cardiac program, and many other classes for all ages and abilities. In fact, one of the local community-based programs for individuals with developmental disabilities is planning on coming in the afternoons to swim and do weight training. As Joan becomes more familiar with the diversity of individuals she'll be working with, she begins to feel unsure of her skills. In fact, she's never worked with young children or individuals with disabilities. Her only experience with disability was in an athletic training class she took working with athletes to rehab injuries to knees and ankles. As she begins to think about the classes she needs to offer, she's not sure how to organize them—by activity, age, disability, or a combination of these. In addition, she's wondering how she'll hire and train her staff to work with this diverse population.

1. What particular model of disability do you think Joan has been exposed to? Why do you think so?

2. How might you organize classes if you were Joan? How would you justify your decisions?

3. What critical issues might Joan want to address in her staff training?

4. Do you think Joan could use role extension, reflective practice, and restructuring as it relates to classes for this new facility? Why or why not?

Scenario 1.2

Darren is an elementary physical education teacher at Ponderosa Elementary School. He has just learned that his district is taking over all the special education programs. Students previously in separate classrooms run by the county will now be in the district classes with their peers. What this means for Darren is that he'll have two students in his second-grade physical education class next year who have been identified as having a disability. Darren is a little nervous about this, but he thinks he'll be able to meet these students' needs. In fact, the current students in his class come from a variety of socioeconomic and ethnic backgrounds. He has 20 students in his class, and next year he'll have an additional aide from special education coming to provide additional support. One of the new students has cerebral palsy and uses a power wheelchair and a computer to communicate. The other student has a short attention span and difficulty in problem solving and learning. Darren knows that each student in his class has different skills, and he tries to use this to his advantage. In fact, in his class a lot of cross-teaching occurs, with students helping each other. He often puts students into heterogeneous groups and gives them roles or jobs that meet their level of skill for a given activity. In this way, each student can contribute to the game or activity. Darren is excited to have these two new students in his class and feels they'll contribute to the classroom dynamic. He's eager to learn more about their experiences and the services they might have been receiving through special education so that he and his students can benefit from their expertise.

1. How could the IMAPA assist Darren in providing an inclusive second-grade physical education class for all his students?

2. How has Darren used capability shifting to promote learning in his classroom?

3. What benefits might be gleaned by both students and teachers who participate in Darren's class?

Overcoming Barriers to Inclusive Physical Activity

Learning Outcomes

After completing this chapter, you should be able to

» recognize barriers in the access to and accommodation of participants in physical activity programs;

» distinguish among person-, context-, and task-related barriers that can hinder involvement of participants in physical activity; and

» discuss strategies to overcome barriers and promote inclusive physical activity programs.

INCLUDING ALL INDIVIDUALS

For a few years Brian White has worked as the fitness program coordinator at his community's fitness club. Through a survey of members, he has recently been reminded that his club doesn't offer programs for people with special interests in certain activities; nor does the club involve members who have identified themselves as needing individualized program plans. Most of his club's members are 25 to 45 years old and exercise during regularly scheduled times and programs.

Brian believed it was time for his club to accommodate a more diverse membership, including older adults with age-related functional differences, adults with physical or mobility differences, and participants of all ages with learning differences. He began to offer several new alternative programs. For the past four months, the club has offered aquatic programs as well as tai chi and yoga. Unfortunately, no new members signed up for the programs. Given the accessible program schedule and exciting new offerings, Brian wondered why there was no increase in the diversity of new members. What did he need to do to meet his goal of increased and more diverse membership?

A move toward inclusive physical activity requires an understanding of the philosophical foundations underlying inclusive programming, as discussed in chapter 1. Such a move also requires an awareness of the barriers that might exist to hinder the involvement of individuals in physical activity programs. In your view, what factors might have prevented new participants from enrolling in Brian's programs? If you were Brian, how would you overcome such hurdles?

For most of us, which programs we want to join and when we want to be active are the basis for our physical activity decisions. Of course, several factors influence our decisions, such as how much time we have to be active, where the programs are taking place, and when the sessions we're interested in are being offered. Nonetheless, our interests, needs, and preferences should be, and usually are, the primary reasons behind our physical activity choices.

Although barriers to physical activity participation exist for all individuals across the life span, many more factors exist that deny individuals with differing abilities the freedom to choose or participate in activities that are available (Smith, Austin, & Kennedy, 1996). Barriers are present at many levels in the realization of all-inclusive programs—from initially accepting individuals with different movement capabilities and providing access to physical activity programs to finally accommodating individuals once they join. As much as possible, a person's involvement in physical activity should be based on individual choice rather than on such factors as what's available or accessible. If physical activity professionals are going to work toward providing access and accommodation in physical activity programs, they must broaden their understanding of the breadth and depth of barriers that preclude inclusive physical activity and work toward overcoming them.

Barriers to inclusive physical activity involve one of three categories: (1) context-related barriers, which are external and arise from people and places of physical activity programs; (2) person-related barriers, which are internal to the individual participant; and (3) task-related barriers, which are directly related to the activity and serve as the foundation for the programming effort. Each of these barriers can influence the acceptance of, access to, and accommodation of all individuals in physical activity programs (figure 2.1).

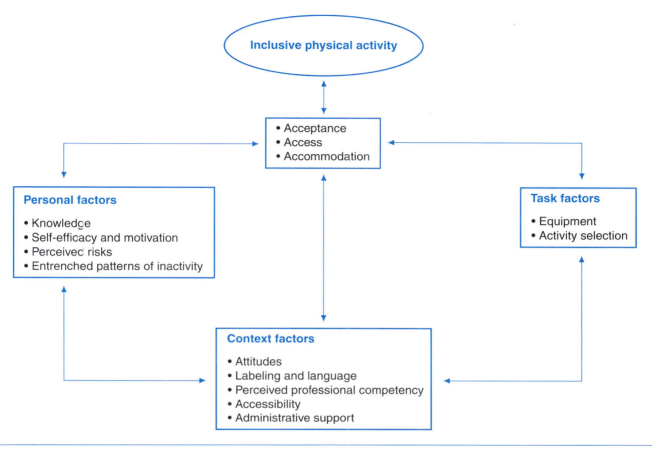

Figure 2.1 Many barriers exist singularly or in combination that might prevent full access to and accommodation of all individuals in physical activity. These barriers might be related to the person, context, or task.

THINK BACK

Think back to the choices you've made regarding your own participation in physical activity.

1. What activities have you participated in?

2. What factors allowed you to make these choices?

3. Did any factors prevent you from making certain physical activity decisions? If so, what were they? How could these factors have been changed?

CONTEXT-RELATED BARRIERS AND STRATEGIES

Many of the barriers to inclusive physical activity exist within the very walls of the communities, schools, and physical activity facilities in which individuals live and are involved. These contextual or environmental barriers are imposed on the individual by others in those settings or the way in which the setting is constructed. For instance, context-related barriers might include negative attitudes, the use of labels and inappropriate language, lack of professional confidence and competence, inadequate accessibility, and lack of administrative commitment and support.

Attitudes

The attitudes and perceptions of others are among the most significant factors preventing individuals with diverse abilities from participating in many activity programs (Heward, 2000). Attitudes are generally based on learned beliefs and commonly reflect the extent to which someone or something is favorably or positively regarded (Brehm & Kassin, 1996). Personal experience, familiarity with others, knowledge, and prevalent views of significant others combine to shape a person's belief system. These beliefs in turn might also influence behavior toward and relationships with those who are perceived as different. Individuals with differing abilities might be perceived negatively, treated as being incapable of making decisions, or even devalued and ignored completely.

Effects of Negative Attitudes

In physical activity programs, the way practitioners, administrators, and program directors view and react to individuals whom they perceive as different or less able significantly affects the success of inclusive efforts. For example, research supports that teachers' attitudes toward students with disabilities influence interactions and successful inclusion for school-age children in physical education (Block, 2000). Also, a relationship exists between a teacher's attitudes toward inclusive programming and the type or severity of a child's disability. Research suggests that the more significant the difference in ability, the less favorable the practitioner attitude (Block & Rizzo, 1995). In addition, students with learning differences were viewed more positively than those with behavioral or cognitive differences (Rizzo & Vispoel, 1991).

Practitioner attitudes also play a role in inclusive practices for individuals of all ages including adults involved in recreation and leisure activities (Smith, Austin, & Kennedy, 1996; figure 2.2).

A lack of acceptance by program participants toward individuals with disabilities also inhibits inclusive physical activity programming. Research has shown that attitudes of schoolchildren toward their peers with significant ability differences play a part in their intention to participate with them in physical education (Verderber, Rizzo, & Sherrill, 2003). As is true of professionals, participants develop attitudes based on what they experience around them and what they see in those to whom they look up to for leadership or guidance. In other words, the level of acceptance displayed by professionals subsequently affects the attitude, acceptance, and behavior of peers or participants in the program. Practitioners who don't exhibit positive behaviors and attitudes toward participants with ability differences might negatively influence peer acceptance and attitudes toward those same individuals.

The effects of attitudinal barriers on individuals with different abilities are considerable and are among the most difficult to overcome (Smith et al., 1996). They are especially influential in physical activity programs, in which communication, cooperation, and teamwork are important prerequisites to group participation and individual achievement.

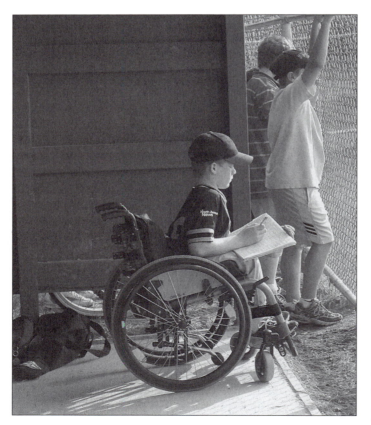

Figure 2.2 Negative attitudes of practitioners toward participants can decrease the level of physical activity involvement and inclusiveness of programs.

Strategies for Promoting Inclusive Attitudes

Because attitudes are most critical in determining who will and who won't have the opportunity to participate in particular programs, efforts aimed at promoting positive perceptions and attitudes take priority over considerations of access and accommodation. If attitudinal barriers are likely to be the most significant, how can people come to accept and support individuals perceived as different and with whom they have had very little exposure? The answer involves changing perceptions through increased knowledge, awareness, and experience (figure 2.3).

Attitudes toward people with greatly differing abilities are highly affected by social, physical, and experiential factors. Such attitudes can be influenced by significant others including parents, teachers, friends, and family members. They might develop from past experience or might arise from current ideas or beliefs. For instance, if children grew up in a community in which there were no other children with great differences in ability, the children in this community might come to believe that people with differences are unlike themselves and don't belong in the community. Or they might be afraid of the "different" children because of their lack of exposure

Figure 2.3 Changing perceptions and promoting positive attitudes can significantly influence the level of physical activity involvement of people with differences in ability.

to them. Had the school or neighborhood been more inclusive, the beliefs and attitudes of the children would likely have been quite different. What then are the strategies that foster positive, more accepting attitudes?

Preparing peers and participants for inclusive programming is an important step in the process. The peers of participants with differing abilities need to understand the nature of ability differences, and, more important, increase their awareness of similarities. In general, attitude change is elicited in two ways: through exposure to information and through experience. Strategies that expose people to information include educational presentations, guest speakers, and instructional units infused into a program's curriculum. Educational programs must be positive; they must show that individuals with differing abilities are active agents in change; and they must emphasize the *whole* individual, not the medical characteristics and challenges the individual faces (Wright, 1980).

Simulation activities can also increase awareness and information about differences in ability. These simulations are designed to enable students to experience an ability difference through the use of special equipment and instruction. Although simulation activities might seem an ideal way to share information about what it's like to have a significant ability difference, some people ethically question the use of simulations (Behler, 1993). They argue that simulations might expose participants to feelings and experiences that individuals with differences in ability have only *some* of the time or under *some* circumstances. In fact, they maintain, participants in simulation activities can't truly understand what it's like to have a particular disability label or difference in ability.

Research has also failed to offer equivocal support for the effectiveness of simulation activities in promoting positive attitudes (Ellery & Rauschenbach, 2000). A decline in positive attitude as a result of these activities might be associated with increased awareness of perceived limitations or with peer acceptance based on athletic ability. For these reasons, simulation activities

Figure 2.4 Peers involved in a simulated goal-ball game can deepen their understanding of the skills and capabilities individuals with differences in vision possess during a competitive physical activity or sport.

should not be used as introductory activities; rather they should be used only after participants have been taught the abilities and coping skills of people with differences in ability (Wood, 1998). Wright (1980) recommends a constructive view of simulations that promote a deeper understanding of "disability" by including activities that portray people with differences in ability as active agents for change, focusing on the skills they require and possess rather than on any deficit they might have (figure 2.4). Through simulations, "disability" can be exposed as a function of environmental barriers and simulation activities can highlight contextual modifications that foster improved performance and increased success.

Direct contact can further promote positive attitudes. However, if negative stereotypes and fears are reinforced, such contact can also cause negative feelings to develop. Because the type of setting and contact can have different effects on attitudes, interactions must be planned and intentional. The experience must demonstrate that the person with ability differences is participating within his or her capabilities rather than highlighting his or her inadequacies. In addition, direct contact promotes favorable attitudes when the experience is perceived as voluntary and enjoyable. Change in attitude occurs when shared enjoyment takes place and when accommodation becomes a natural part of the process (Wright, 1980). Contact alone does not positively change perceptions and acceptance. A social climate in which value and respect for individual similarities and differences exist is essential.

Labeling and Language

Associated with the concepts of attitudes and acceptance is the notion of labeling. We all have many labels attached to us. Some labels are used to denote relationships (e.g., mother, sister, nephew, mentor, friend, colleague), while others can also give us insight into roles and responsibilities (e.g., teacher, student, advisor, director). When we use these labels, there is an underlying assumption that the labels assist in only *partially* defining or helping us understand someone. Generally, people realize that a person wears many hats and that these hats can and do change from one time to another and from one place to another. No one is *only* a mother or *only* a teacher—we know these people are much more as well.

Problems With Labels and Language

Unfortunately, labels can be negative and generalized to represent the whole person regardless of place and time. People with perceived differences in ability have endured a countless number of derogatory labels over the years for the sole purpose of excluding them from everyday activities, services, and privileges (Heward, 2000). Often people's intolerance toward those from whom they differ is displayed through their language and words. Research examining the everyday language used in conversations about individuals with disability labels showed that "disability" is typically equated with abnormality and that individuals with such labels are frequently devalued (Danforth & Navarro, 1998).

Two opposing perspectives relate to labeling individuals with "disabilities". Some professionals believe that labeling serves a purpose to the benefit of those being labeled. Labels are often a prerequisite to receiving services, funding, and legal clout and are required for access and accommodation in certain programs (Kauffman, 1998). Other professionals argue that labels used to classify or categorize individuals perpetuate stereotypes and exclusionary practices (Stainback & Stainback, 1991). Despite some valid arguments that support labeling, labels tend to focus attention on differences rather than similarities and on individual deficits rather than societal and contextual factors that create ability differences. The most cited disadvantages of labeling include the following:

- Labels reduce individuality and ignore the uniqueness of each participant, classifying individuals solely by group membership. The label becomes the primary identifier of the individual rather than the many other possible labels, such as teacher, mother, sister, employee, or friend. Labels don't attempt to convey the total essence and nature of an individual.

- Labels lead to stereotyping and overgeneralizations about ability or inability that in turn encourage limited expectations.

- Labels are usually disability-based rather than ability-based. They focus attention on what an individual can't do rather than on what he or she can do.

- Labels are often viewed as permanent, emphasizing stability rather than change.

- Labels are sometimes used inappropriately to relieve responsibility of practitioners for changing contexts or situations that could allow successful participation of the individual. It may be easier for some practitioners to attribute a participant's failure to his disability rather than the lack of time and effort given to reflecting on and revising activity plans to accommodate the participant's ability differences.

Regardless of the physical activity setting or the age of the participant, labels that deemphasize the abilities of an individual and devalue his or her skills can't possibly encourage acceptance. Such labels do little to promote high expectations, successful inclusion, or individual accommodation.

Strategies for Promoting Acceptance Through Language

The words we use to label or define someone influence how he or she is viewed and subsequently treated. The first step toward fostering acceptance and respect is changing the language we choose. Terms such as "handicapped" or "crippled" previously evoked images of inability, pity, or fear and tended to group all people together regardless of their needs, strengths, and individuality. Recent perspectives favor the term "disability" and, for the most part, the use of person-first language. For example, we should say "a child with a disability" rather than "a disabled child." This seemingly small difference emphasizes the individual rather than the disability and is person-centered, not group focused. Here are other guidelines for using terminology and language choices that help shift our language toward being more positive and accepting:

Table 2.1 The Preferred Language of Inclusive Practices

Preferred term	Avoid
Head injury	Brain damage
Deaf or hearing impaired	Deaf and dumb
Nonverbal or without speech	Mute or dumb
Blind or visually impaired	Sightless
Developmentally delayed	Slow
Uses a wheelchair	Confined or bound to a wheelchair
Person who has …	Afflicted with, suffers from, or victim of
Mental illness or emotional disability	Crazy or insane
Congenital disability	Birth defect or defective

- Avoid using a disability or label to refer to someone. For example, say "the man who lives down the street in the green house" instead of "the blind man who lives down the street."

- Emphasize the uniqueness of each individual. When we use person-first language and focus on roles and other social labels, we avoid defining people by their disabilities (e.g., Susie, a second grader with a learning disability).

- When it's important to distinguish between individuals with and without "disabilities," use the phrase *people without disabilities.* Avoid using the terms "normal" or "healthy" to indicate those individuals without disabilities.

- Jargon such as "challenged" or "differently abled" are not always helpful in promoting acceptance and empowering others. The disability is not a challenge by virtue of itself but rather because of other people's views and how contexts have been constructed.

- Avoid using words such as "crippled," "defect," "afflicted," and other terms that are negative or devaluing. Restrict your use of the noun "patient" to hospital settings. Table 2.1 lists other preferred terms and phrases and those that should be avoided.

Although it's important to communicate with and about people with disabilities in positive and respectful ways, simply changing the language we use will not automatically lead to greater acceptance and inclusion. Using positive language must be accompanied by changed societal attitudes and values critical for creating inclusive physical activity environments.

Did You Know?

Some groups prefer to claim their identity through their difference and are empowered by rejecting the person-first concept. Deaf individuals prefer to be called "deaf" or "hard of hearing" rather than "a person with a hearing impairment."

Perceived Professional Competency

Although some practitioners feel quite comfortable and capable working with individuals with very different abilities, many do not. Often, programs and activities are planned for individuals who are similar in ability or for those who fall within the middle range of skill level. It's both common and valid for professionals to feel inadequate to meet the needs of all individuals, including those participants with significantly different abilities. Many times, practitioners charged with the responsibility for teaching, coaching, or instructing have had little exposure and experience involving people with significantly different learning, movement, and behavioral capabilities. Their fears are often based on their lack of knowledge about various person-related conditions, and their own perceived competence to teach individuals with diverse abilities.

Barriers Created by Lack of Perceived Professional Competency

In educational settings, barriers to inclusive programming include lack of teacher collaboration and inadequate training of practitioners (Liu & Pearson, 1999). Particularly in physical education settings, research has shown that practitioners' attitudes toward teaching students with disabilities in general physical education is most influenced by the practitioner's perceived competence to do so (Block & Rizzo, 1995; Rizzo & Wright, 1988). As a result of this lack of professional preparation, teachers often have limited expectations of students with disabilities in the general physical education setting (Lieberman & Houston-Wilson, 1999). Perceived professional competence might also play a role in whether practitioners in community-based exercise or activity programs choose to include adults with differing abilities. Inadequate coaching and training has also been cited as a barrier for women with disabilities in terms of sport participation (Grimes & French, 1987).

Professional knowledge and perceived competency are critical for programs to be inclusive of all individuals interested in lifelong physical activity participation. Without them, many individuals will continue to be excluded from physical activity opportunities.

Strategies for Enhancing Perceived Professional Competence

Staff development and training are necessary for creating successful inclusive physical activity programs (figure 2.5). The effects of training on teacher attitudes toward inclusion show that in-service training leads to more favorable attitudes (Dickens-Smith, 1995). College courses and academic preparation can also help promote positive attitudes (Rizzo & Vispoel, 1992) and perceived competency (Kowalski & Rizzo, 1996) among preservice practitioners. Collaborative strategies must be developed and skills and resources shared across all facets of activity programs in order to benefit all participants. In chapter 3 we'll provide an in-depth look at collaboration as a means of obtaining information and developing professional competency.

Figure 2.5 Conferences and in-service workshops related to inclusive physical activity can help increase perceived competency of practitioners working with individuals of diverse abilities.

Elements of Effective Practice

- Increase active learning and practice time of participants.
- Promote high rates of success for participants through task and context variation.
- Set high but realistic expectations for participants.
- Assist participants to learn from observation and self-reflection.
- Allow individual and group input into the process (e.g., suggested modifications).

- Engage in ongoing reflective and critical thinking—be a problem solver.
- Promote participant self-responsibility and decision-making.
- Provide a supportive and accepting climate for all participants.
- Garner support and use all available resources to support professional practice and participant involvement.

Rink, J.E. (1998). *Teaching physical education for learning* (3rd ed.). Boston: McGraw-Hill.

Effective instruction that meets the needs of *all* participants includes a hierarchy of pedagogical practices in which organization, instruction, and management form the basis of the physical activity environment. Participant success is the ultimate goal.

The success of an inclusive physical activity experience involves the realization of participant and practitioner goals and the amount and quality of the participant's involvement. The degree of success achieved depends not only on the participant's ability level but also on the practitioner's beliefs about his or her own ability and effectiveness to run the inclusive program and meet everyone's needs.

Accessibility

When we think of accessibility, we typically imagine someone in a wheelchair unable to enter a building with stairs or attend an activity session held on the second floor of a building without an elevator. It's true that these kinds of architectural barriers can hinder an individual's involvement in physical activity programs, but there are many other accessibility factors that can limit participation. Accessibility barriers constitute anything that prevents an individual's equal access and opportunity to facilities and programs, including communication obstacles, transportation constraints, and economic limitations.

Barriers Related to Accessibility

Architectural barriers, the most glaring of the accessibility hurdles, involve structures that present obstacles or make a building unusable by individuals with differences in ability. Even when a ramp leads directly to an entrance, a person using a wheelchair might not be able to use the facility if there's no accessible parking or if the front door is too heavy to open. Other common barriers include the lack of handrails, doorknobs difficult to operate, or doorways too narrow for a wheelchair. How rooms or spaces are arranged might also affect accessibility. Extraneous equipment can impede the movement of people with mobility or balance difficulties; exercise equipment might be too close together, preventing individuals who use wheelchairs to move between or beside them.

Beyond the facility design, barriers related to communication might hinder access to buildings and programs. In particular, people with disabilities frequently cite poor signage as hindering accessibility (Kaye & Longmore, 1997). Examples include lack of Braille to identify specific rooms or offices and abstract signs that can confuse individuals with learning needs who want to use the facility.

Even if a facility is accessible in the broadest of definitions, individuals might still be denied access if they're unable to get to and from the facility or program. Whether it's a parent trying to take her infant to a class or an older adult wanting to get to a community exercise program, transportation barriers continue to hamper attempts by individuals with ability differences to participate in physical activity programs. Individuals living in more rural areas might not have access to public transportation. For others, public transportation might exist, but the specific transportation system might not accommodate individuals with ability differences. For instance, the law requires public transit agencies to include wheelchair lifts on buses or railway cars, but this law applies only to new equipment. Although most public buses currently do have lifts, they're often broken or drivers receive little training in how to operate them (Kaye & Longmore, 1997). Some communities have implemented specially arranged accessible transportation services for certain individuals, but critics condemn the practice as separate and unequal. The schedule, restrictions, and cost associated with these services might prevent individuals from using the service and further hamper individuals from joining physical activity sessions. For example, in some locations individuals are allowed to use the special services bus only for appointments to the doctor, not for any kind of recreational or leisure activity, and they must call at least two days in advance to make an appointment for the service. These types of restrictions could certainly prevent someone from attending a physical activity class or going out with a friend to participate in a special event.

Did You Know?

Nationally, 40 to 45 percent of buses used by public transit systems have no wheelchair lifts (Kaye & Longmore, 1997).

The freedom to participate in physical activity means not only that individuals can physically enter a program but also that they can financially access the program. Economic barriers exist for many people, but they're even more common for individuals with differences in ability. Although there are indications that employment levels for people with "disabilities" are increasing, the data have shown a widening gap in income levels for those with disability labels compared to those without (Kaye, 1998; LaPlante, Kennedy, Kaye, & Wenger 1996). Those who are employed often find themselves in low paying positions. This situation, compounded by higher than average expenses such as medical needs and special transportation, often puts the cost of health and fitness clubs or community programs out of reach. In fact, the cost of exercise programs has been cited as a major obstacle to physical activity participation (Rimmer, Rubin, & Braddock 2000). Financial barriers exist not only for adults interested in exercise programs but also for those interested in sport participation. Sophisticated new equipment for individuals with ability differences allows greater freedom and better performance, but costs may be prohibitive for many aspiring athletes (Hamel, 1992). In addition, travel expenses for competitions can be expensive, and businesses are less likely to sponsor athletes with disabilities because of the lack of media coverage to sell their products.

Did You Know?

Individuals with disabilities have a much higher poverty rate. One fourth of children with disabilities are poor. Nearly one third of adults with disabilities live in poverty. Although employment rates vary according to nature and severity of disability, only about one in four individuals with disabilities is employed (Kaye, 1998).

Despite greater awareness and improvement in reducing architectural barriers for individuals with ability differences, equal access to buildings and programs in the broadest sense of accessibility hasn't yet been realized.

Strategies for Overcoming Accessibility Barriers

Over the past two decades, equal access to programs and services for all individuals, including those with differences in ability, has improved. This trend toward increased inclusion has come about mainly through a heightened awareness and legislation calling for an end

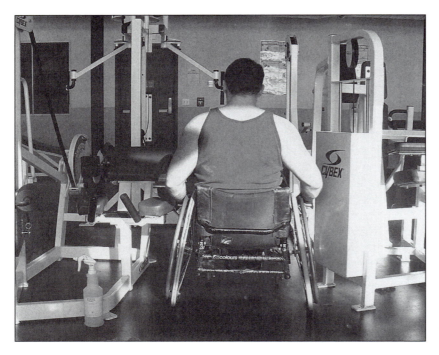

Figure 2.6 Beyond ramps and elevators, the spacing of equipment in fitness facilities can further improve accessibility and the opportunity for all individuals to exercise.

to discriminatory practices in all aspects of daily life, including physical activity opportunities. One of the most important steps in ensuring this equality came with the passage of the Americans with Disabilities Act (ADA) in 1990. The law provided a clear mandate to eliminate discrimination and afford equal access so that all individuals could participate more fully in society's activities and benefit from various programs and services. As a result, health clubs, exercise and recreational programs, and other community-based physical activity programs became more accessible to individuals with disabilities (figure 2.6).

School-based accessibility issues were addressed with another significant piece of legislation, the Education of All Handicapped Children's Act of 1975, now called the Individuals with Disabilities Education Act (IDEA). As part of the IDEA, students with disabilities are to be provided a free public education alongside their peers to the maximum extent appropriate. Consequently, more and more children have had access to, and the necessary supports in, general physical education programs within their schools. See appendix D for specifics related to this law and other critical legislation supporting inclusion over the past three decades.

Accessibility to physical activity programs and activities, however, doesn't occur simply with the passage of laws. Practitioners need to advocate for both access and accommodation for those with whom they work. They must become familiar with the legislation and how components of the laws affect their programs and services. Practitioners should also understand the philosophical underpinning of the laws and be clear about how their programs must be nondiscriminatory in practice, policy, and attitudes (Smith et al., 1996). Practitioners who are more aware of the barriers that limit access can implement strategies to allow more participants to be involved in their programs. Possibly, they can provide or assist with transportation, offer sliding scale memberships, secure sponsorships from local businesses to offset participant costs, or choose more accessible locations for their activities. A practitioner who's also familiar with the range of adaptive devices or modified equipment available will further facilitate the move toward more inclusive physical activity programming (figure 2.7).

Although legislation has been helpful in promoting awareness and increasing access to programs, true equality hasn't been realized. Continued efforts must be made in educating others and informing them of the laws. Unfortunately, though, we can't legislate change in attitudes and acceptance. Such change must come from increased commitment on the part of practitioners and those overseeing their programs to ensure the intent of the laws is realized.

Administrative Support

Many practitioners have favorable attitudes toward including individuals with significant differences in abilities in their programs, but they lack the support and commitment of others involved in the decision-making process. A teacher might feel positive about having a student

Figure 2.7 Specialized equipment available at many ski resorts has increased access to the slopes for individuals with differences in ability.

with a cognitive difference enter her physical education class but not be provided the supports needed by the administration in order for her to do this effectively. A fitness practitioner might welcome individuals with mobility differences into his exercise class but lack the support of the program director when it comes to accommodations and support. Administrators and directors must value the philosophy of inclusive practices and be committed to providing a supportive and effective place for inclusive physical activity to occur. Without such a commitment, the best of intentions can go astray.

Lack of Administrative Support

Some of the barriers to inclusive physical activity programming extend beyond the practitioner directly responsible for the program and might even seem initially beyond the practitioner's control. Administrative issues related to facility availability and scheduling, finances needed for equipment or increased support services, or time for increased training and professional development might further hinder the opportunity for inclusive programs to exist. For instance, in the public schools, many educators contend that a lack of time significantly impedes their ability to include students with ability differences into their classes (Liu & Pearson, 1999). In addition, teachers might not be provided with enough collaborative planning time to include students in the general physical education program (Lytle & Collier, 2002). Scheduling conflicts prevent needed collaborative meetings from taking place in which strategies and modifications are to be planned. Support personnel are not always available to assist within the program, and when they are they might not be adequately trained in how to assist most effectively. Similarly, practitioners might feel the need to gain knowledge and skills necessary to assist with the inclusion of children or adults with differing abilities in physical activity and exercise programs. However, for this to occur there must be a commitment and time available to attend

← **THINK BACK**

Think back to Brian White's situation.

1. Which of these contextual barriers might have played a role in the lack of new members joining his programs? Why might these have existed?

2. What would you suggest Brian do in light of these factors?

3. What strategies might he use to increase participation in his programs?

conferences or workshops. This often takes practitioners away from their daily responsibilities, which might in turn cost supervisors additional money for training fees as well as substitute personnel. Regardless of the setting or program activity, administrative support is critical in any physical activity environment for inclusive practices to be realized.

Strategies for Gaining Administrative Support

One of the most critical factors in the continued success of any inclusive model is the availability of adequate support to assist practitioners in developing and implementing inclusive programs. Initially, program personnel must commit to the time and energy required of collaboration, program planning, and reflection for including individuals with diverse needs in established physical activity programs. Practitioners must then advocate for what they need in terms of support to ensure that inclusion of all individuals can occur. This includes educating administrators or supervisors about the philosophical and legal basis for their inclusive efforts, barriers that might exist, and potential strategies to overcome them. The importance of administrative or supervisor support can't be overlooked in efforts to provide inclusive physical activity programs. Not only can they affect necessary administrative procedures to accommodate individuals with diverse needs in inclusive settings (financial resources, scheduling, matching of participants and practitioners, and providing needed time for planning and collaboration), but they can also provide access to necessary training opportunities for practitioners and staff members who are implementing programs and modifications. As discussed earlier, perceived professional competency of those implementing physical activity programs is key to attitudinal change and future professional practice. After training, practitioners should also be provided with ongoing support to facilitate the inclusive program. Ongoing support might be needed in the form of follow-up conferences or training sessions, reduced class or group size, release time for planning, additional support personnel, or other such assistance. In addition, practitioners can promote inclusive programming through parent support, special events, and high visibility of their programs. Every individual who works in the environment must make a commitment to the philosophy of inclusion, including practitioners, participants, and administration staff. Each must believe that every individual in the program deserves respect, access, and meaningful participation. In chapter 3 we present a collaborative approach useful in gaining administrative commitment and support.

▶ PERSON-RELATED BARRIERS AND STRATEGIES

Along with external barriers related to physical activity opportunities, there are also obstacles to physical activity participation that are internal to the participants and related to their own knowledge and behavior. These person-related or intrinsic barriers can further limit choices and behavior regarding physical activity (figure 2.8).

Knowledge

To make a choice about participating in a physical activity, an individual must first be aware that the program exists. Many people don't participate in physical activity programs because they have limited knowledge about the programs. Individuals with ability differences might be unaware of program availability, their legal rights to access programs, and the benefit of participation in physical activity.

Barriers Related to Knowledge

A lack of knowledge regarding program availability might be the reason some people don't participate in physical activity. For example, the parent of a child who's beginning to show delays in reaching motor milestones might not be aware that early intervention programs exist or how to access them. An adult with joint pain and limited range of motion might not know that the local YMCA has a heated pool and conducts low-impact water exercise programs. Rimmer and colleagues (2000) found that not knowing where to exercise was one of the primary barriers (along with cost and transportation issues) to exercise participation for African-American women with physical differences in ability. Although organized sport and fitness opportunities are growing for individuals with ability differences, many still don't know about the array of opportunities available to them (Hamel, 1992).

Figure 2.8 What participants know and believe about themselves and their involvement in physical activity influences their participation in physical activity programs.

Even when people with ability differences know that a program exists, they might not know about their legal rights to access these programs. Parents of a child with an identified disability might be uninformed about educational laws and their child's legal right to participate in an inclusive physical education program with necessary supports provided. An adult wanting to join a community-based activity program might be unaware of laws that guarantee accessible transportation and program access.

In some cases it's not a lack of knowledge about programs or legal rights that prevents people from gaining access to exercise programs. Rather, the primary barrier for some people is their lack of education regarding the benefits of physical activity. Beliefs and attitudes toward physical activity and the awareness of its importance for health and quality of life significantly influence activity participation and exercise choices. Parents might believe that their child with a mobility difference can't possibly benefit from physical education, especially in classes with more highly skilled peers. For older adults, a lack of knowledge about the benefits of exercise at an advanced age has been cited as a barrier to physical activity (Conn, 1998).

Strategies for Increasing Knowledge

Individuals with differing abilities can increase their knowledge of program availability in several ways. They themselves can seek out information regarding program options, or practitioners can gather information to help educate potential participants about activity opportunities. For example, the Internet is a great source of information about activities available for individuals interested in disability sports programs (see appendix C for disability sport Web sites). Many sites describe competitions, rules, and trainings. Community recreation programs should also be able to inform people about the many diverse programs available within the community. A phone call to the community exercise facility might reveal that they have special features to encourage individuals with diverse abilities to join their facilities, such as heated therapy pools, water aerobics classes, spacious facilities that allow for greater mobility, and knowledgeable staff to assist with all skill and ability levels. Community recreational facilities might have alternative equipment available, such as a monoski or guides at the ski slope. Contacting facilities directly and inquiring about physical activity opportunities can be a simple first step toward opening the door to inclusive participation.

Lack of knowledge concerning legal rights prevents some individuals from making informed choices and might restrict participation in many aspects of society, including physical activity opportunities. Individuals with differences in ability must advocate for themselves and learn advocacy-related skills that facilitate their involvement (Wolfe, Ofiesh, & Boone, 1996). They need either to become self-informed or be educated by others about their legal rights. Friends, family members, teachers, and practitioners all carry the responsibility to serve as advocates and assist individuals with differing abilities to become empowered by the legislation in place to serve them and create equitable environments.

For individuals to adopt and adhere to physical activity and exercise, they must first believe that such involvement is beneficial. Providing potential participants with literature and materials describing the benefits of physical activity might be enough to spark their interest in joining. Another strategy is to involve health professionals as sources of information and support. For school-based programs, teachers might prepare parents and their students by discussing the benefits, both physical and social, that result from inclusive physical education classes.

Finally, people won't participate in physical activity programs if they don't know the program exists, that they have a right to join, and that the activity is important for them. Educating individuals is essential to expanding their opportunities for inclusive physical activity.

Self-Determination, Self-Efficacy, and Motivation

Motivation to be physically active is another significant determinant of physical activity behavior. Individuals are motivated to participate for many different reasons. Some might be encouraged by others or externally pressured to be involved, whereas others might choose to engage in an activity out of self-interest, personal commitment, or intrinsic value. Motivation might be based on an internal factor, such as participating because the activity is enjoyable and brings pleasure, or it might be that the activity allows social interaction with friends. Ultimately, intrinsic motivation will influence an individual's decisions in terms of involvement in a task or activity. The higher one's motivation, the more apt he or she is to try an activity, put forth effort while participating, and stay with it, even when it becomes challenging. According to Bandura (1977), intrinsic motivation has its roots in a person's self-efficacy or belief about his or her capabilities to perform a specific activity or attain a desired outcome. The greater an individual's self-efficacy or self-perceptions about ability in a specific task, the greater the motivation to participate and adhere to the task. But perceived competence isn't the only factor that plays a role in one's motivation to engage in activity. Many factors contribute to whether a person is self-motivated. Self-determination of behavior involves internalization or regulation of extrinsic motives as well as perceived locus of causality (Ryan & Deci, 2000). Based on this premise, practitioners must realize that social contexts and conditions can either enhance or diminish positive motivation and understand their role in establishing settings that foster autonomy, competence, and connectedness.

Barriers to Motivation

Some people lack the confidence to participate in a physical activity or exercise program and are consequently unmotivated to join. If individuals with differences in ability believe that they won't be able to do the activity or achieve success as others in the program do, they are less likely to be interested in joining or motivated to stay in the activity after starting it. These kinds of efficacy expectations have been shown to influence the exercise behavior of older adults (Resnick, 1998) and adults with physical disabilities (Cardinal, Kosma, & McCubbin, 2004). Individuals with high self-efficacy begin exercising and stay with their programs longer than those with lower self-perceptions of ability. Research also shows that, for adults with long-term mobility differences, those with increased motivation and higher exercise self-efficacy have a higher probability of staying with the program (Kinne, Patrick, & Maher 1999). For children, a lack of confidence is among the primary barriers impeding the inclusion of children with visual differences in general physical education programs (Lieberman & Houston-Wilson, 1999). Regardless of age and program type, motivation and confidence are necessary prerequisites to program participation. In terms of self-determination to engage in physical activity, alienation, a lack of connectedness, and less than optimal challenges can create further barriers to activity for participants of varying abilities.

Strategies for Increasing Confidence and Motivation

The key to increased participation and meaningful involvement in physical activity programs is to ensure that participants are internally motivated to join and be physically active. Programs must be perceived as enjoyable and nonthreatening. Participants need to believe they have the skills to join and be successful. As such, activities must be designed to include a wide range of skill levels with optimal challenges and success planned. Making this happen involves finding out what needs to be manipulated or modified in any activity (e.g., equipment, instruction, physical setting) so that everyone involved can participate. Practitioners must provide positive reinforcement and feedback so that participants feel more confident in their abilities to perform a task or engage in the activity. By modeling a program that is inclusive of all individuals, other participants might too believe they will be accepted and successful. Chapter 6 offers many strategies for individualizing physical activity programs and increasing participant success and confidence.

Perceived Risks

Whenever someone contemplates participating in a physical activity, he or she weighs the benefits of being physically active, such as improved physical and psychological well-being, against the risks of participating, such as possible fatigue, soreness, injury, and embarrassment. If the perceived benefits of being physically active outweigh the perceived risks, the individual is more likely to engage in physical activity. However, when the perceived risks are greater than the perceived benefits (whether the perceived risks are real or not), one isn't likely to choose to participate.

Barriers of Fear and Perceived Health Risks

For many individuals with varied abilities, this cost–benefit analysis can be further complicated by increased symptoms related to a medical condition, increased energy demands to participate in the activity, or feelings of inadequacy compared to others in the group. It has been suggested that sedentary living occurs when people believe that the risks of physical activity exceed the benefits. Such benefit-cost comparing has been shown to influence many adults' decisions to be physically active (O'Brien-Cousins, 2000; Rhodes, et al. 1999). Specifically, fear of injury and concerns for safety and suitability of exercise are cited as barriers to exercise in older adults (Dishman, 1994). The potentially unpleasant sensations, such as fatigue or pain, associated with exercise further limit the adoption of physical activity for many older adults (Nies, Vollman, & Cook, 1998).

Regarding children with ability differences, parents might make decisions about their children's involvement in inclusive physical activity programs with similar concerns in mind. They might prevent their children from participating in group physical education classes because they are concerned about safety or fearful of social isolation or ridicule by peers. Young people with differing abilities might also choose not to participate in physical activity because of their own perceived limitations.

Strategies for Overcoming Fears and Perceived Risks

Although fears and perceived risks might be unfounded, they're valid and real to those who experience them. As with other person-related barriers, education and insight are critical in helping individuals overcome these concerns. For some, information about what constitutes physical activity might be necessary. The old saying "no pain, no gain" might dissuade some people who believe that exercise, to be beneficial, must be of high intensity, prolonged over time, and painful. Exercise and fitness practitioners could share recommended guidelines from organizations such as the American College of Sports Medicine (ACSM) and the Council on Physical Education for Children (COPEC) that offer recommendations for healthy and appropriate activity. Many professional organizations have resources describing the nature of physical activity and set guidelines for best practice. Practitioners might want to provide parents and children with the standards developed by the National Association of Sport and Physical Education (www.aahperd.org/naspe). This organization offers information regarding essential components of quality physical education programs, how programs should be developed and implemented, and the competency of practitioners involved in the programs. Practitioners working with adults who have differences in ability may recommend the National Center on Physical Activity and Disability (www.ncpad.org) that offers information and guidelines on a variety of activities. Programs must be well planned, adhere to professional standards and guidelines, and consider individual differences and needs. Providing potential participants (or those guiding their physical activity decisions) with such material gives them a better understanding of the critically reviewed and professionally developed program guidelines and also demonstrates that the practitioner is aware and knowledgeable about well-established standards in the field.

To further alleviate fears, participants should have the opportunity to observe and speak with others of similar ability and concerns. Through dialogue and observation, they might find their fears to be based more on fiction and misinformation than fact. They will learn that physical activity modifications and related accommodations can serve to prevent injury, equalize participation, and promote a fun, exciting, and safe experience.

Entrenched Patterns of Inactivity

Many experts believe that past experiences contribute to present and future behavior. If an individual was physically active as a youngster, he or she is more likely to live a physically active lifestyle as an adult. Individuals who don't engage in any regular physical activity might be inactive simply out of habit. These entrenched behaviors remain influential on physical activity habits throughout the life span.

The Barrier of Inactivity Habits

As we've seen, many barriers influence physical activity choices and involvement. The inactivity that might result from context and person-related obstacles in turn becomes an additional barrier to participation. Despite known benefits of exercise, only 30 percent of older adults exercise regularly (Elward & Larson, 1992). Low-income, racial and ethnic minorities, and populations with identified disabilities are more likely to be sedentary than the general population (Taylor, Baranowski, & Young, 1998). The type of disability is another factor influencing habitual physical activity levels among young people (Longmuir and Bar-Or, 2000). The population as a whole is at significant risk for inactivity and the associated health risks that go along with it (see the report of the surgeon general on physical activity and health at www.cdc.gov/nccdphp/sgr/sgr.htm).

Strategies for Overcoming Inactivity Habits

Just as there are many reasons for people being inactive, there are many ways to promote their adoption of and adherence to physical activity. Many of the strategies already discussed to overcome context-related barriers and those that speak to increasing individual knowledge and motivation can be used to change behavior and foster increased physical activity. In addition, practitioners can offer unique events to introduce potential participants to new activities, such as community "fun run–walks" or bicycle–wheelchair "fun rides." Local health and fitness clubs can identify groups through organizations and send out specialty mailings with advertisements, such as "exercise with a friend," "two for one," or "three free sessions" to try to help individuals overcome the inertia of inactivity. The extent of ways to educate and motivate individuals to become physically active is limited only by the creativity and commitment of the practitioner. Once participants become active, practitioners need to continue their efforts to provide enjoyable and accommodating programs so that all participants can continue to succeed.

THINK BACK

Think back to Brian White and the local fitness club.

1. What person-related barriers have you faced in your own exercise experiences?

2. Do you believe that some of the person-related barriers might have prevented potential participants from joining?

3. What steps should Brian take to overcome these barriers?

▶ TASK-RELATED BARRIERS AND STRATEGIES

We've discussed the many potential barriers related to the context and individual, but aspects directly associated with an activity might also present barriers for involvement. These task-related barriers have considerable influence on the motivation levels and self-confidence of participants, as well as on the attitudes of significant others. Task-related barriers interact with contextual and individual barriers to further intensify the exclusion of individuals of diverse abilities. Such barriers include activity selection and features of equipment used in the activity. Although equipment is really part of an activity context, we'll discuss it here because it's closely related to the task and the successful accomplishment of the task.

Equipment

Many physical activities require some form of equipment. For an infant, it might be a squishy ball. For a school-aged child, it might be a playground ball, jump rope, or bicycle. An adult might use several pieces of sport-specific equipment or fitness and weight-training equipment. Regardless of the activity, the equipment selected for a task can serve to increase or decrease accessibility for individuals with diverse abilities.

Equipment Barriers

We don't generally think of equipment as a barrier to physical activity involvement. Rather, we view it as a necessary component to participation in an activity. For example, if an individual wanted to go downhill skiing, she would need skis, boots, and poles. However, for an individual who is nonambulatory, this equipment alone would not afford the opportunity to participate. In another example, a child in the first or second grade might not find a standard height basketball hoop accessible for learning how to shoot baskets. In this case, the child doesn't have the strength needed to be successful with this equipment. These examples show how either the lack of availability or the lack of appropriateness of equipment can serve as a barrier to physical activity participation.

Strategies to Overcome Equipment Barriers

The physical activity practitioner in any setting must consider the variability of participants' needs when planning and preparing equipment for activity sessions. In our skiing example, the

Figure 2.9 The right bike allows this youngster with a difference in balance and body awareness the opportunity to engage in physical activity.

adult could participate in downhill skiing quite proficiently with the appropriate equipment, such as a monoski. For the child who wants to learn to shoot a basketball, a shorter hoop or lighter ball can be used. The use of varied equipment or adapted equipment can make all the difference in creating access for participation. Most accommodations require little or no specialized equipment, just a variety. For example, when children are learning to dribble a ball with one hand, the teacher should provide several sizes and types of balls for children to select from. Some children will need a larger playground ball to practice, and others might be ready for an actual basketball. In an adult stretching class, some people might be able to reach their toes easily to hold a particular stretch, and others might want to use a firm band to extend their reach to complete a stretch. All individuals want and need to feel successful. By providing equipment options, practitioners can make success more likely for everyone (figure 2.9).

Activity Selection

The tasks included in physical activity programs, whether skills in physical education class or exercises in physical fitness programs, must be chosen with consideration for the meaningfulness, age-appropriateness, and functional value they have for participants. For example, an elementary class might be practicing the skills of catching and throwing in order to use these skills in games, whereas seniors in a water aerobics class might be working to improve strength and range of motion and promote better balance. Barriers might exist within these and other types of activities when consideration for participant age, ability, and future involvement in physical activity are not taken into account.

Barriers Presented by Activity Selection

One potential barrier to participation of individuals with differing abilities in physical activity programs is the meaningfulness of the activities available. An increasing number of adults and students with diverse abilities and capabilities are included in prestructured physical activity programs. In school settings, curriculums are set, units developed, and traditional activities implemented. In communities, exercise programs are offered within typically organized facilities, often with set routines and group exercises implemented. Besides the limited activities to choose from, there's a risk that participants or parents will find little meaning in the activities offered and thus devalue the physical activity experience. The result will be avoidance of or little enthusiasm shown for the activity. For instance, if a high school physical education program offers team sports only one semester, those students who find individual or leisure activities more meaningful and satisfying might avoid taking additional physical education credit once they've met graduation requirements. Likewise, adults who find aquatics classes more meaningful might avoid exercising if only step aerobics is offered at noon during their lunch hour when they want to exercise.

Another factor concerning the inclusion of individuals with diverse abilities into physical activity programs is the appropriateness of the activity. Some individuals' physical or developmental capabilities are not the same or even similar to others of the same age. An adult, for instance, whose intellectual capabilities are not commensurate with other adults might have difficulty understanding complex rules and strategies in some team-oriented recreational activities or have trouble understanding the concept of pacing while jogging. For this reason, practitioners often avoid age-appropriate activities and implement activities geared to much younger individuals or children. For example, it wouldn't be appropriate for a high school teacher to have his or her high school students with developmental delays participate in a game of "London Bridge" to practice walking or skipping to music. Walking for exercise could be practiced in the community or with age-appropriate music and dancing. The absence of age-appropriate physical activity can be connected to a lack of training and competency by professionals and tends to perpetuate stereotypes and lowered expectations by other individuals.

Although equipment might or might not be considered a barrier to participation, how the equipment is used in an activity can be. Activities with equipment that fosters age-inappropriate participation can also serve as barriers to inclusive programming. A beach ball might be an appropriate piece of equipment for a youngster with limited strength and range of motion in his or her arms, but using a beach ball with a 15-year-old simply throwing the ball to a hoop target is age-inappropriate. It would be more appropriate for this participant to use the beach ball in a modified volleyball game given that her peers also engage in this activity. How equipment is used and in what context can be the difference in promoting inclusive attitudes and perceptions or not.

Another possible barrier to physical activity participation is beliefs about whether the activity serves a functional purpose for the individual. Concerns over whether students with diverse abilities should participate in general physical education classes have centered on whether the tasks or activities in that program are of functional value. Will the physical activity program help the individual with vocational skills, daily life skills of dressing and grooming, and so on? While this question is not asked about most children entering a physical activity program, it is commonly asked of those with significant differences in ability. The importance an activity has for enhancing functional capabilities in adults with ability differences is also a concern for some. Although lifting weights might improve fitness, an individual with balance problems might feel that weight lifting is unimportant because it doesn't directly improve balance and the functional skill of walking.

Strategies for Appropriate Activity Selection

Effective physical activity programs usually spring from well-planned and organized plans. Of course, curriculums and program guides also offer guidance in this regard. However, these should be viewed as general guides, not program mandates. Regardless of setting or participant age, program activities should be derived from meaningful goals and objectives for the participant. For school-aged children, the physical education curriculum or activities within curricular units must be adapted to meet the unique learning outcomes important for the student. Adapting the curriculum in physical education is a key strategy to inclusion (Block, 2000). For some children with ability differences, we shouldn't assume that the general physical education program is nonfunctional. In fact, the general physical education program can be functional for all students in the promotion of lifetime physical activity. In fact, research shows that both functional and age-appropriate skills are more likely to be reinforced and maintained when they are taught in the natural environment (Horner, Dunlap, & Koegel, 1988).

Community-based activity programs must also include opportunities for adults to self-select meaningful activities. Participants could be offered such recreational activities as canoeing or bowling, which they may be more likely to participate in than team-oriented recreational activities such as volleyball or basketball. Adults in exercise programs should have individualized exercise plans that consider outcomes of functional independence rather than simply strength gains in isolated muscle groups.

Activities and the goals within them are chosen based on participant interests, needs, age, and availability of resources. Consideration is given to skills needed in present settings of physical activity and future settings of intended activity. Activities should be planned with thought for the potential of continued involvement in the activity. For instance, adults in exercise programs might be taught how to do resistance exercises with rubber tubing rather than free weights because free weights might not be available at home when they exercise outside of program sessions. Children in schools might not have aquatics as part of their program if there are no swimming pools in the community and instead learn to ride bicycles or cross-country ski.

For practitioners to promote physical activity involvement for all individuals, activities should be considered personally meaningful by the participants. They also need to be age-appropriate and functionally important if life-long physical activity and associated health benefits are to be realized.

THINK BACK

Think back to your own experiences in physical activity programs.

1. Can you think of an experience you had in which there were task barriers that prevented you from successful participation? Was the task too easy or too difficult for you?

2. What strategies could have been used to create a more optimal challenge for you?

Now, think back to Brian White's ideas as the fitness coordinator.

1. What kinds of task-related barriers could have prevented participation?

2. If you were Brian's consultant for creating inclusive environments, what ideas might you give him?

SUMMARY

Although barriers of all kinds can influence the inclusion of all individuals in physical activity programs, there are many ways to overcome such hurdles. The key to overcoming obstacles is a step-by-step approach of deconstructing traditional ways of knowing and doing and, more important, reconstructing a program where all are valued and respected.

Inclusive physical activity should be seen not as a method of programming but as the ongoing development of relationships and social networks for diverse individuals. It's the responsibility of practitioners to consider the context, the person, and the task in order to create accessible programs in which every participant is valued, respected, and empowered to meet his or her physical activity goals.

What Do You Think?

1. Which barriers do you think are most limiting when it comes to inclusive physical activity? Why?

2. Do you believe the physical activity programs you know about or have experienced consider these barriers in the planning of the programs? Do you think they could? How?

3. Which barriers do you believe are the easiest to overcome? Why do you believe this?

What Would You Do?

Scenario 2.1

Maria and Juan are a happy young couple with a new baby boy, their first child. They're planning on having a big family. Little Juanito is a beautiful 11-month-old baby. He was born in April and will soon be having his first birthday. His family is very excited and is planning a big party for him. Maria recently visited her sister, Angelita, whom she hadn't seen since the birth of Juanito. Angelita has three children of her own and is helping Maria plan Juanito's birthday party. During the visit Maria put little Juanito on a blanket on the floor to play with his cousins while she and Angelita talked. While they were talking, Angelita noticed that Juanito had not rolled over or moved from his place. She remembered when her children were that age they were all over the house and pulling up on the furniture. After they finished planning the party, Angelita asked Maria if Juanito was rolling over yet. Maria said no but that he did roll from his side to his back and seemed to be a very happy baby. Later, while driving home, Maria wondered if she should be concerned. Juanito had always been a perfect baby and hardly ever cried. He seemed happy and content. The only challenge they had ever had was a very long labor when he was born. Other than that, he had been a healthy baby, and they hadn't had to return to the doctor since coming home from the hospital.

1. What possible context-related barriers are presented in Maria's situation?

2. What person-related barriers are present for Maria and Juanito?

3. What strategies might help Maria overcome these barriers?

Scenario 2.2

Marsha is a new recreational therapist who works at a live-in senior facility. This is the first time this facility has hired a recreational therapist. Most of the individuals who live at the facility are relatively independent, with some using assisted living and others 24-hour nursing care. Marsha is really excited because at her previous job for the city recreation program she worked with adults with developmental delays. Many of the programs were poorly attended because of a lack of transportation. She found this frustrating because she spent many hours preparing lessons and activities, and it was disappointing when only two or three people showed up. Marsha is really excited about her new job, knowing that transportation will not be an issue. Most of the activities take place on site in a nice new recreation room, and she has also been provided with a facility van to take people off site to special events. She decided her first program for the residents would be to offer tai chi every day. But at the end of the first week, Marsha was sorely disappointed. Very few people attended the tai chi sessions. Transportation was not an issue, so what was the problem? Marsha scheduled a meeting with her boss to discuss her concerns. Assume the role of Marsha's boss.

1. What barriers might you identify with Marsha as potential reasons for the lack of attendance in the tai chi classes?

2. What suggestions would you give Marsha to confirm what the possible barriers are?

3. What strategies could you suggest to Marsha to help her overcome the barriers once they were confirmed?

Inclusive Physical Activity Program Planning and Implementation

Lifelong physical activity involvement is essential to the quality of life and health of all individuals. Encouraging and fostering this participation are the responsibility of all physical activity practitioners. With the basis for inclusive physical activity explained in part I, part II provides a systematic approach to planning and implementing appropriate programs for individuals of varying abilities.

For inclusive settings to be successful, practitioners must have the necessary supports and skills by which to include everyone. Chapter 3 discusses the need for effective communication and a team approach for creating successful inclusive programs. Different models of consultation and several collaborative strategies are presented to assist team members in working collectively when offering inclusive programs.

Before any programming takes place, practitioners must consider the needs and interests of participants and the meaningfulness of the activities offered for each individual. Chapter 4 considers the focus of physical activity programming across the life span. Since initial assessment and ongoing evaluation are critical components of any effective program, this chapter also discusses the many purposes of assessment in inclusive physical activity. Specific issues and considerations related to assessment as well as insight into specific assessment strategies are presented.

A sequential process is offered in chapter 5 to help practitioners develop inclusive and age-appropriate programming. The practical approach described is then applied to three age groups: infants and toddlers, school-age children, and adults. Issues and strategies regarding access and accommodation are discussed within each age group.

Chapter 6 takes a functional approach to programming by examining factors related to the person, context, or task that influence movement skill and performance. Analysis of both tasks and movement performance is explained and the process of creating opportunities for success is discussed. This is achieved through the functional approach to modifying movement experiences (FAMME) model, which offers a range of modifications that can be used to accommodate participants with varying skills. Emphasis is placed on the individual's capabilities rather than limitations and the matching of skill to a particular movement situation.

Teaming and Collaboration

Learning Outcomes

After completing this chapter, you should be able to

» define a person's frame of reference and understand how these vary across disciplines;

» discuss the elements of effective communication;

» describe the members of a professional team and their roles;

» explain the process of collaborative consultation and the steps for effective problem solving;

» identify the benefits and barriers to consultation; and

» identify strategies for effective collaborative consultation.

INCLUDING ALL INDIVIDUALS

Brooks Middle School, a brand new facility, has recently hired all its faculty and staff members. Emily Booth has been hired as the new physical education teacher, joining many other new teachers and professionals at the school. Emily is very excited about her job and loves working with middle school children. She teaches six periods a day of coed physical education in classes that include children of wide-ranging levels of ability. Several of the students in her classes have individual education programs (IEPs) and have a team of professionals who help plan their programs. Emily has never served on a collaborative educational team and is a little uncertain about her role in the process. Several of the team members have come into her classes to observe her students, including the physical therapist, occupational therapist, and adapted physical education teacher. They have come at different times, asking many questions about her curriculum, equipment, and the behavior of students in the class. Emily wants to meet with the adapted physical education specialist to question her about several of the students in class and to get ideas for variations to the activities she's presenting. In fact, there's one particular student she's having trouble with, Maddy, who doesn't seem to want to participate in any of the activities. Emily is concerned she's not reaching this child; she's not sure if Maddy can't do the activities, is not interested, or is having trouble adjusting to the class. An IEP meeting has been scheduled in two weeks to discuss her program.

Who will attend this meeting, and what are their roles? What is Emily's role within this group of professionals? She's about to become part of a collaborative team. Effective inclusive practice requires that professionals examine their own beliefs, as discussed in chapter 1, and work toward creating accessible inclusive settings for individuals of all abilities, as discussed in chapter 2. This process requires effective communication and collaborative practice. How will Emily become a contributing part of this team? What will she be able to share?

The need for a team approach to inclusive physical activity planning is clearly documented in the Individuals With Disabilities Education Act (IDEA). This landmark federal law describes the need for educational teams to serve individuals from birth through their transition into adulthood in community-based physical activity programs. No one individual is expected to have the expertise necessary to teach all individuals of varying abilities. The collaborative process allows for professionals to come together in a creative problem-solving process to design the best possible physical activity experiences for individuals with diverse abilities and needs (Friend, 1988; Stainback, Stainback, & Ayres, 1996; Villa, Thousand, Nevin, & Malgeri, 1996). However, merely being part of a professional planning team doesn't make the team effective. One of the key features of a collaborative team is that each member brings a unique perspective to the table. This perspective is known as the person's *frame of reference*. Frame of reference is based on individuals' previous experiences, beliefs, values, and training; this frame is the lens through which each individual views the world. These lenses shape an individual's view of others' abilities as well as their attitudes, as discussed in chapters 1 and 2.

The concept of frame of reference is analogous to the story of the three men who were blind and were feeling an elephant for the first time. The first man held the tail and proclaimed that the elephant was like a rope. The second man felt the side and said that the elephant was like a wall. The third man tried to reach around the elephant's leg and said that the elephant was like a tree trunk. Each of these men had a piece of information about the elephant but not the whole picture. They could choose to spend their time arguing over whose perspective was accurate,

Figure 3.1 "Knowing in part may make a fine tale, but wisdom comes from seeing the whole." (Young, E. 1992, p. 36)

or they could respect and value each other's view and listen carefully, thereby gaining a better understanding of the elephant as a whole. Obviously, the latter choice would make them a more effective team (figure 3.1).

Highly effective teams include such elements as clearly defined roles, respect for other members, social support, shared understanding of expected behaviors, and effective communication (Friend & Cook, 2000; Lytle & Bordin, 2001). To be an effective team member, one must continually practice these skills. For this reason, we'll discuss communication first in this chapter and follow that with more details on the team members, the collaborative consultation model, the collaborative process, and the collaborative strategies for teachers and community-based practitioners.

THINK BACK

Think of two teams or groups that you've worked with, one that was effective and one that was ineffective.

1. List the characteristics of each group.

2. What characteristics made the effective group a positive experience?

3. What is your frame of reference? What do you value in others and in yourself as team members? How might your values support or hinder your interactions with others?

4. Think back to Emily. What information might she need about her role as a team member?

EFFECTIVE COMMUNICATION

Communication is the process of creating shared meaning and can be defined as "occurring when someone attributes meaning to another person's words or actions" (Martin & Nakayama, 2000, p. 61). All professionals need effective communication skills, not only for working with their students but also for working in collaborative teams with other professionals, parents, and family members. Communication is a complex process that involves many elements, including listening, questioning, making statements, and using methods of nonverbal communication.

Listening

We'll discuss listening first because it's the most critical aspect of communication and in establishing a positive rapport with others. The two types of listening are passive and active. Each serves an important purpose. The two types are often used together in a dialogue with another person. Passive listening involves listening without saying anything and is frequently

Figure 3.2 (a) Ineffective and (b) effective listening.

used when the speaker needs to vent frustrations or explain something in detail. In this case the listener's job is to listen attentively without making any comments. Three positive aspects of communication can result from passive listening. First, it allows the speaker to talk without interruption or interference from another's ideas or thoughts. Second, the process of talking about an issue can often reduce the frustration (which is why we call it "venting"). Third, people sometimes find solutions to their own concerns through talking about them out loud.

Active (or reflective) listening is the process of sharing with the speaker that you have heard what he or she is saying and might involve paraphrasing, clarifying, questioning, or perception checking (Thomas, Correa, & Morsink, 2001). The listener should attend fully to what's being said and listen for the content and emotion of what's being shared. The listener can then paraphrase for the speaker what he or she heard and try to correctly process the content of the interaction. Figure 3.2 illustrates the difference between ineffective and effective listening.

Regardless whether passive or active listening is being employed, it's critical for the listener to enter the interaction with empathy (Covey, 1990). In other words, the listener should intend to fully understand the other person emotionally and intellectually without projecting his or her own ideas, thoughts, or feelings into what's being shared. This type of listening is a wonderful tool in gathering accurate information about another's perceptions, concerns, and ideas. Effective listening establishes rapport, shows concern and a desire to comprehend, and demonstrates accurate understanding.

Questioning

Another important skill for effective communication is questioning. How someone asks a question and the type of questions he or she asks can influence an interaction either positively or negatively. Questions are used to seek information, provide information, or clarify or confirm information. How a person gathers information is important because some questions can be perceived as intimidating. People should maintain professional equity in their interactions and not create a feeling of interrogation through the way in which questions are asked.

Questions that seek information are typically straightforward, such as, "What time should I meet you at the health club?" But questions that provide information can be intimidating, or irritating, particularly if they're stated in a way that suggests the other person should already know the information or if advice is being given (figure 3.3). Consider how you might feel if another professional said to you in a somewhat condescending tone, "Didn't you call the physical therapist already?" suggesting that you should have already taken care of this, or "You weren't using the smaller racket, were you?" after seeing the child with a small racket in a class setting. Questions such as these are really providing information about what an individual should or shouldn't have already done. Other examples might include, "Don't you think the parents will be upset if we don't try the behavior strategies here that they are using at home?" or "His wife won't allow him to get in the pool without assistance

Figure 3.3 Questions can enhance or inhibit communication. How do you think this question affected communication?

will she?" In the first question the person is really stating that she thinks the same behavior strategies should be used in the physical activity setting that are used at home. In the second question the person is saying that the wife does not let the husband get in the pool without assistance. Perhaps a better way to provide this information would be to say "Let's talk with the parents about what behavior strategies will work best in this setting. What do you think might work?" or "I believe his wife shared that she likes him to have an aid when getting in the pool. Perhaps we should talk with her about any concerns she might have with him getting in the pool by himself. What do you think?" In each example the question has been changed to a statement that is then followed up with a question that allows the other person to provide more information about their thoughts. This shift in how the information is provided allows both individuals to share information freely without feeling intimidated or like they should or shouldn't have known or done something.

Finally, questions are used to clarify information. These types of questions are used frequently and can be very helpful to ensure you're in agreement about what's expected. For example, "You're going to bring the modified equipment next week?" or "Do you do agree with me that Levia is ready for this activity?"

The most effective uses of questions are to seek information or clarify information. Questions used to advise or provide information should be used cautiously, and the speaker should be clear about the intent of the question before asking it.

You can categorize questions by whether they seek, provide, or clarify information. You can also group them by whether they're open or closed (table 3.1). A closed question requests a "yes" or "no" answer. An open question allows for elaboration and requests the responder to give more than just a "yes" or "no" response. When you ask open questions, you're likely to get more information (sometimes more than you need). In general, phrase your questions with your purpose in mind. Use closed questions when you're seeking quick,

Table 3.1 Open Versus Closed Questions

Closed question	Open question
Does Jerry like physical education?	How does Jerry feel about physical education?
Can Jackie complete the mile run?	What is Jackie's fitness level?
Are you having trouble with balance?	What are your concerns about your balance?

efficient information. Otherwise, give people a chance to express themselves more fully by asking open questions.

Making Statements

Statements are critical to effective communication and allow people to share ideas, thoughts, feelings, concerns, and perceptions. Statements can provide information, explain a process, give suggestions, provide direct commands, or indirectly request information. Statements that provide information are often descriptive in nature, describing an event, situation, or behavior (Friend & Cook, 2000). Descriptive statements are based on what's perceivable and usually don't include an evaluation of the event. Evaluative statements give the perceiver's "take" on what has been perceived. Contrast the following two statements. Which is descriptive and which evaluative?

1. Maddy ran over, pushed Carolyn on the arm, and kicked the ball across the playground.
2. Maddy was mean to Carolyn and took the ball away from her.

The descriptive statement (1) gives details of what happened without assessing the behavior described. The evaluative statement (2) presents an opinion of what happened and does not describe the complete behavior. Clear and accurate descriptive observations and communication can be effective in problem-solving teaching and learning situations with other professionals. Removing the evaluative nature of the event allows us to be objective and open to the possible causes and solutions without seeming to pass judgment. For example, Maddy might have pushed Carolyn for many reasons, so jumping to the conclusion that the push was mean spirited is premature.

Other types of statements explain a process or offer guidance to others. Teachers frequently use this form of communication when instructing individuals about how to complete a task or perform a skill. In this process the speaker typically describes the steps in detail and gives examples of what to do. For example, in a badminton class the teacher might describe the steps in completing an overhead clear and then demonstrate the skill for the class.

Other forms of statements are suggestions or direct commands. Suggestions are softer than commands, such as, "One idea is to reduce the weights for Susan" or "Maybe some stretches for the hamstrings would help Joey." Suggestions are meant to allow the listener the option of accepting or rejecting the idea. Commands are more forceful statements and suggest that the person being spoken to should do as he or she is told, such as, "Reduce the weights for Susan" or "Joey, stretch your hamstrings." Such statements don't intend to allow for alternatives and often suggest that the one making them has authority. Effective teachers and other practitioners generally avoid stating commands.

Finally, statements sometimes request information. These statements are really questions and are generally spoken as an invitation for comments from another. They are indirect in nature and can help to prevent the feeling of interrogation during a discussion or interview. "I wonder what the recreational therapist is doing with him" and "I'd like to know how they transferred him on the last field trip" are examples of statements that are inviting information. Such statements allow individuals to share freely as they choose. The speaker intentionally takes the risk of not getting the information he or she wants. When receiving information is the primary goal, it's often best to ask questions directly rather than phrase them as statements.

Using Nonverbal Communication

You've heard the expression "a picture is worth a thousand words." In fact, some people have suggested that up to 90 percent of communication occurs not through words but through nonverbal messages (Thomas, Correa, & Morsink, 2001). Nonverbal communication, which

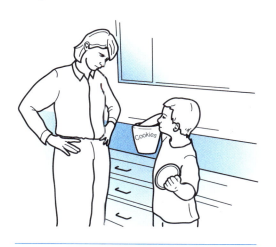

Figure 3.4 Body language can be much more efficient than words.

includes facial expression, posture, gestures, eye contact, proximity, and tone of voice, is a powerful mode of expression that people use at both conscious and subconscious levels.

You can tell a lot about what people are thinking or feeling by their facial expressions. Most of us have had someone give us "the look," meaning pay attention or quit doing whatever it is we're doing (figure 3.4). We have also witnessed the expressions of individuals attempting to perform a task that's difficult for them. Such a look that conveys so much—frustration, despair, self-consciousness, embarrassment, guilt, regret—is indeed worth the many words it would take the learner to try to describe the complexity of his or her feelings.

Posture can also tell us a lot about a person's feelings or attitude. During a meeting, when people are sitting with their arms crossed against their chests, an observer might interpret that they're resistant or closed to the ideas being shared. Of course the observer could

Cultural Differences and Nonverbal Communication

In North American culture, eye contact during communication sends the message that we are listening and paying attention. But in some Asian cultures too much eye contact is a sign of disrespect. In fact, gazing downward when speaking to a person in authority might show greater respect.

How close people are when they're talking is also a factor in communication. For example, in the Hispanic culture people tend to stand closer and touch more than they do in Asian cultures. An early intervention teacher might receive hugs when entering a Hispanic family's home and receive a head bow when entering an Asian family's home. Practitioners should be aware of an individual's comfort level in relation to proximity when interacting and respect these differences. Often facial expression or other nonverbal behaviors will tell the practitioner if he or she has overstepped the boundaries. Keen observation skills are important to quality communication.

THINK BACK

1. How does the tone of voice and body language change the meaning of the words in the following statements?
   - "That family is really wonderful." (Spoken with a smile, positive tone, and while looking the person in the eye.)
   - "That family is really wonderful." (Spoken flatly with no enthusiasm while rolling the eyes.)

2. Emily Booth (from our chapter-opening scenario) is about to meet with her professional team members. Write two open-ended questions that she might ask at the meeting. Create two statements that would provide information to Emily if you were one of the team members.

3. As a friend of Emily, what suggestions would you give her to make sure that her body language in the meeting presented her as an open, interested, and willing team member?

4. Identify two elements of communication you'd like to work on in your own professional interactions. How might these skills help you be a better communicator?

be mistaken—it could just be that the air in the room is too cold. Practitioners need to be aware of these kinds of gestures and try to read them correctly based on the environment, the individuals, and the context.

Bear in mind that for individuals with differing abilities, elements of communication might be altered. For example, a person with craniofacial muscular dystrophy might appear expressionless even when very happy; someone who has had a stroke might experience partial paralysis that affects his or her facial expressions and voice tone. When working with individuals with disabilities, practitioners should be aware of possible variations in communication style and sensitive to how they might affect communication or interaction. They also need to be in tune with the overall mood or tone of their participants without being oversensitive to the point of seeing messages in nonverbal communication when the messages aren't there.

▸ TEAM MEMBERS

Now that we've discussed effective communication, we should consider the roles of the diverse team of individuals who communicate together to provide programming for individuals with disabilities. Such team members come from diverse disciplines, and it's this diversity that helps them form a complete perspective. A team is defined as two or more individuals who form an interdependent, coordinated group that through good communication and clear procedures work toward a common goal, in this case providing quality physical activity programming for individuals of differing abilities (Friend & Cook, 2000).

The members of a team are determined by the needs of a learner as well as the context in which he or she will be participating in physical activity. Team members of a school-based program might differ from those who serve in a sports program or community-based program. In any case, a combination of the following individuals might be involved: the student or participant, the parent or care provider, physical therapists, occupational therapists, speech and language pathologists, special education teachers, administrators, psychologists, nurses, and the adapted physical education specialist. Each of these individuals plays a role that contributes to the understanding of the individual as a whole. Roles are expected behaviors generally agreed on by members of the group or by society as a whole (Brehm & Kassin, 1996). In the following sections, we'll give a brief description of each of the individuals who might serve on a team along with an example of how he or she might interact with the physical activity practitioner.

Individuals

Of highest importance is the individual you're serving. Address this person's desires and needs first. When possible, the individual participant or learner should be a part of the program planning team. Whether this works well often depends on the age of the individual and the preferences of his or her parents or family members. In many cases, individuals know their needs better than anyone and can often share them clearly and effectively. They can identify their own strengths and limitations and many times make their own adaptations to achieve success in a given situation. When working with adults, ask them what works best for them and what their desires and goals are in planning programs and interventions. When working with young children or learners with more limited abilities, you might need to facilitate the process by identifying needs and goals and letting the learner respond to them.

Family Members

Family members usually know the most about the individual and see him or her on a daily basis. Parents or caregivers have researched the needs of the learner and often interact with all of the team professionals. In most cases, the parent or family member also knows the individual's family history and medical history. These members might have specific desires for the learner that should be addressed. For example, family members might want the physical activity practitioner to teach their child how to ride a bicycle as a lifetime recreational skill and for transportation later in life. Or they might want the individual to practice getting up from the floor and transferring in and out of a chair. In any programming, the desires of the individuals and their families should be paramount to instructional planning (as well as meet educational standards and guidelines for individuals within the public schools).

Adapted Physical Education Specialists or Adapted Physical Activity Practitioners

The adapted physical education specialist is the one responsible for physical education curriculum for individuals with disabilities who qualify for services within the public schools. This person should have teacher training in physical education as well as special education and adapted physical education. Currently, several states require a specific adapted physical education (APE) specialist credential for teaching APE in the public schools. This credential usually requires university coursework in the area of adapted physical education and supervised student teaching experience. Other states require a teaching credential in physical education with an endorsement in APE. Many states with no credential or endorsement requirements use the adapted physical education national standards (APENS) exam as their requirement for adapted physical education specialists.

In examination of the roles of the adapted physical education specialist in the public schools, a recent national survey by Kelly and Gansneder (1998) found that 59 percent of adapted physical education teachers provided some form of indirect services. These indirect services were defined as " . . . itinerant or consultant . . . you provide information, assessment, or other assistance but do not teach the children directly. The actual physical education services are taught by another person" (Kelly & Gansneder, 1998, p. 146).

The roles of the adapted physical educator within the public schools are very diverse. They might teach independent of the general and special education teachers or in collaboration with them. Roles of the adapted physical educator include advocate, educator, courier, resource coordinator, and supporter or helper. These five roles have been identified by Lytle and Hutchinson (2004), but there are likely many other roles APE specialists play that haven't been clearly defined or identified yet. Although APE specialists in the public schools are available as valuable resources for general and special educators, community college and university faculty who specialize in adapted physical activity can also be excellent sources for practitioners in the field. Most community colleges hire adapted physical activity instructors, and many university faculty members have a specialty in this area. These individuals can be excellent resources for community-based programs. Figure 3.5 illustrates the many diverse roles that adapted physical education specialists play in the schools.

Physical Therapists

Physical therapists (PTs) are medical health care professionals with scientific training in understanding the human body and how it functions in order to remediate dysfunction. Specifically, the focus of the PT is on mobility, balance, posture, and the activities of daily living as they pertain to motor control and coordination of movement. Physical therapists are also trained in the use of environmental and assistive devices to facilitate function in daily living. A practitioner might consult with a PT in regard to specific positioning for optimal performance in an activity. PTs might also consult with practitioners about gross motor function, exercises, and activities to facilitate abilities following the termination of physical therapy. Termination might be based on the learner no longer needing therapy or on the lack of medical coverage. In adult exercise programs, physical activity practitioners often pick up programming when therapies terminate.

Role of the Adapted Physical Educator

Advocate. An advocate is defined as one who pleads another's cause. APE teachers often serve as advocates for the students or individuals they work with. An example includes helping parents in times of transition as a student moves from one grade to another or one school to another. In this case the APE teacher is often the person who knows the student best and might have worked with the child for many years. APE teachers might also serve as advocates for students to facilitate inclusion or get services or programming within the community.

Educator. APE teachers also serve as educators. In this role they give information to others such as teachers, instructional assistants, parents, and others based on the training from their discipline. In the educator role, APE teachers share such things as curriculum ideas, sample lesson plans, ideas for modifications, and equipment; they also demonstrate teaching episodes. They might assist an individual or an entire group. APE teachers often serve groups of teachers or parents through in-service trainings or conference presentations.

Courier. Couriers obtain information from one source and share it with another. This information is usually outside of their domain of expertise. An example of playing a courier role is getting medical information about an individual to share with a general physical education teacher about possible contraindications of an activity or obtaining behavioral information from the special education teacher to share with the classroom teacher to make sure the interventions are consistent.

Resource coordinator. This role includes obtaining services or coordinating facilities. An example of this role is providing information to parents about community programs and activities. Responsibilities could include scheduling to bring in outside organizations for assemblies such as disability dance troupes or wheelchair basketball teams. In this role, APE teachers need to work closely with custodial and secretarial staff for scheduling and planning of events.

Supporter or helper. This is the role that APE teachers often play when they're first working with a general physical education teacher or classroom teacher. It's the role they play when establishing rapport and in helping to maintain positive relationships with individuals they consult with. In this role, APE teachers give positive feedback, help with equipment, and assist the general physical education teacher in any way necessary. In this role, APE teachers are often serving within the context of someone else's general physical education program. They might also assist with general education students and students that are on the APE caseload.

Figure 3.5 Five roles of the adapted physical educator as identified by Lytle 2004.

Occupational Therapists

Occupational therapists (OTs) are medical health care professionals who deal with the remediation of dysfunction. Their focus is on interventions for activities of daily living and stress adaptability (Pratt & Allen, 1989). OT training emphasizes sensory motor integration, activities of daily living, fine motor skills, positioning, assistive devices, and adapting behavior or equipment to help perform such tasks as eating, dressing, playing, and working. A practitioner might want to consult an OT about adapting the grip of an implement (e.g., racket, paddle, or golf club), facilitating an individual's participation in physical activity, or using devices that might improve performance.

Speech and Language Pathologists

Speech and language pathologists (SLPs) focus on the development of speech, language, and hearing. Physical education practitioners collaborate with speech pathologists on how to communicate with individuals. Goals and objectives among the two disciplines can often be inte-

grated quite easily. For example, language is inherent in movement activities, and practitioners can easily integrate speech and language goals from the SLP into the motor programming. The SLP might also find it helpful to integrate gross motor goals during speech because motor activities are often motivating and fun for children. In some cases, the SLP and the adapted physical education teacher might even present lessons together, which can be particularly effective when working with young children in a play-based approach.

General Educators

General educators include teachers within the public school system who aren't special education teachers, such as classroom teachers, elementary physical education specialists, or general physical education teachers. The general education teacher is often the one in the school setting who knows the child best. This teacher typically sees the child on a daily basis and has a good understanding of his or her learning style and strengths. The general education teacher is often familiar with how the child interacts with peers in different settings, including the classroom, playground, lunch room, and perhaps elsewhere. This teacher also knows particular behaviors the student might have and understands the curriculum being taught and how it will be presented. This is important information in team planning and problem solving, such as when determining modifications or variations for instruction.

Psychologists

Psychologists are frequently part of individual educational planning teams for students within the public school system and provide a variety of services, including expertise in development, learning, counseling, and assessment. They serve on teams aimed at meeting the educational needs of students having difficulty in the school system, as well as on collaborative service delivery teams within the community. One of the roles of the psychologist on such teams is helping to assess the child's achievement and abilities to allow for successful and educational planning. School psychologists also consult with teachers, parents, and other team members to help them address the development or behavior management of a child. School psychologists might also engage in district-wide work, such as serving on curriculum committees, planning and evaluating programs, and doing in-service training. In addition, they might contribute to classroom education on emotional awareness, coping skills, social skills, and other topics.

Nurses

Nurses are often helpful in providing necessary medical information for programming and in alerting practitioners and others about precautions that should be taken. Nurses might also contribute by explaining medical protocols for standard procedure for an individual with a disability or in an emergency. Individuals with severe allergies, medications, or other health concerns might have a nurse who is part of their individualized education plan or individual home program. Most nurses are experienced with medications and their possible side-effects. They are also valuable connections to the medical community and sometimes a practitioner's best resource for medical information or in making medical referrals. In an infant program, a discharge nurse from a neonatal intensive care unit (NICU) might assist a family in connecting with early intervention services. For seniors, a community health care nurse might assist in caring for individuals who need daily assistance in the home.

Physicians

Other important players on the team might include general practitioners, neurologists, orthopedists, endocrinologists, or other specialists who work with participants within a physical activity program. Physicians are likely to serve as a referral source for community-based programs.

They also provide information regarding restrictions to physical activity participation, and their medical records can supply important information about a participant's medical history. Although, because of their schedules, physicians might not be a part of typical program planning meetings, their information and expertise can be helpful to the team and shouldn't be overlooked.

Recreation Therapists

Recreation therapists (RTs) plan, organize, and direct recreational programs for individuals with disabilities. They are often excellent resources for community activities and programs for individuals of all abilities. Depending on the interests and needs of the individual, RT programs are typically for such activities as social interaction, games, aquatics, gardening, arts and crafts, and expressive arts. RTs work in many settings, including hospitals, rehabilitation centers, schools, community parks, recreational departments, and correctional institutions.

Music Therapists

Music therapists are trained to use music to promote the physical, cognitive, psychological, and social needs of individuals of all abilities. They use the creative forms of singing, moving to, or listening to music to promote general health and well-being. Music therapists work in such settings as hospitals, community and mental health agencies, rehabilitation centers, day care facilities, nursing homes, and schools. Some practitioners collaborate with a music therapist to incorporate music into their physical activity programs. The presence of music enhances learning and motivation for some individuals.

Orientation and Mobility Specialists

Orientation and mobility (O&M) specialists provide one-on-one instruction to individuals who are visually impaired. Their role is to help individuals achieve independence and confidence in traveling in and through their environments. Mobility is the ability to travel from one place to another, and orientation is understanding one's position in space as it relates to other objects or people within the environment. O&M specialists might provide assessment, instruction, consultation and collaboration, family support, or in-service training. They can assist the physical activity practitioner in examining an environment's accessibility and helping to develop appropriate goals for learners.

← **THINK BACK**

1. Which professional role might you play in your future career? Describe three key professionals and how they might help you in providing services to an individual.

2. Think back to Emily Booth's IEP meeting about Maddy. What team members might be present at Maddy's IEP meeting? Why do you think these members would be important to the team in getting a holistic picture of Maddy?

Figure 3.6 shows examples of strategies to help team members connect and stay connected.

▶ MODELS OF CONSULTATION

Now that we've seen the range of individuals who might serve on the multidisciplinary team of physical activity programs, we can examine the process through which these team members interact. The terms "consultation" and "collaboration" have both been discussed in the literature. Consultation is typically defined as one professional assisting another professional. The dynamic often involves an unequal relationship between individuals,

1. Call your local community college and ask for the coordinator of their adapted physical activity program.
2. Ask for the names of the special education staff at your school, including the APE, PT, OT, psychologist, and SLP.
3. Make weekly or monthly calls to parents or family members of participants.
4. E-mail or call physicians every six months to a year to check health records and receive updated information.
5. Invite other team members to present a workshop or lecture within your program.
6. Invite a team member to team or co-teach with you.
7. Ask other team members to observe your program and make recommendations.
8. Use worksheets to discuss issues or needs when it's difficult to find time to meet.
9. Keep notes, minutes, or a communication log.
10. Ask for feedback from team members regarding your services.

Figure 3.6 Strategies to increase connections between team members.

with the consultant serving as the "expert" (Coben, Thomas, Sattler, & Morsink, 1997). Collaboration, however, involves a process of two equal individuals defining and solving a problem together.

Collaboration is ". . . a way to humanize the service delivery system. It improves the outcomes for children with special health needs and their families. Collaboration facilitates satisfying and effective relationships" (Bishop, Woll, & Arango 1993, p. 11). This need for more collaborative relationships in the consultation process emerged in the 1980s, and the term "collaborative consultation" became prevalent in special education literature (Coben, Thomas, Sattler, & Morsink, 1997). Collaborative consultation, as a model, evolved from three previous models: mental health consultation, behavioral consultation, and process consultation (Conoley & Conoley, 1988).

Mental Health Consultation Model

Mental health consultation is concerned with relationships among people. In this model, the consultant focuses on the teacher's needs and doesn't work directly with the student except to model a possible instructional strategy or technique for the teacher. Premises of this model include equal status of participants, voluntary participation, supportiveness, and interactions based on the consultee's needs. The role of the consultant is to be supportive and prevent coming across as the expert by seeking the consultee's input, not taking credit for ideas, and emphasizing equal status. Additional strategies used by the consultant might include discussion, use of parables, confrontation, and exploration of feelings. The focus of this model is on teacher attitudes and behaviors and establishing a trusting relationship.

Behavioral Consultation Model

Behavioral consultation was developed by school psychologists out of the need to assist teachers in dealing with behavioral problems in the classroom (Gutkin & Curtis, 1982). The focus of this model is to change the individual's behavior by changing the teacher's behavior. The behavioral approach to consultation is directive in nature and focused on identifying the problem behaviors of individuals and designing strategies for remediation through the teaching of new skills and knowledge to the teacher or instructor. The behavioral consultation approach is linear and involves the following five steps: problem identification, data collection, solution selection, intervention, and evaluation (Dustin & Ehly, 1984; Conoley & Conoley, 1988; Friend & Cook, 1996; Gutkin & Curtis, 1982; Gutkin, 1996). Included in this process is systematic data collection for problem identification and evaluation done by either the consultee or the consultant. Because of the documented evidence of positive change through systematic data collection, behavioral consultation is the most widely used model of consultation in the schools (Conoley & Conoley, 1988). However, this model is also used in adult community-based programs and adult-supported living settings.

Process Consultation Model

The process consultation model is different from the previous two models in that it focuses on the system or group (Friend & Cook, 1996; Conoley & Conoley, 1988) and emphasizes the process rather than the product or outcome. Process consultation stems from the need for teachers to interact on many levels, including leading groups, setting agendas, solving problems, managing conflict, communicating, and giving feedback. Success in these interactions depends primarily on effective communication skills. The process-oriented consultant is interested in group dynamics, how groups function, and interpersonal skill building. This approach requires administrative support and a belief that better interactions result in better learning environments. Example strategies in the process consultation model include needs analysis, data collection and feedback, and simulations. A possible advantage of the process consultation model is that it is a systems approach and focuses on the entire group rather than on an individual teacher or learner. By affecting the group as a whole, a greater number of individuals are influenced. However, this model might fail to remediate a specific individual's needs and concerns within a given class or program.

Collaborative Consultation Model

Collaborative consultation is a model of consultation that combines elements of three other models: mental health, behavioral, and process consultation. Elements of the mental health model include the need for equal status, trust, establishing positive relationships, and the modeling of strategies for change. In addition, the stages of consultation as defined by the behavioral model are also present in the collaborative consultation model. These include needs identification, data collection and analysis, solution selection, implementation, and evaluation (Bradley, 1994; Friend & Cook, 1996; Idol, Paolucci-Whitcomb, & Nevin, 1995; Pugach & Johnson, 1995). Finally, collaborative consultation takes from the process consultation model the need for effective communication and interpersonal skills. Figure 3.7 shows the models of consultation that have contributed to the model of collaborative consultation.

Friend and Cook (1996) define collaboration consultation as " . . . a style for direct interaction between at least two coequal parties voluntarily engaged in shared decision making as they work toward a common goal" (p. 6). This model of consultation is based on several assumptions (Friend & Cook, 1996; Idol et al., 1994):

- That each individual engages in collaboration voluntarily
- That all parties have equal power and equal value
- That individuals agree on a common goal
- That all share in responsibility and decision making
- That resources and information are shared freely among participants
- That individual team members are equally accountable for outcomes

Effective collaborative consultants recognize that the input of several individuals allows for greater creativity regarding solutions and acknowledge the complexities of setting goals

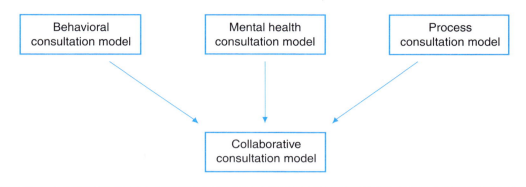

Figure 3.7 Aspects of the mental health, behavioral, and process consultation models contribute to the collaborative consultation model.

(Pugach & Johnson, 1995). Collaborative consultants are reflective about their own personal practices and enjoy the social interactive process. In addition, they don't judge others but are open and receptive and value the thoughts and ideas of others. Information brought by all professionals is equally valued and has equal status in addressing learners' individual needs (Friend & Cook, 1996). The collaborative consultative model recognizes the interchanging roles that team members play. For example, the general physical education teacher might be the consultant regarding what a student's behavior is like during active dynamic situations that the classroom teachers might not see. In another instance, an individual with a disability might be the consultant by sharing perceptions on his or her needs and possible interventions (Dettmer, Dyck, & Thurston, 1999). The collaborative consultation model acknowledges the complexities of setting goals, recognizes that each person in the process has valuable information to contribute, and values the input of several individuals because it allows for greater creativity in finding solutions (Pugach & Johnson, 1995).

In addition to acknowledging that each member of the team has valuable and critical knowledge to contribute, members are also comfortable with "role release." Role release means that team members are willing to share ideas from their knowledge base that are implemented by other team members. For example, a physical therapist might train a practitioner on stretching exercises for a learner to work on during an activity program; a speech pathologist might show an adapted physical educator some speech and language goals to integrate into the physical education program.

In summary, the collaborative consultation model is a wonderful blend of the best aspects of the mental health, behavioral, and process models of consultation. It focuses on effective communication, equal value, equal status, role release, and respect for all team members in providing the most effective programming for individuals of differing abilities. Because of the inclusive nature of the collaborative consultation model and its predominant use in special education literature, we highly recommend the collaborative consultation model.

▶ COLLABORATIVE TEAM PROCESS AND ISSUES

Teams are generally formed to assist in determining needs, writing individual goals, designing programs, and tracking progress. The members of the collaborative team are determined by the needs of the individual and family members. Desirable characteristics of effective team members include being open, caring, warm, understanding, positive, task-oriented, enthusiastic, calm, flexible, and respectful of others' points of view (Kampwirth, 2003). Each member brings to the team his or her perspective and skills, which contributes to a holistic view of the child or individual. The team's purpose is to develop a shared framework, create a unified set of goals, engage in problem solving, and evaluate their effectiveness.

Five Phases In Becoming An Effective Team

Teams typically go through the following five phases in becoming an effective team. Some teams move through this process quickly, and others might never reach the later stages. Teams that do reach the later stages might revisit the other stages as the needs of the team change.

1. Forming—members examine their task, learn more about each other, and clarify their reason for existing as a team.

2. Storming—members resolve issues of power, leadership, procedures, and goals.

3. Norming—teams establish role relationships and define leadership roles and procedures for accomplishing their work.

4. Performing—members align themselves and work toward achieving the team's goal.

5. Adjourning—having completed its task, the team disbands.

From Friend and Cook *Interactions,* 3e. Allyn and Bacon, Boston, MA. Copyright © 2000 by Pearson Education. Reprinted by permission of the publisher.

Collaborative Teams

- Have established group norms
- Promote the idea that we "sink or swim together"
- Develop and support goals together
- Share resources, ideas, and knowledge freely
- Have face-to-face interaction
- Share successes and recognize each other for positive work
- Hold each member accountable for the group process

Many factors can influence the success of the team and this collaborative team process. These include the decision process; quality of documentation; willingness of professionals to share their professional territory, skills, ideas and resources; communication skills of team members; and the identified benefits and barriers to successful collaborative consultation. In the following sections we'll discuss each of these issues in detail.

Collaborative Consultation Decision Process

When the collaborative process is used, all individuals on the team benefit. Individual participants profit from the expertise of several individuals as well as their own critical input into the decision process. Team members gain greater knowledge through the process of sharing ideas with other members, which leads to greater professional expertise, satisfaction, and reduced isolation. The collective team process generally follows five steps (Bradley, 1994; Friend & Cook, 2000; Idol et al., 1995; Pugach & Johnson, 1995):

1. Needs identification
2. Data collection and analysis
3. Solution selection
4. Implementation
5. Evaluation

Let's briefly look at each of these steps one at a time.

1. *Needs identification.* For example, a student is having trouble participating in physical education with his peers or an adult is having balance difficulties while engaging in a physical activity program. The first step in the process is to identify the cause of the problem and what needs to be done to solve it. Once the needs have been identified, the team can begin to collect

valuable information (step 2) to assist in the process of deciding how to address the problem. Depending on the age of the person, the setting, and the team members, needs might be identified by the individual learner, a single team member, or by a combination of members.

2. *Data collection.* This step includes all kinds of resources, including a possible individualized assessment with both formal and informal procedures. These might include standardized tests; observation; interviews with teachers or practitioners, parents, and learners; review of health records; and any other method that might provide insight into the needs of the individual. During this step, the team seeks to discover as much information as possible to determine what the strengths and concerns are for the individual. Once all available information is gathered, the team discusses possible solutions (step 3). As much as possible, the learner should be a part of this process. The individual and his or her family are important members of the team.

3. *Solution selection.* This step begins with a review of the data and involves the process of determining what intervention will best assist the individual in meeting his or her goals for successful participation. Only after a review of all the available information can the team begin to generate solutions. A short brainstorming session is a great way to start this process, and all ideas should be considered. Following the brainstorming session, ideas can be evaluated for effectiveness, adapted, and narrowed to determine the best solution possible. Solutions or interventions could be anything from changing the setting or equipment to adjusting instruction to working on specific skills. Possibilities for intervention are limited only by the creativity of the team. The data-collection and solution-selection steps involve the input of the entire team in an attempt to gain a complete picture of the individual.

4. *Implementation.* Once solutions have been selected, they need to be implemented. The implementation phase includes the initiation of services and the beginning of programming or changes. Implementation doesn't necessarily require the entire team. In fact, it might be one individual, or several, who implements the intervention. In a physical activity setting, the practitioner, general education teacher, adapted physical education teacher, instructional assistant, peer, or family member might be responsible for implementation. In many cases, a combination of individuals work together to provide a quality program.

5. *Evaluation.* This step is one of the most critical steps in the process. It's through continued data collection and evaluation that practitioners can determine if specific interventions or ideas are working. Data alone are useless, so it's up to the collaborative team to determine the meaningfulness and accuracy of the data collected. Data collection might include both formative (ongoing) and summative (final) methods, as discussed in chapter 4. Documentation of data and evaluation is critical to determine the success of a program.

Documentation

Documentation is one of the most critical aspects of the consultation process, partly because the practitioner isn't always the one who implements the plan. For this reason, it is critical for the practitioner to have all the necessary records for collecting or tracking progress. This information can be collected by the teacher, an assistant, a family member, the individual, the adapted physical educator, the community practitioner, or another team member, as long as the progress is documented in a systematic way. Documentation should be consistent with the goals and interventions determined by the team and should track how much progress is made. If no change occurs, the team can identify this early and reconvene to determine possible alternatives. Simple methods of data collection include notes from daily observation, activity logs, systematic observations of behavior, checklists, and rubrics. We'll discuss data collection more in chapter 4.

However, all of the above steps to effective consultation cannot be accomplished unless effective positive relationships have been formed. For many professionals that are itinerant (travel from place to place) this can be challenging because each environment has it's own culture and climate. Itinerant professionals have to be good at reading environments and communication signals to establish rapport, build relationships, and thus work collaboratively together to meet the needs of individuals within a variety of physical activity programs or settings.

Professional Territory and Skills

Practitioners serving as itinerant consultants often work for a district, county, or special program. These professionals usually provide services to several different locations. A survey of adapted physical education (APE) teachers in California showed that the range of sites served was from 1 to 30, with an average of 6 (Lytle & Johnson, 2000). Itinerant professionals, such as adapted physical educators, physical therapists, occupational therapists, and recreation therapists, usually have an office at a single site and serve individuals at several locations. Most general physical education teachers or physical activity professionals have their own gyms, rooms, and fields that make up their professional home. This space might be shared with a few other individuals in their department or program. Itinerant consultants should keep this in mind when they enter another professional's territory. They are a guest in that environment, whether it's a family's house or a professional's office, and must be aware of the expected behaviors and climate of each school or community environment. Depending on personalities, frequency of interaction, and many other factors, it can take several weeks, months, or even years for consultants to establish rapport with teachers or professionals they collaborate with. The importance of establishing rapport, using effective communication, and being aware of the environment in which professionals work can't be overstated.

Skills identified as necessary to be an effective consultant for physical activity are shown in table 3.2 (Lytle & Collier, 2002). Ideally, skills include good communication and listening, good people skills, strong content knowledge in general and adapted physical education, respect, and

Table 3.2 **Top Rated Descriptors of APE Consultants and Number of Votes by Six APE Specialists**

Great consultant	Skills	Attitude	Knowledge
People skills (5)	People skills (5)	Disability awareness (4)	Content in GPE/APE (6)
Communication skills (5)	Can modify and adapt (4)	Professionalism (4)	Assessment (4)
Knowledge of APE and motor skills (4)	Organizational skills (3)	Flexible (4)	Writing goals, objectives (3)
See others' point of view, how they are thinking and feeling (3)	Problem solver (2)	Self-motivated (2)	Program planning (3)
	Communication skills (2)	Enthusiastic (2)	IEP process (2)
Sense of humor (3)	Big bag of tricks (2)	Teamwork (2)	California Framework (2)
Good listener (2)	Smile and be pleasant (2)	Cooperative (2)	Task analysis (2)
Respect (2)	Quick thinker (1)	Personality (2)	Motor skills (2)
Positive (2)	Punctual (1)	Collaborative attitude (1)	Understand law (1)
Flexible (1)	Time management (1)	Be able to let things go and not bother you (1)	Knowledge about disability (1)
Easy going (1)	Respect (1)	Even tempered (1)	Know what is feasible (1)
Consistently there (1)	See others' point of view (1)	Reflective (1)	Professional library (1)
Gain trust (1)	Adapt how you approach people (1)	Approachable (1)	Developmental skills (1)
	Physical skills (1)	Diplomatic (1)	
	Attention to detail (1)	Positive (1)	
	Know where to find information (1)		
	Perspective (1)		

APAQ 2002, 19(1).

a sense of humor (Emes, Longmuir, & Downs, 2002; Horton & Brown, 1990; Knoff, McKenna, & Riser, 1991; Lytle & Collier, 2002). For many teachers, communication and interaction skills must be learned on the job. However, many preservice training programs are starting to integrate effective consultation training into their curriculum (Yocum & Cossairt, 1996).

Benefits and Barriers

Collaborative consultation can be a highly effective way to provide services for individuals of all abilities. First, it allows individuals to be educated with their peers or colleagues in a natural setting (Block, 2000; R.K. Lytle, 1999). Second, it can provide parents or caregivers with a sense of comfort, knowing they have a collaborative team for support and services. Third, collaborative teams provide a holistic view of the individual. Fourth, collaborative teams provide greater accountability for progress because all members are responsible for outcomes. Fifth, all team members gain professionally by learning from each other, which reduces the possibility of professional isolation. Finally, collaborative consultation allows for creative problem solving.

Along with the many benefits of the collaborative approach, some challenges do exist. The two primary barriers to effective consultation are (1) not having enough time and (2) resistance among participants on the team (Karge, McClure, & Patton, 1995; R.K. Lytle, 1999). The demands placed on professionals in all capacities are tremendous, and consultation is often added on top of their typical responsibilities. It can be challenging for team members to find the time to meet for discussion. Adapted physical education teachers often find themselves contacting general educators during their prep period, lunch, recess, between classes, or after school. Communication also frequently takes place via written notes, letters, documents, e-mails, and telephone calls. However, the most effective planning takes place when individuals have time to meet face to face, even for only 10 to 20 minutes. Most professionals relish the opportunity to talk with others and share ideas. However, time might be wasted on complaints, school politics, stories, or other issues. It's important for professionals to listen and recognize this need. Collaborative team members might need to set aside a few minutes for informal discussion and then move to a more structured planning time. It can be helpful if practitioners come to the meeting with upcoming curricular activities and related instructional plans. Then the actual meeting time can be spent reviewing the curriculum and discussing possible modifications, adaptations, or how the material will be split if coteaching or other collaborative teaching methods are to be used. The adapted physical educator can follow up by making any modifications to the curriculum or supplying needed materials. This model can help professionals be more efficient with their time.

Although adapted physical education teachers might have some flex time built into their schedules, the challenge in collaboration might involve general educators who don't have release time. Adapted educators have to be flexible in finding ways to meet with teachers. Administrators and facility supervisors can often assist teachers in finding time for consultation. When time becomes available, teachers must be well prepared and efficient in their use of the precious minutes. There never seems to be enough time for the kind of collaboration professionals desire (Friend & Cook, 2000).

Aside from time, the other major challenge for effective collaborative consultation is working with people who are resistant or lack proper understanding of physical activity curricula. As we mentioned earlier, it's important for practitioners to be able to share their curriculum and program focus with team members so they can collaborate on planning methods. For example, if a classroom teacher isn't providing physical education or is only providing inappropriate activities, it can be very challenging for the adapted physical education teacher to brainstorm modifications. Consultants hear comments such as, "We don't have time for PE" or "We've been playing dodge ball and kickball." In such cases, the adapted physical education teacher has to both consult on how to modify the teacher's activities and also provide some educating and curriculum ideas for the teacher—as well as supply in-service training (figure 3.8)! When

Figure 3.8 Consultation can also assist teachers in changing instructional strategies that limit student participation and skill practice.

team members don't appreciate the value of physical activity, consultations can be challenging. Regardless of the situation, professionals must first establish a trusting relationship and positive rapport before anything can be accomplished. Circumstances might require informing team members of the importance of physical activity and providing examples of how to create developmentally appropriate activities and programs. Physical activity practitioners might need to provide sample lessons and model instructional techniques for others. Regardless of the situation, team members have a responsibility to do whatever they can to work effectively to provide quality physical activity for all individuals.

Collaborative Connections

There's often some confusion about how adapted physical activity, physical therapy (PT), and occupational therapy (OT) interface. To what extent do they provide the same services? Although they're all based on the scientific foundation of human movement, these three fields are in fact very different disciplines. One key element that makes adapted physical education very different from PT and OT is that physical education is a curriculum area that all children in the public schools must receive and is defined as a direct service under special education law IDEA. Although "adapted" physical education is not required for all children, physical education is required. Adapted physical education should be viewed as an academic content area, just as reading and math are content areas of education. On the other hand, PT and OT are considered related services under IDEA and aren't required for all children. PT and OT are provided to students only if deemed "educationally necessary," which means if the child needs PT or OT services in order to participate or access the educational program. For example, a child might need OT services to help with modifications and adaptation for fine motor skills so he or she can complete assignments and writing tasks on time. In another example, a child might need sensory integration training to help with focus and attention to tasks.

1. Think back to Emily's first IEP meeting with Maddy. What will be the process in identifying the needs for Maddy?

2. What documentation might the team use in this process?

3. What are some of the benefits of the team process for Maddy?

4. What are some of the challenges the team will face in this process?

For adults, adapted physical activity can serve as a means to lifelong health and wellness with a focus on prevention, maintenance, and well-being. OT and PT are medical services that can be a valuable resource for program planning and design within any physical activity program. Team members should recognize that these three disciplines aren't interchangeable. Yes, they all deal with motor abilities, but each has a specific body of knowledge and expertise to assist in planning and programming for individuals of differing abilities. These three disciplines, when collaborating, can provide the best possible services to all individuals.

COLLABORATIVE STRATEGIES FOR TEACHERS AND PRACTITIONERS

Many collaborative strategies exist for practitioners to use to help individuals with disabilities be successful in physical activity settings. We'll discuss a few of these strategies here, including methods for creating time for communication, developing positive relationships, and implementing coteaching techniques.

Strategies to Create Time

As we've mentioned, time is one of the primary challenges to effective collaborative teaming. For this reason, it's critical to have strategies to help create face-to-face meetings. The first and easiest strategy is to have built-in meeting times. For example, establish that the first Friday of every month the team will meet at a designated time and place. This method is frequently used for faculty or staff meetings and can be used effectively for teams that consistently work together. However, team members often don't have similar schedules, so weekly meetings aren't realistic. In such as case, it might be necessary to hold meetings at nontraditional times, such as Monday evenings or Thursday mornings before school. Community programs might also schedule meetings at nontraditional times, such as Saturday afternoons or late in the evening after a community program. Ideally, collaborative teams should meet monthly on a regular schedule—face to face, if possible. If face-to-face meetings just can't be worked out, another form of regular communication must occur; communication is critical to collaboration. Each member should have all the information of the group so that planning isn't fragmented. By using such methods as weekly e-mail,

Ideal Meeting Schedule

1. Entire team meets face to face at least every three months.

2. Weekly e-mail updates on progress and questions are sent to all team members.

3. Each member keeps a daily log of activity, interactions, and questions for team reference.

4. Each member visits or observes other team members at least once a month. In some cases it might be necessary to observe or work as coteachers once or twice a week.

communication journals, phone messages, and 5- or 10-minute interactions or observations with individual team members, the group can be highly effective and efficient. Within the public school system, many districts have created specific release days or minimum days to create time for teachers to meet. Within community-based programs, scheduling should be more flexible.

Strategies to Create Positive Relationships

Establishing a positive rapport is paramount to effective teaming. Certainly this begins with effective communication skills and ensuring that other team members feel listened to and heard. Listening and reflecting on the other professionals' ideas or concerns can be very helpful. Finding things another team member is doing that are helpful and effective and commenting on them helps to promote a positive relationship. This can be done verbally, in notes, or through writing a letter to the other team member's employer, commenting on how helpful their program is. Other ideas include the following:

- Honor each member's style of interaction.
- Acknowledge caseloads or class size and the demands that accompany this workload.
- Honor each member's teaching and management style.
- Invite others to visit your program.
- Bring snacks to share.
- Write frequent thank you notes.
- Invite families of other professionals to participate in special events, such as open house or other activities.

Coteaching

Coteaching occurs when two professionals serve a diverse group of learners in a single setting. Traditionally, coteaching involves two teachers, but it could involve more. In a school-based physical education setting, coteaching typically includes the general physical education teacher and the adapted physical education teacher working together to provide instruction to an entire class of diverse learners. In a community-based setting, two or more practitioners might work with a group of individuals in an activity program. Coteaching provides a host of benefits to the learners and practitioners involved, including the following:

1. Eliminates the need for students to leave the gym or facility for extra help
2. Allows for increased engaged time in physical activity
3. Ensures correlation of physical activity content for all students
4. Allows all students to benefit from the instruction of two teachers
5. Increases learner–teacher interaction
6. Prevents stigma of being pulled from activity for special help
7. Allows for development of social skills
8. Promotes positive interactions and acceptance of all individuals
9. Allows for individualized support and modifications within a heterogeneous group
10. Provides for the sharing of ideas and resources to enhance the knowledge base for all team members involved in the program

In the following sections we'll briefly discuss several styles of coteaching, including one teaching, one observing; station instruction; parallel instruction; and team instruction.

One Teaching, One Observing

In this instructional style one person is primarily responsible for the instruction, and the other is the observer. The role of the observer is generally determined by the coteaching team and might include watching a single individual, a small group, or the group as a whole. The observer has the opportunity to look for specific behaviors or skills. As we mentioned earlier in this chapter, it's extremely important to document observations with specific coding forms and observation notes.

The observer might also assist individual learners as needed and move about the workspace to ensure success for every participant. The advantage of this approach is that it doesn't require a lot of joint planning time. However, care needs to be taken that no one person is feeling that he or she is carrying the burden. Both members of the teaching team may play either role. It's a good idea to vary this, at least occasionally, so that team members have the opportunity to appreciate each other's role and to learn how perspectives and insights differ from different teaching perspectives. For example, in a community volleyball program one person might serve as the instructor for the lesson and the other roam around the instructional space and provide individuals cues, feedback, and assistance to aid in participant learning.

Figure 3.9 Stations can support learning for individuals with a differing abilities.

Station Instruction

This approach allows for a variety of skills to be taught and for participants to break up into smaller groups (figure 3.9). For example, in an elementary class, teachers might have motor stations for balance, locomotor skills, throwing, and catching. In a community-based setting, there might be stations for weight training, stretching, and aerobic activity. Coinstructors each take a station to assist learners with instruction. When it isn't possible for an instructor to be at each station, then some of the stations can be set up to review familiar skills. Learners can work at these stations alone, and instructors can assist at the stations that include new skills. Volunteers, family members, university students, or cross-age peers are all good sources for additional support when using a station approach to instruction. However, be sure to train inexperienced staff prior to their supervision of activities.

Parallel Instruction

In this approach, coteachers break the group in half, and instructors deliver the exact same content simultaneously. Coteachers must plan lessons jointly. The main

Figure 3.10 Here one teacher serves as the facilitator and the other as the recorder.

benefit of this approach is that teachers work with smaller groups. However, both teachers must know the content. How the group is divided depends on the purpose of the instruction. Groups might be divided based on competitive levels or to create heterogeneous groups so that individuals can teach each other throughout the lesson. An example of this technique might be during the beginning instructional phase of a new unit in which teachers want to provide specific feedback to students. The smaller groups allow for better observation and more feedback from the teacher.

Team Teaching

In a team-teaching environment both teachers are responsible for the planning and implementation of the instruction, just as they are in parallel instruction. However, during the actual lesson they take turns giving instruction, providing feedback, demonstrating, or facilitating (figure 3.10). This differs from the "one teaching, one observing" approach in that each teacher or facilitator plays both roles in a single lesson. Each facilitator provides some instruction as well as moving about the instructional space to assist learners. In a community-based program, one teacher might instruct the group while the other helps an individual with modifications or physical assistance, as necessary; the teachers might then switch roles for the next phase of the lesson.

Although coteaching can be time consuming, it's a highly effective means of enhancing instruction for diverse groups of learners. Regardless of which coteaching method is employed, both individuals are responsible for the success of the class and the individuals within it. Which method works best depends on the nature of the learners in the program and the content to be taught.

← THINK BACK

1. Think back to Emily Booth, the new teacher at Brooks Middle School. How might the adapted physical educator, physical therapist, or occupational therapist work toward developing a positive rapport with Emily? What strategies might the team use to create an effective team environment that supports the individuals in Emily's program?

▶ SUMMARY

Teams are made up of two or more individuals working toward a common goal. Each team member brings to the team their frame of reference, which comes from their training, beliefs, and background. These varying frames of reference, or perspectives, allow for a holistic view of an individual as the team begins to plan appropriate programming. Paramount to the teaming process are effective communication skills in order to create a common vision, determine appropriate goals, share ideas and resources, and problem-solve issues and needs. Team members must respect each other and value the diverse perspectives of others. Members of the team include the individual and family, as well as (possibly) the PT, OT, adapted physical educator, speech pathologist, general educator, psychologist, nurse, physician, or other activity leaders. Although there have been many models of consultation, the collaborative consultation model is the most current and desired model for professionals in educational and community settings. However, for effective collaboration to take place, professionals must establish team norms and make time for effective planning and communication.

What Do You Think?

1. Think about your personal and professional history and your previous experience with individuals with differing abilities. Describe your personal frame of reference. How might you interact with professionals in other disciplines?

2. Think of someone you respect and enjoy talking with. Referring to the types of communication described in this chapter, identify what and how this person uses communication effectively when talking with you.

3. What professionals from the team have you interacted with? Interview one of them about his or her background, training, and experiences to better understand his or her frame of reference and how you might interact with this discipline in the future.

What Would You Do?

Scenario 3.1

1. Following is a dialogue between two professionals. Can you identify the types of communication the listener is using during each of her responses?

   Practitioner: I'm excited about working with Jackie in my program, but I'm really nervous about whether we can meet her needs. We've never had someone with her level of abilities before, and I'm a little worried about working with someone with autism (see appendix A).

   Listener (Response 1): So, are you saying you have some concerns about her participation?

   Practitioner: Yes, I'm afraid the program might be too difficult for her. I'm not sure how to modify all the activities. Some of them I'm sure will be no problem, like swimming and aerobics, but I have no clue about kickboxing and tennis.

   Listener (Response 2): You're concerned about how to adapt for kickboxing and tennis but feel pretty comfortable with swimming and aerobics?

Practitioner: Yes, the individual activities will be fine, but I'm really concerned about the partner activities. Jackie might get injured, and that could be a liability issue for the program.

Listener (Response 3): It seems as though you're very concerned about Jackie's safety during these activities. Is that right?

How did you do? Check your answers.

Response 1: Clarifying the content of what was shared

Response 2: Paraphrasing or summarizing what was said

Response 3: Perception checking of the emotion behind what was shared

2. Who might be on the team of individuals working with Jackie?

3. Describe the five steps to the decision process as it relates to Jackie's physical activity setting.

4. What types of collaborative strategies might be helpful in providing appropriate physical activity programming for Jackie?

Scenario 3.2

Bob has decided to begin a new exercise program at the community YMCA. He's committed to maintaining his fitness and abilities for as long as possible and has determined that the better physical condition he's in, now that he has retired, the better he'll be able to deal with his diagnosis of Parkinson's (see appendix A). Bob loves to play golf and has recently retired in Arizona to a home on the golf course so he can play regularly and enjoy the benefits of the great winter weather. In the summers, when it's really hot, he plans on staying at his cabin in the mountains of Oregon, not too far from where he worked for more than 30 years. There he enjoys fishing and walking. Bob has a new doctor at the Mayo clinic in Scottsdale and has been working with a PT. On Bob's first visit he met a trainer at the YMCA named Steve. Steve will be designing an individualized program for Bob.

1. What team members should Steve talk with as he begins to develop a program for Bob?

2. What questions would Steve want to ask each of these team members? Indicate whether each question is open or closed.

Program Focus and Assessment

Learning Outcomes

After completing this chapter, you should be able to

» describe how the purposes of assessment differ across various inclusive physical activity contexts;

» explain the factors that influence the assessment process and discuss assessment strategies effective in providing meaningful assessment data;

» discuss the difference between formal and informal assessment approaches and implications for individuals with diverse ability levels; and

» identify the focus of inclusive physical activity programming across the life span and explain the connection between curriculum and assessment.

INCLUDING ALL INDIVIDUALS

Terrance just obtained a job teaching adapted physical education for Jackson County schools. In his new job, he'll serve as an itinerant teacher for several rural schools. He has just received his caseload and discovered he has students from preschool through high school. In his role, he'll be providing direct instruction to students as well as consulting with general education teachers and other professionals who might be collaborating on educational programming for certain students. Terrance is also teaching yoga two nights a weeks at a local recreation facility to earn extra money to help pay off his school loans. He's very excited about his new job with the schools; he has recently reviewed the files on all his students and has visited the school sites he'll be working in.

To create quality programs for each of the individuals he works with, Terrance will need effective skills in three key areas: (1) assessing individual strengths, (2) evaluating the demands of a task or activity, and (3) understanding environmental variables and how they affect learning. Assessment, defined as the process of collecting information about an individual and making decisions based on that information (Smith, 1997), usually includes two phases: measurement and evaluation. Measurement is the process of assigning a number to a characteristic (Burton & Miller, 1998). For example, if we measure someone's range of motion using a goniometer, we might find that her elbow flexion score is 90 degrees. In another case we might measure throwing accuracy to a target and get a score of 10. In each case, we end up with a number that represents a characteristic for the individual—in the first case flexibility and in the second case accuracy. However, this number is meaningless by itself. During evaluation—the second and more important aspect of assessment (Burton & Miller, 1998)—the numbers derived from measurement are interpreted in context of the environment and the individual. It's the ability to see the "big picture"—all the aspects of the individual, environment, and task and how they interact—that's most critical to a meaningful evaluation.

Our purpose in this chapter is to provide a brief overview of assessment as it relates to individuals with differing abilities. We surely don't intend our discussion to be a comprehensive or in-depth look at the many issues relating to assessment. What we do hope to accomplish in this chapter is to identify the meaningful skills for individuals to learn based on their abilities, settings, interests, and future plans. Identifying what's critical, functional, and relevant for the individual is the first step in determining which skills to assess. Assessment is the cornerstone to effective teaching.

▶ PURPOSES OF ASSESSMENT

Assessment is an integral part of effective physical activity instruction and must be incorporated into any quality program. It's an ongoing process that takes place before, during, and after programming and aids the practitioner in answering many important questions, such as the following:

- What are the individual's current abilities?
- What types of activities are appropriate for this person?
- What skills and abilities should be assessed for this person?
- What are his or her interests now and what might they be in the future?

- How effective is the program in meeting the needs of this person?
- Is the individual benefiting from participation in this program?
- What new skills and abilities has he or she learned?
- How can instruction be enhanced for this person?
- What skills and abilities has he or she learned through participating in this program?
- How has his or her quality of life been improved?

These are just a few of the many possible questions asked during an assessment process. Physical activity professionals must become competent and knowledgeable in the purposes and use of assessment. In the next section of this chapter we'll briefly discuss several of the important reasons for assessment, including legal requirements, screening, support decisions, planning and instruction, progress, and sport classification (Burton & Miller, 1998; Choate & Evans, 1992; Horvat & Kalakian, 1996).

Legal Requirements

The Individuals with Disabilities Education Act (IDEA) mandates assessment of individuals with disabilities from birth through 21 years of age. These requirements include "assessment to determine if there is a need for specialized educational services," to report progress on those receiving special services, and for re-evaluation at least every three years.

The IDEA Categories of Disabilities

- Autism
- Deafness
- Deaf or blind
- Hearing impairment
- Mental retardation
- Multiple disabilities
- Orthopedic impairment
- Other health impairment
- Serious emotional disturbance
- Learning disability
- Speech or language impairment
- Traumatic brain injury
- Visual impairment, including blindness

Individuals with a suspected disability or who are at risk for a disability are entitled to have an assessment completed by their local special education program. However, just because someone has a disability or a risk for a disability doesn't necessarily mean that they'll receive services; they must also show a discrepancy in abilities that demonstrates their need for services. Anyone in the community or school can make a referral to the local education program for an assessment on an individual from birth through age 21. Once a referral has been made, the local education agency is obligated by law to follow through by informing the parents of the referral, obtaining parent or guardian permission, and completing a formal assessment to determine possible areas of need. At the completion of the assessment, an individual family service plan (IFSP) or an individual education program (IEP) must be completed. For individuals older than 21 there are no legal requirements for assessment. However, assessment for adults is usually connected to a community-based program with a focus on one of the following areas: screening, setting decisions, planning and instruction, progress, or sport classification.

Screening

Screening is primarily used to determine if further evaluation is needed. In a school environment, students are generally screened as a group, which doesn't require parental permission. However, a child *may not* be pulled from his or her peers and given a test that no other student is given unless a parent (or other caretaker) has first granted permission. For the process to be considered a screening, all students in the program must participate in the same activity. For example, in the past, junior high school students were screened by the school nurse for scoliosis;

each student was evaluated by the nurse to determine if there was a need for further testing. In physical education, screenings are often set up as stations including such areas as balance, eye–hand coordination, eye–foot coordination, and locomotor skills. Screening is typically designed as a pass–fail protocol. If a student is found to need individual testing, then parental permission is required, and at this point the process becomes an individualized assessment.

Screening is also used for adults to determine if a particular program is appropriate. For instance, adults interested in joining an aquatic exercise class might be initially screened to determine what kind of aquatic experience they have or what aquatic safety skills they possess. An initial screening might also be completed by a physical activity practitioner to determine if any existing medical conditions, such as high blood pressure or cardiac problems, need to be considered before an individual participates in certain exercises.

Support Decisions

When screening reveals that individuals need further assessment, they are subsequently assessed to determine their areas of strength and areas of need; programmatic decisions are then based on this information. Through individual assessment, practitioners attempt to answer questions such as these: What support services might this individual need? How might the individual's needs best be met? How should programs be implemented? For example, a toddler who has motor delays might need physical therapy, occupational therapy, or adapted physical education. The interdisciplinary team must also decide (with the family) what, when, where, and how these services will be received. Services might be provided in the home, at an infant childcare center, or both. For the public school age child, assessment decisions will determine if the child needs adapted physical education services and, if so, how and where these services will be provided. Some students might be assessed to require smaller group instruction rather than participating in a larger general physical education group. Students with differing abilities can

Figure 4.1 Decisions about physical activity should be based on the individual's skills and interests.

work together in these smaller groups to accomplish motor goals and social development. For an adult, support decisions are based on the individual's skills and interests as well as what programs are available in the community (figure 4.1). Such programs might include adult classes at the YMCA, community recreational classes, health club programs, or competitive sports programs. We'll discuss programming and support decisions for physical activity programs in detail in chapter 5.

Planning and Instruction

Once support decisions have been made, programming can begin. In any physical activity setting, it's important at the onset of programming to determine the current level of performance for the individual. Once his or her current level of performance has been identified, the physical activity practitioner can plan the curriculum or program based on an ecological approach, as discussed in previous chapters. Programs will vary depending on the age and interests of the participant, the professional standards and guidelines set forth by the organization or educational board, and the availability of the physical activity opportunities and resources in the community. For example, the California Physical Education Challenge Standards state in Standard 1, grade 2, "The student will be competent in many movement activities . . . Students who meet this standard will be able to skip, hop, gallop, jump, and slide in a variety of situations" (California Department of Education, 1998, pg. 9). Based on this standard, the focus of the curriculum should be on activities that help develop these skills. On the other hand, an adult who wants to work on personal fitness might not have a formal curriculum or document to guide the planning phase. In this case, the program depends entirely on the interest of the individual and which options are available. If programs are available, he or she might choose quad rugby, wheelchair basketball, a walking program, swimming, or weight training, depending on his or her interests and personal goals. More detailed information on planning and programming is presented in chapter 5.

Progress

Once programming begins, assessment is critical to determine if the individual is benefiting from involvement. The evaluation of progress allows the practitioner to determine if the goals set for the individual are being met. Documentation of this process is critical to determine what the next steps should be. For example, an adapted physical education practitioner working with an infant might set a goal for the child to pull to a stand independently and maintain upright posture. The practitioner needs to document the activities and interventions that are being completed as well as the progress the child is making. This way, as soon as the child meets a goal, a new one can be established. The evaluation of change over time is critical to the assessment process. The documentation of both the intervention and the progress informs the practitioner that the instruction is effective or not. When a child is not making satisfactory progress, this is discovered early through the documentation process, and the intervention can be changed to promote greater improvement. The same process is necessary for adults involved in physical activity programs or activities. It's always important to assess if an exercise regime or activity program is benefiting a participant so that the program or protocol can be modified as necessary. For instance, in a walking program documentation would include the distance an individual walked each day. This information would show what progress occurs in strength and endurance over time.

Assessment is an ongoing process that should be embedded within instruction. It should be done continually, not only at the end of an activity or unit. Ideally, assessment should take place hourly, weekly, monthly, and yearly. During each moment of instruction, the practitioner is continually interacting with participants, observing and giving feedback, changing instruction to meet the needs of the learner, and adjusting to the ever-changing environment. On an hourly or daily basis the instructor reflects on the process—what's working, what's not working, and what needs to be done in the next session. Documentation of progress made toward goals and objectives should be done daily, monthly, quarterly, and annually. Annual reports give an overall picture of the individual in the movement context, including progress, new skills, behaviors, concerns, and goals for the future. Through a continual dynamic interaction among the participant, the task, the practitioner, and the environment, the participant comes to acquire new skills.

Sport Classification

Practitioners also use assessment to classify individuals for sport competitions. Sport classification, used to equalize competition, is often based on functional ability, medical evaluation, or both. For example, in Special Olympics, athletes are classified based on their age, gender, and skill level. In a 100-meter heat, participants might be between 8 to 10 years of age, all female, and have similar qualifying times. In wheelchair basketball (figure 4.2), a player classification point system is used to equalize skill level among teams. This system classifies the players by functional ability during shooting, passing, rebounding, pushing their wheelchair, and dribbling. Such elements as trunk stability, force, and balance are evaluated, which vary depending on the degree of injury to the spinal cord. Athletes are categorized by ability, and the point values assigned to each player on a team are totaled so that no team exceeds a certain number of points on the court at any one time. Typically, the sport organization responsible for governing the event is responsible for determining who and what will be used to determine

Figure 4.2   Assessment is used to classify athletes for competition.

classification and for maintaining records on athletes. Those who take part in the classification of athletes might include medical doctors, occupational therapists, physical therapists, or other individuals who have completed specialized training. This use of assessment for sport classification ensures that competition is equitable and challenging for all. You can find more information on sport classification at these Web sites:

> www.iwbf.org/ International Wheelchair Basketball Federation
> http://edweb6.educ.msu.edu/kin866/ Disability Sport Web page, Michigan State
> www.paralympic.org/ International Paralympics Committee
> www.ciss.org/about/reg.html Deaf World Games
> www.cpsport.org/ CP Sport (sports for people with cerebral palsy)
> www.specialolympics.org/ Special Olympics

◀ THINK BACK

Think back to Terrance, who works with individuals from birth through adulthood. How might you help Terrance answer these questions?

1. Terrance's neighbor has a daughter named Julia who is 19 months old and is having trouble learning to walk. What can Terrance do to assist his neighbor? How might assessment be used to assist Julia in learning to walk?

2. Terrance has just started teaching his yoga class. Most participants are between the ages of 30 and 60. What purpose might assessment provide for Terrance in this setting?

3. Terrance is working with a student at the high school who's very interested in wheelchair racing. How might Terrance use assessment with this student?

▶ ASSESSMENT CONSIDERATIONS

For practitioners to obtain the most complete and true picture of an individual's level of performance or functioning, several questions must be answered. What factors need to be considered when selecting the best evaluation instrument? What type of assessment will provide me the most useful information? How do I know the information I have gathered is trustworthy and accurate? What factors might influence assessment data?

General Test Characteristics

To make the assessment process as meaningful as possible, practitioners should always select the most appropriate instrument for gathering performance data. When choosing an evaluative instrument, tests should be examined based on certain characteristics that either render the test suitable or unsuitable for the particular situation. Baumgartner and Jackson (1995) and Horvat and Kalakian (1996) suggest that several test characteristics be considered when selecting assessment tools.

1. *Is the test appropriate for the purpose?* Some instruments have been developed for the sole purpose of screening and don't provide the comprehensive information necessary for support decisions or programming decisions. Other tests are developed specifically for fitness. A practitioner wouldn't want to use a fitness test to evaluate motor development or a test designed for 3- to 10-year-olds for a high school student. Knowing the purpose of the assessment is critical to test selection.

Validity asks, Does the test truly measure what it says it measures?

Reliability asks, Are measurements consistent? Would you get the same results if you performed the same test twice under like conditions?

Figure 4.3 Clearly this teacher will not get the best performance from this child on this particular day. What person-related facture will influence the validity of this assessment?

2. *Is the test reliable and valid for the individual and performance being assessed?* Because the assessment provides the foundation for justifying and making important decisions regarding physical activity involvement, practitioners must know that these decisions are based on accurate and trustworthy information. The test must be examined for validity; external factors that influence whether the information is trustworthy must also be analyzed. Test validity and reliability are usually discussed in the introductory chapters of any quality standardized assessment tool and should be reviewed before the tool is chosen. However, the validity of test results might be influenced by several factors both intrinsic and extrinsic to the individual. Person-related factors (intrinsic factors) include such aspects as the participant's mood, level of motivation, fatigue (figure 4.3), anxiety about the assessment, medication, and attention span.

Among extrinsic factors that might also affect test results are modifications to standardized test instructions, the setting in which the test is administered, and the communication style used to convey instructions. For example, a test might require that directions are given in a certain way using exact specified language. The individual might be able to perform the task but doesn't understand the terminology of the test protocol. If the physical activity practitioner changes the language to help the student understand the directions, this change affects the validity of the test results. There are many other extrinsic factors beyond those we've mentioned that can affect assessment results. Although no test or test situation is perfect, practitioners must try to ensure that the information they're gathering best represents the individual's performance abilities by considering the nature of the assessment, the individual performing, and the setting in which the assessment is conducted.

3. *Is the test sensitive enough to detect changes in performance or discriminate among individuals?* There are many tests available for several different purposes, and not all tests have the same ability to detect variations in performance. The ability of a test to discriminate between small variations in performance is critical to test selection. Skills, or components of skills, must be broken down into measurable parts small enough to determine a score. For example, table 4.1 compares two test items for the overhand throw.

In sample 1, if participants could project the ball forward in any manner, they would score a Y (yes) and pass the test. Many participants would be able to pass this test, and we wouldn't be able to distinguish differences in their performance. However, in sample 2 we'd be able to discern variations in performance because of mechanical differences and variations in the distance the ball was thrown. Sample 2 provides much more information and allows for distinguishing among variations in performance among individuals as well as measuring changes in performance within an individual over time. The ability of a test to measure small variations in performance is a key factor in test selection.

Table 4.1   Two Test Items for the Overhand Throw

Sample 1 Overhand throw			Sample 2 Overhand throw with softball		
Throws a softball forward	Y	N	Steps with opposition	Y	N
			Elbow back	Y	N
			Downward arc in preparation for throw	Y	N
			Follow-through toward target	Y	N
			Transfer of weight	Y	N
			Hip rotation	Y	N
			Distance _____	Y	N

4. *Is the assessment or test safe for the participant?* Safety is an important concern when working with people in a movement context. Here are a few simple safety suggestions to keep in mind when planning and implementing a motor assessment:

1. Select a testing instrument that's appropriate, valid, and reliable for the individual you're testing.
2. Review medical history with the family or individual before completing the assessment. Check for medical concerns or activities that are contraindicative for the individual.
3. Make sure that the equipment is safe for the individual to use based on his or her ability.
4. If the individual fatigues easily, break the assessment into multiple sessions.
5. Start with activities that provide success and gradually work to more challenging tasks.
6. Never put participants in a situation that could be detrimental to their health or well-being. Yes, this is common sense, but it's important to keep in mind when attempting to establish the limits or range of an individual's skills and capabilities.

Assessment Strategies for Obtaining Meaningful Data

As stated earlier, if the information gleaned from the assessment process is to be worthwhile, the many factors that influence the data must be carefully and conscientiously considered. Practitioners can use several strategies to obtain useful information. A three-pronged approach to effective assessment considers these facets: the administration of the assessment, the practitioner's skill in carrying out the assessment, and the participant's abilities to perform. Table 4.2 lists many of the considerations in conducting assessments.

From an administration standpoint, practitioners should choose their assessment tools based on how well the instruments match the purpose for which they're intended. Instruments developed for specific ages and groups should be used for those groups. There are several low-cost, easy-to-administer assessments that can provide important information. In addition, practitioners might choose to create observation checklists or rubrics that supply valuable data specific to the information they desire. Examples of informal tools will be discussed in more detail later in this chapter, and sample rubrics are provided in figures 4.7 and 4.12. Many physical education texts also provide checklist examples, criteria for exercises or skills, and tools for evaluation (Best-Martini & Botenhagen-DiGenova, 2003; Graham, Holt-Hale, & Parker, 2001; Wessel & Zittel, 1995).

Table 4.2 Assessment Considerations in Selection of Tools

Administration considerations	Practitioner considerations	Individual considerations
• Ease of administration • Cost • Time • Individual vs. group • Purpose of assessment • Relationship of test content to teaching and learning environment • Age range • Population	• Skills • Knowledge and experience with tool • Knowledge of student • Knowledge of context and learning environment • Curriculum knowledge	• Age • Time of day • General health • Medication • Interest • Motivational level • Learning style • Comprehension • Previous experience

Considerations related more to the practitioner also require thoughtful assessment planning. Initially, practitioners should review assessment instruments thoroughly and understand the tool's intent, how to use the tool, and how to interpret the measurement data. Next, to ensure that the assessment process is appropriate, practitioners must understand the participants' needs and the context in which the participants will perform the tests. Finally, and most important, the practitioner should know which skills and activities are most meaningful for each participant and focus assessment on these priorities. In chapter 5 we'll present guidelines for identifying program priorities for individuals in inclusive physical activity programs.

The third part of the process of obtaining accurate and trustworthy assessment data pertains to the participant and his or her ability to accommodate individual differences in the assessment process. For instance, some individuals might show smaller gains or increments in improvements over time than anticipated. In rare cases, skills might actually decline; for example, after an eight-week fitness program, a participant might perform fewer sit-ups than he or she did before completing the program. However, in such cases, the practitioner might be assessing more than just an improvement in performance; perhaps he or she is testing for the level of independence gained or a reduction in prompts needed by the participant to complete the task. Because of the variability in performance of participants, practitioners should assess performance on multiple occasions rather than rely on a single test session. Many factors—motivation, fatigue, blood sugar level—can result in fluctuations in performance levels. Table 4.3 identifies participant variables that might influence assessment outcomes and suggests strategies for practitioners to follow to obtain reliable and valid assessment results.

Formal Versus Informal Assessment Tools

A formal assessment tool is designed to yield the same results regardless of who's administering it (assuming the protocol is followed). Many people are familiar with the scholastic aptitude test (SAT) and the graduate requirement exam (GRE) and have experienced taking standardized tests at some point during their education. These tests are designed with very specific directions and specifications that allow for consistency across administrators. All standardized tests are formal tests. In many cases, a standardized test might be administered to determine eligibility for special education services within a public school system.

Informal assessments are tools designed to evaluate progress or performance but which don't adhere to the strict guidelines of a formal test. Examples of informal assessment tools include checklists, observations, questionnaires, interviews, rating scales,

Did You Know?

A formal test involves a standard set of motor activities that require a response. This response elicits a numerical representation or measurement.

Table 4.3 Assessment Strategies Related to Participant Variables

Participant-related consideration	Assessment strategy
Small improvements in performance	Levels of prompting/independence gained
Unfamiliarity with tester or test items	Familiarization period
Optimal movement pattern nonexistent	Practitioner-made rubric
High variability in performance	Multiple assessment sessions Observe decreased variability pattern
Distractibility	Removal of distractions
Motivation	Peer support/verbal encouragement
Medication	Scheduling of assessment
Attention span	Multiple assessment sessions
Individual disposition	Determine motivators from parents or teachers
Learning style	Use most appropriate learning style (e.g., visual, kinesthetic, musical, and the like)

Figure 4.4 Sometimes informal observation of children in their natural environment elicits a more reliable performance than a standardized test.

or teacher-made tests. Informal assessments can be extremely valuable for program planning and ongoing evaluation. In some cases, a teacher might be able to elicit a greater performance from a student in a more natural setting than when following a protocol (figure 4.4). Standardization often doesn't allow for the playful nature of individuals and might not always elicit the best possible performance from an individual.

On the other hand, informal instruments allow instructors to create tools specific to the curriculum and environment in which they teach and to incorporate more meaningful or functional skills or tasks. In assessing an individual, it's often necessary to combine formal and informal methods to get a complete picture. We'll discuss methods of informal (authentic) assessment later in this chapter.

Norm-Referenced and Criterion-Referenced Tests

Many types of assessment instruments are available to document performance, each serving its own purpose. Some assessment tools, known as norm-referenced tests, are used to compare individuals to their peers. Normative data comes from the product measurement of a particular skill, such as the number of sit-ups in 20 seconds. From a large sample of individuals, statistics are applied to determine averages. However, it is important to remember that the "average" statistic for that measurement came from a whole range of

Gallop

1. Arms are bent and lifted to waist level at take-off.

2. Take a step forward with the lead foot followed by a step with the trailing foot to a position adjacent to or behind the lead foot.

3. There's a brief moment when both feet are off the floor.

4. Maintain a rhythmic pattern for four consecutive gallops.

Figure 4.5 Test of gross motor development 2: sample criteria for the gallop.

Adapted, by permission, from D. Ulrich, 2000, *Test of gross motor development*, 2nd edition (Austin, TX: Pro-Ed Publishers), 18..

scores from individuals. In any third-grade class would all the children be reading at the third-grade level? All computing math at the third-grade level? All writing at the third-grade level? Would they all have the same motor skill level? Even within the domain of motor skills, some individuals will be good at balancing whereas others excel at eye–hand coordination skills. While norm-referenced tests often are scored based on the product or outcome of a skill, such as the number of sit-ups done in 30 seconds, other types of assessment tools might look at the process of the skill or how it's performed, such as how someone catches a ball. For example, are the arms bent and relaxed in ready position? Is the ball caught and controlled with the hands? Although norm-referenced tests can be very helpful in determining how one learner compares to peers, most norm-referenced tests are not based on individuals with disabilities. This can make the use of a norm-referenced test inappropriate, depending on who is being tested and the purpose of the assessment. In many cases, it might be more appropriate to use a criterion-referenced test or another procedure, such as an authentic assessment method.

Criterion-referenced tests are an example of a process assessment. They are used to compare an individual against predetermined criteria. Figure 4.5 shows an example of criteria for the performance of galloping from the Test of Gross Motor Development (Ulrich, 2000, p.18). In this example, it is the process of the performance that is most important, not the product.

In another example, the Brockport Physical Fitness Test (table 4.4) uses a criterion reference for minimum and maximum heart rates for aerobic functioning. In each case, a performance standard is set for the individual to meet (Winnick & Short, 1999, p. 78).

Considerations for individuals with differences in ability may also exist with criterion-referenced tests. Note that what's mechanically efficient for one person might not be the most efficient movement for another. For example, someone with spastic cerebral palsy (appendix A) might find that the best way to throw for distance is to throw over the shoulder and backward. Another individual might find stepping with the opposite foot, using trunk rotation, and following through in the direction of the target to be most effective. Always recognize individual variability in performance. The challenge for the reflective practitioner is to find out what works best for each individual and help him or her develop those skills to optimal capacity. In many cases, traditional pre-made standardized tests aren't appropriate. In such cases, authentic assessment methods can be an appropriate alternative.

Authentic Assessment

Authentic assessment has many advantages over traditional formal or standardized methods of assessment, primarily in that it connects assessment to curriculum (Joyner & McManis, 1997; Smith, 1997). Many standardized tests include content that has little relation to the actual curriculum. For this reason it can be challenging to write goals and objectives for a student's IEP or activity program based on

Table 4.4 Brockport Physical Fitness Test—Minimum and Maximum 10 s Heart Rate Values

Aerobic functioning	Minimum	Maximum
General	23	30
Quadriplegic (C6-C8)		
Resting HR <65	14	17
Resting HR ≥ 65	(Resting HR + 20)/6	(Resting HR + 30)/6
Arm-only exercise	22	28

Reprinted, by permission, from J.P. Winnick and F.X. Short, 1999, *The Brockport physical fitness test manual* (Champaign, IL: Human Kinetics, 78.

formal assessment results. For example, a learner might be asked to balance on one foot as part of a standardized test. The child might have some difficulty with this static balance task, but he or she might not have any trouble with dynamic balance activities, such as galloping or skipping, and can use these in dynamic physical activity. Authentic assessment techniques allow teachers to evaluate students on an ongoing basis in ways that connect to the curriculum and standards. Although reliability and validity of authentic assessment methods might be lower, they still provide valuable information about a learner. Physical activity teachers can improve reliability and validity by making sure the tasks align with the curriculum. According to Joyner and McManis, "If the assessment is not related to the content taught in class and the way that it was taught in class, the assessment will not provide a true indication of student ability" (1997, p. 39). Quality authentic assessment methods have several components, including the following (Block, Lieberman, & Connor-Kuntz, 1998; Lund, 1997):

- Tasks are based on real-world settings.
- Tasks require higher-level thinking and application.
- The criteria for performance are presented in advance.
- The assessment is part of the curriculum and embedded in the instruction.
- Teachers and learners work together in the process, supporting each other and providing feedback.
- Learners often perform work publicly.
- Learners demonstrate skills in a variety of situations.
- An evaluation of the process is included, as well as the product of learning.

Did You Know?

Authentic assessment is defined as evaluation of student performance in natural or more "real life" situations (Block, Lieberman, & Connor-Kuntz, 1998; Choate & Evans, 1992; Melograno, 1994).

Figure 4.6   Journals can be a valuable tool in assessing student understanding.

There are many types of authentic assessment methods, including task sheets, systematic observation, written essays, journals (figure 4.6), interviews, exhibitions or performances, and portfolios (Lund, 1997; Pike & Salend, 1995; Smith, 1997).

Again, the most important component of any authentic assessment tool used is that it reflects the standards and outcomes or IEP goals and objectives to be reached by the individual learner. One way to ensure the standards or objectives are being met is by using rubrics.

Rubrics can be developed for any type of authentic assessment and should reflect the outcomes of the program. Outcomes are based on designing down from the standards—to the program, to the course, to the unit, to the lesson (Hopple & Graham, 1995). Although standards are appropriate for many students, how they're tailored and how the associated benchmarks are developed determines if they're inclusive of all children. Benchmarks are typically written to focus on a predetermined movement form and might exclude some students from achieving the desired criteria by virtue of their ability differences. Inclusive benchmarks incorporate the criteria necessary to attain the goal of the skill while allowing learners the opportunity to meet the benchmark in different ways (Johnson, Kasser, & Nichols, 2002). Figure 4.7 shows the connections among a national

Throwing Competency Rubric—Grades 3 & 4: NASPE Standard 1

Standard 1—Demonstrates competency in many movement forms and proficiency in a few movement forms.

Standard 1 benchmark—Throwing with appropriate form, controlling accuracy and force.

Sample objective from an IEP—By May 6, 2001, Joe will demonstrate an overhand throw by orienting his wheelchair sideways to the target, moving his trunk forward with his throw, and following through toward the target in four out of five trials, as observed and recorded by his teacher.

Needs work: Meets some or all of the criteria in 1A or 1B

Competent: Meets all of the criteria in 1A or 1B, all of the criteria in two other assessments, and some of the criteria in the remaining assessment

Exceeds standard: Meets all of the criteria in 1A or 1B and all of the criteria in the remaining assessments

Assessment 1: (Form A)

Student demonstrates

• A preparatory motion of the throwing arm (arm brought back to initiate throw)	Yes	No
• Body orientation appropriate for optimal release of the ball	Yes	No
• Weight shifts forward toward target	Yes	No
• Follow-through that's beyond the release of the ball	Yes	No

Assessment 1: (Form B)

Student demonstrates

• Downward arc of throwing arm initiates windup	Yes	No
• Rotation of hip and shoulder to point where nondominant side faces target	Yes	No
• Elbow up and back	Yes	No
• Weight transferred by stepping with opposite foot	Yes	No
• Follow-through beyond point of release diagonally across body	Yes	No

Assessment 2: (Spatial accuracy)

Student demonstrates

• Ability to hit a stationary target (two square feet) from a distance of ___ feet	Yes	No
• Ability to hit a stationary target (two square feet) from a distance of ___ feet	Yes	No

Assessment 3: (Spatial and temporal accuracy)

Student demonstrates

• Ability to throw an object to a moving target so that the object is catchable (moving target is no more than ___ feet away)	Yes	No

Assessment 4: (Force)

Student demonstrates

• Ability to throw ball with appropriate force so that it is catchable from a distance of ___ feet	Yes	No
• Ability to throw ball with appropriate force so that it is catchable from a distance of ___ feet	Yes	No

Figure 4.7   Example of related standard, objective, and inclusive rubric for the overhand throw.

← THINK BACK

1. Remember Terrance from the chapter-opening scenario? What are some of the test characteristics that Terrance would need to consider when selecting tools for individuals within his program?

2. How might Terrance use both formal and informal tools to assess his students?

3. In working with individuals with diverse abilities, how might Terrance use norm-referenced, criterion-referenced, and authentic assessment methods to evaluate participants in his many programs?

standard for physical education, an IEP objective, and an inclusive rubric for the skill of throwing.

▶ ASSESSMENT ACROSS THE LIFE SPAN: WHAT ARE WE LOOKING FOR?

Assessment is an important component to any inclusive physical activity program, and knowing where to direct assessment efforts is critical. As we mentioned earlier, assessment shouldn't involve every skill or activity possible. This would be too cumbersome for even the most efficient practitioner. Assessment should focus on the skills and activities most meaningful for participants in terms of their age, physical activity opportunities available, and possible future physical activity involvement. At different times across the life span, practitioners will focus on various aspects of movement. Table 4.5 lists the skills and abilities often focused on and assessed in physical activity programs for individuals across the life span.

Although in this chapter we discuss general trends for evaluation and assessment across the life span, assessment priorities aren't entirely exclusive to one particular period. For example, reflexes are generally examined during infancy, but they might also be assessed later in life in relation to neurological concerns. The same is true for walking. An individual's ability to walk might be re-evaluated following a head injury or stoke. Likewise, many adolescents and adults participate in the same activities, and the assessments approach might be similar.

In addition to the identified movement skills and activities listed in table 4.5, assessment might also include gathering information on communication skills, social skills, on-task

Table 4.5 Focus of Programming Across the Life Span

Infants and toddlers	Early childhood (preschool)	Elementary school	Adolescents	Adults
• Spontaneous movements • Reflexes • Motor milestones	• Fundamental motor skills • Orientation skills • Play participation • Locomotor • Object control • Water readiness	• Locomotor skills • Nonlocomotor skills • Object control skills • Movement concepts • Rhythms and dance • Aquatics • Fitness • Leisure activities	• Sport-related skills • Fitness • Leisure activities • Aquatics • Activities of daily living	• Leisure activity • Fitness • Activities of daily living • Aquatics • Sport skills

behavior, and other behaviors. Practitioners should consider the related aspects to physical activity involvement that might need to be addressed and developed for successful participation. A practitioner might also need to assess the settings in which inclusive physical activity programs might exist. These environmental assessments or surveys might focus on the accessibility of the site, or they might be directed toward particular activities to determine which skills or tasks must be taught so that participants can more successfully access the program activity. The focus of physical activity participation and related assessment priorities for individuals across the life span are described in the following sections. However, although the following sections are separated based on age groups, the ultimate decision about the focus of a program is based not on age but on the current needs and abilities of individuals in their current settings as well as the skills they will need in future settings. Separating information by age groups is merely convenient for organizational purposes.

Infants and Toddlers

Individuals who work with infants and toddlers in the motor domain must work with a cross-disciplinary team of professionals and the family to provide appropriate assessment and programming for the infant or toddler. An occupational or physical therapist often provides motor assessment and programming for early intervention teams. However, the adapted physical educator is often called on to serve infants and toddlers as part of their teaching caseload (Cowden, Sayers, & Torrey, 1998; Cowden & Eason, 1991). Physical and occupational therapists along with the adapted physical education specialist work collaboratively with the rest of the early intervention team to provide the best possible evaluation and programming for the infant and his or her family. The focus of assessment and programming at this stage in life is on spontaneous movement, reflexes and reactions, and motor milestones (figure 4.8).

Spontaneous movements are movements that appear to serve no specific purpose, such as reciprocal kicking and arm movements. However, these movements are quite similar to patterns used later in life and might really be quite purposeful. For example, research shows that infantile supine (on the back) kicking is a rhythmical and coordinated movement similar to upright walking (Thelen, 1995; Thelen, 1985; Ulrich & Ulrich, 1995). Thus, these early movements tell the practitioner something about the child's future potential as a mover.

Reflexes and reactions are involuntary movements often observable in infants. The persistence or absence of reflexes outside of their general developmental time period can be a sign of neurological concerns. In such instances, reflexes are often seen across the life span (table 4.6). For example, the retention of the symmetrical tonic neck reflex might inhibit an individual's ability to tuck the head to the chest to perform a forward roll, or the startle reflex might affect a person's ability to focus in a gym where there are many sudden loud noises.

For the developing infant, reflexes tend to disappear shortly before voluntary motor patterns begin. Research suggests a strong connection between reflexes and voluntary movement patterns. By changing environmental conditions, the persistence of reflexes and an earlier onset of a motor pattern can be influenced. For example, in one study infants' stepping reflex was elicited daily for the first eight weeks of life. This practice actually increased the stepping reflex, and these infants began showing the signs of walking earlier (Zelazo, Zelazo, & Kolb, 1972a, 1972b).

Figure 4.8 Early physical activity programs focus on the acquisition of motor milestones.

Table 4.6   *Infantile Reflexes and Reactions*

Reflex/reaction	Starting position (if important)	Stimulus	Response	Time	Warning signs
Primitive reflexes					
Asymmetrical tonic neck reflex	Supine	Turn head to one side	Same-side arm and leg extend	Prenatal to 4 mo	Persistence after 6 mo
Symmetrical tonic neck reflex	Supported sitting	Extend head and neck	Arms extend, legs flex	6 to 7 mo	
		Flex head and neck	Arms flex, legs extend		
Doll eye		Flex head	Eyes look up	Prenatal to 2 wk	Persistence after first days of life
Palmar grasping		Touch palm with finger or object	Hand closes tightly around object	Prenatal to 4 mo	Persistence after 1 yr; asymmetrical reflex
Moro	Supine	Shake head, as by tapping pillow	Arms and legs extend, fingers spread, then arms and legs flex	Prenatal to 3 mo	Presence after 6 mo; asymmetrical reflex
Sucking		Touch face above or below lips	Sucking motion begins	B to 3 mo	
Babinski		Stroke sole of foot from heel to toes	Toes extend	B to 4 mo	Persistence after 6 mo
Searching or rooting		Touch cheek with smooth object	Head turns to side stimulated	B to 1 yr	Absence of reflex; persistence after 1 yr
Palmar-mandibular (Babkin)		Apply pressure to both palms	Mouth opens, eyes close, head flexes	1 to 3 mo	
Plantar grasping		Stroke ball of foot	Toes contract around object stroking foot	B to 12 mo	
Startle	Supine	Tap abdomen or startle infant	Arms and legs flex	7 to 12 mo	
Postural reactions					
Derotative righting	Supine	Turn legs and pelvis to other side	Trunk and head follow rotation	From 4 mo	
	Supine	Turn head sideways	Body follows head in rotation	From 4 mo	
Labyrinthine righting reflex	Supported upright	Tilt infant	Head moves to stay upright	2 to 12 mo	

(continued)

Table 4.6   (continued)

Pull-up	Sitting upright, held by 1 or 2 hands	Tip infant backward or forward	Arms flex	3 to 12 mo
Parachute	Held upright	Lower infant toward ground rapidly	Legs extend	From 4 mo
	Held upright	Tilt forward	Arms extend	From 7 mo
	Held upright	Tilt sideways	Arms extend	From 6 mo
	Held upright	Tilt backwards	Arms extend	From 9 mo
Locomotor reflexes				
Crawling	Prone	Apply pressure to sole of one foot or both feet alternately	Crawling pattern in arms and legs	B to 4 mo
Walking	Held upright	Place infant on flat surface	Walking pattern in legs	B to 5 mo
Swimming	Prone	Place infant in or over water	Swimming movement of arms and legs	11 days to 5 mo

Reprinted, by permission from K. Haywood and N. Getchell, 2001, *Lifespan motor development.*, 3rd edition (Champaign, IL: Human Kinetics), 90..

Finally, motor milestones are typical voluntary motor behaviors observed in infants and toddlers. Although individuals might vary in when they reach these motor milestones, they generally follow the same sequence (e.g., lifting the chin when lying on the stomach, lifting the chest when lying on the stomach, rolling over, sitting, standing with help, creeping (stomach up), standing alone, and walking (Haywood & Getchell, 2001).

Individuals who work with infants and toddlers need a strong educational background in motor development to understand how reflexes and reactions can influence motor behavior throughout life. The Hawaii Early Learning Profile is an excellent user-friendly developmental checklist for evaluating motor performance in infants and toddlers. Table 4.7 illustrates a portion of the gross motor section of this tool. In addition to the evaluation checklist, this tool also provides curriculum to assist in the development of skills and ideas for parents as they interact and play with their children. For a more complete list of formal tools, please see appendix E.

When assessing infants and toddlers, we need to understand what motor skills are important as well as the context in which the child is developing—that is, we need to see the "big picture." Infants and toddlers don't function in isolation but within the context of their family. For this reason, assessment at this level focuses on the entire family. What are the family's strengths, and how is the family and environment supporting the growth and develop-

Table 4.7   Sample Items From the HELP Checklist

3.09	Extends both legs
3.10	Rolls side to supine
3.11	Kicks reciprocally
3.12	Extensor thrust inhibited
3.13	Flexor withdrawal inhibited
3.14	Assumes withdrawal position
3.15	Holds chest up in prone, weight on forearms
3.16	Rotates and extends head
3.17	Rolls prone to supine
3.18	Holds head beyond plane of body when held in ventral suspension

Reprinted, by permission, from VORT, 1997, *HELP Checklist* (Palo Alto, CA: VORT Corporation), 10.

ment of the infant or toddler? Are there areas in which the family needs support? Here are some questions that might be asked:

- What is the child's medical and health history?
- What kinds of things does the family like to do with the child?
- What types of support services are in place for childcare, medical care, and so on?
- What are the family's perceived needs?
- What are the family's perceived strengths?
- What are the family's goals for their infant or toddler?
- What types of playgroups or parent support groups are available?
- How does the infant or toddler interact with the primary caregiver?
- How does the infant or toddler interact with others?

These are just some of the questions that can provide insight into the strengths and needs of the family and child. Appendix E provides a more complete list of assessment tools for infants and toddlers.

In addition to formal tests that might be helpful in determining an infant or toddler's current motor abilities, there are also many informal ways to gather information to provide a more holistic picture of the child. These might include interviews with the parents or caregiver, informal observations, questionnaires, or checklists of skills or activities. For example, here are some questions that might be asked of the parent during a home visit and informal observation (figure 4.9):

Figure 4.9 An informal interview can provide valuable information about a child and his or her family.

1. Can you tell me about your son, Trent?
2. What kinds of things does Trent really enjoy doing with you or other members of the family?
3. What are Trent's strengths?
4. Can you share a little bit about Trent's siblings?
5. How does Trent move about the house or play space?
6. What are your concerns for Trent?
7. What does a typical day for Trent look like?
8. What would you like to see Trent doing a year from now?
9. What kinds of things do you like to do as a family?

Such questions will elicit much information not garnered through the standardized test instrument, such as what the child likes and dislikes, how he or she interacts with others, and what the family's goals are. This information is just as critical to the overall assessment as information gathered through use of standard tools and will assist in determining outcomes for the Individual Family Service Plan. Combining formal and informal data gives the practitioner the best assessment information for planning.

THINK BACK

Terrance just learned that he will be working with three toddlers who attend a center-based special education program two days per week. He'll be seeing them once a week at the facility.

1. What will be the focus of his assessment with these toddlers?

2. What types of information would Terrance want to gather from the center before beginning his programming?

3. What information might he want to gather from the parents of these children?

Figure 4.10 Gross motor playground skills are important for development.

Preschool to High School

Although it's important to understand the context and general program of activities for any age group, such understanding is just a foundation for the more important issue of knowing how to assess the skills an individual has and needs in order to participate in a particular setting or program. To be successful in program planning, practitioners need to be able to assess not only a person's capabilities but also the tasks and environment. As children grow older and leave home for school-based programs, the focus of their physical activity shifts toward the development of playground skills and fundamental motor skills (figure 4.10).

For preschoolers, the general content areas include locomotor skills, orientation skills, object control skills, and play participation and equipment skills (Wessel & Zittel, 1995; Sanders, 2002). Table 4.8 provides a sample for program goals, objectives, and learning outcomes for the young child. Although not all children can meet every program objective in the same way, they can all meet the learning outcomes. For example, examine the first learning outcome in table 4.8: "To demonstrate selected fundamental locomotor skills

Table 4.8   Preschool Program Focus

Program goals and content area	Program objectives	Learning outcomes
Locomotor skills	Roll Crawl or creep Walk Run Jump down Jump over Hop Gallop Rhythmic patterns Wheel	To demonstrate selected fundamental locomotor skills and incorporate them in play and rhythmic activities at school and at home.
Orientation skills	Ascend stairs Descend stairs Climb up a ladder Climb down a ladder Walk on a balance beam Move in pathways, levels, and directions Forward roll Log roll Spatial awareness Body awareness Imitative/expressive movements	To demonstrate selected body management and spatial awareness necessary for participating in play at school and in-home activities.
Object control skills	Track object visually Reach Push object Roll a ball (underhand) Throw a ball (underhand) Bounce a ball (dribble) Kick a ball Strike a ball Throw a ball (overhand) Catch a ball	To demonstrate selected fundamental object control skills and enhance eye-hand and eye-foot coordination necessary to participate in more complex game activities at school and home.
Play participation and equipment skills	Hang from a bar Pull an object Ride in wagon Ride a tricycle or bicycle Swing on a swing Slide down a slide Travel on a scooter board Parachute play	To demonstrate selected play and movement skills necessary to participate in activity settings alone and with others at school and at home.

Adapted, by permission, from J. Wessel, and L. Zittel, 1995, *Smart Start* (Austin, TX: Pro-Ed Publishers).

and incorporate them in play and rhythmic activities at school and at home." A child who uses a wheelchair for mobility might not hop or gallop but can complete locomotion by pushing his or her wheelchair in various patterns and directions independently and can play a game of moving and stopping with music, which would clearly meet this learning outcome.

Figure 4.11 Critical information can be gathered through a play-based approach.

Assessment for the preschool child should focus on the acquisition of the skills listed in the program focus. One frequently used method for assessing young children is the transdisciplinary play-based assessment (Linder, 1996). This method doesn't compare a child to his or her peers but rather allows for the assessment of skills to take place in a natural play setting (figure 4.11). In a traditional assessment approach, each discipline evaluates the child individually; however, in the transdisciplinary play-based approach, one person serves as the play facilitator, and all areas are assessed simultaneously. Members of the transdisciplinary team make recommendations for toys, materials, and activities to elicit desired skills. The play facilitator works with the parent and child to follow the child's lead while respecting the child's desires and wishes. This allows the team to observe the child's learning style, skills, and activity preferences. A play-based approach includes the following benefits:

- Assessment takes place in a natural setting.
- More flexibility is allowed in the testing setting.
- The focus is on the use of toys and play activities, which are a child's natural mode of learning.
- Fewer professionals interact with the child.
- It allows for the use of modeling behaviors or activities.
- Cross-disciplinary interaction is allowed.
- A holistic view of the child is taken.
- Various disciplines are allowed in order to understand how specific areas interface with other disciplines in determining goals for the child.

In addition to the use of formal tools such as the Brigance or Peabody, or the use of a transdisciplinary play-based approach, additional informal procedures help to supplement content and provide a more complete picture of the child. Informal assessments also provide for daily documentation of progress over time. Such informal methods might include anecdotal records, checklists, rating scales, work samples, videos, or rubrics. One such example is a developmental checklist for particular skills. Table 4.9 shows a preschool checklist for the skills of jump over, hop, gallop, and rhythmic patterns (Wessel & Zittel, 1995, p. 236).

Checklists such as these might be developed by the teacher or found in many quality pre-developed curriculums. Figure 4.12 provides another example of a teacher-made rubric for the skill of riding a tricycle. This type of informal tool might be used to supplement the team assessment and document progress.

As a child progresses from preschool to elementary school, the physical activity program focus shifts to movement concepts and skills themes (Graham, Holt-Hale, & Parker, 2001). Movement concepts and skill themes serve as the movement alphabet to make up the skills we use to interact in more complex activities, such as small-group games, dance, aquatics, and sports. Movement concepts include spatial awareness, effort, and relationships. Skill themes include

Table 4.9 Record of Progress   Child _____

Jump over **2 out of 3 times** **Date** _____	**Hop** **2 out of 3 times** **Date** _____	**Gallop** **2 out of 3 times** **Date** _____	**Rhythmic patterns** **2 out of 3 times** **Date** _____
___ Jump forward, 2-foot take-off	___ Hop forward, push off on foot, land on same foot 3 or more times	___ Step forward lead foot, step with rear foot near heel of lead foot	___ Clap or move (stamp, step, tap) 8 consecutive beats; even, moderate tempo
___ Jump forward 12 inches, 2-foot take-off and landing	___ Repeat on other foot 3 or more times	___ Period of nonsupport (hop) as rear foot nears lead foot, 3 or more times	___ Move (run, walk hop) 8 consecutive beats; even, fast tempo
___ Jump forward 24 inches, 2-foot take-off and landing, maintain balance	___ Hop forward on 1 foot, slight forward lean, 5 feet	___ Gallop forward, 1 foot leading, 5 times	___ Clap or move (stamp, step, tap) 8 consecutive measures of uneven rhythm; moderate tempo
___ Prepare to jump forward, knees bent about 90 degrees, arms behind body, take-off angle 45 degrees	___ Repeat on other foot, 5 feet	___ Repeat with other foot leading, 5 times	___ Move (gallop, skip, slide) 8 consecutive measures of uneven rhythm; fast tempo
___ Arms thrust forward, legs extended at take-off, arms lower on landing, knees bent	___ Hop on either foot, elbows bent at waist level, 10 feet	___ Gallop forward 10 feet, either foot leading	___ Clap or move (stamp, step, tap) 3 consecutive measures, accenting first beat of each measure; moderate tempo
___ Jump forward 30 inches, 2-foot take-off and landing, feet contact ahead of body	___ Lift both arms forward with hop, push off	___ Arms bent at sides, lift arms upward with weight transfer to lead foot	___ Move (locomotor) 6 consecutive measures, accenting the first beat of each measure; moderate tempo
	___ Nonsupporting leg bent, foot does not drag	___ Rear knee bent, foot does not drag	___ Move (locomotor) 6 consecutive measures, accenting the first and second beat; moderate tempo

Rubric: Tricycle Riding for Preschoolers

Rider
- Sits on tricycle or in wagon with assistance
- Enjoys riding while another person pushes

Starter
- Needs assistance to mount tricycle
- Can sit on the tricycle and put feet on the pedals with assistance

Mover
- Gets on and off of trike with minimal assistance
- Attempts to pedal with assistance
- Propels self with feet on the ground

Pedaler
- Gets on and off trike independently
- Pedals independently
- Propels self forward without turning

Traveler
- Gets on and off trike independently
- Pedals around obstacles
- Stops independently

Figure 4.12 Rubrics can be informal tools that can supplement more formal tools.

Fundamental Motor Skills (Individual Skills)

Skill themes, movement concepts, aquatics, rhythms

Small-Group Games (Combined Skills)

Corner ball, 4-square, minisoccer, tag, aquatics, beginning dance

Specific Sport-Related Skills and Lifetime Activities (Complex Skills)

Aerobics, archery, basketball, badminton, baseball, canoeing, dance, fencing, golf, hiking, soccer, swimming, tennis, volleyball, yoga

Figure 4.13 A sample progression of skills from elementary school to high school and adulthood.

locomotor skills, manipulative skills, and nonmanipulative skills. In chapter 7 we provide a complete summary of skill themes and movement concepts. Figure 4.13 shows a sample progression of skill focus from elementary school to high school and adulthood.

The individual skills emphasized in public school physical activity programs might be assessed and evaluated in several ways. Often, formal tests are used to determine initial needs, to compare students to a population, to determine individual goals and objectives, and to evaluate progress. Formal tests used in the area of physical activity in the public schools vary significantly. Appendix E provides an extensive list of tools used to evaluate motor skills for individuals from preschool through high school.

Deciding which tool is most appropriate for an individual depends on several questions:

- Why are you assessing the student?
- What skills do you want to evaluate?
- What is the curriculum of the physical education program?
- What are the individual's needs during a testing situation?
- What skills are required in a particular setting?
- What skills will this student need in the future for lifetime physical activity?
- What skills and abilities are important to the family and individual?

Some of these questions, as well as others that might come up as a result of the assessment process, might not be answerable through formal tests.

Standard assessment methods won't provide a complete picture of a child's ability; in some cases, such methods aren't appropriate at all. When this is the situation, informal data collection and authentic assessment methods should serve as the primary means of gathering information—or at least as a supplement to formal testing, as discussed earlier. Many elements can be evaluated through informal measures such as parental interviews, checklists, coding sheets, and observations. Elements of the physical activity environment that can be observed and documented or tallied include time on task, opportunities to respond, peer interactions, appropriate behavior, and successful attempts, just to name a few. Figure 4.14 provides an example of a documentation sheet for opportunity to respond. This tool could be used to determine if a student had ample opportunities to engage in physical activity within a particular setting, such as the game setting in figure 4.15.

Opportunity to Respond Coding From

Date _____

Lesson _____

Time of day _____

Activity or skill _____

Each time the targeted student has an opportunity to engage in the activity (e.g., strike the ball, make a play), place a tally in the box provided.

Student 1:	Student 2:	Student 3:

Questions to ask:

1. Did the students have relatively equitable opportunities to respond during the lesson?

2. Did students have a high frequency of responses during the lesson?

Figure 4.14 Sample coding form.

As the child grows and progresses from preschool to elementary school to middle school and into high school, individual skills are combined into simple physical activities, more complex skills, and lifetime activities. The focus of the program at each grade level should be determined based on the national standards for physical education (NASPE), state standards and guidelines, district or school guidelines, and parent and learner interests and needs. Regardless of the grade level a student is in, the curriculum should be adapted to meet the needs of all learners (as is described in detail in chapter 6). As students enter high school, the focus of their programs should be meaningful to them as individuals and focus on lifelong physical activity participation (figure 4.16) and fitness as well as functional skills. The focus shifts toward how

Figure 4.15 Seeing skills in the context of a game can be critical to the assessment process.

students will be physically active as adults. In the next section we discuss adult programs and assessment in detail. This same content applies to high school students, as they get ready to transition into the adult world.

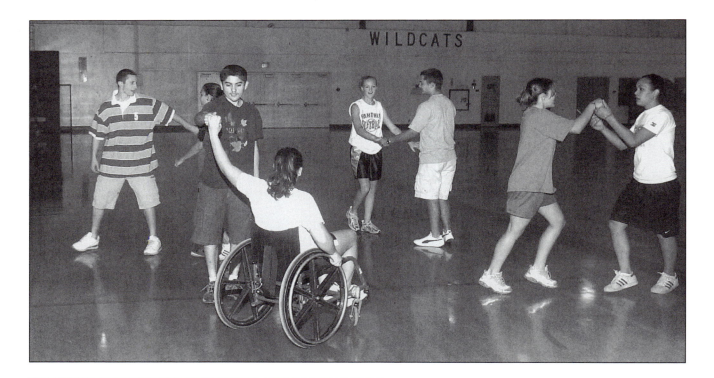

Figure 4.16 Activities must be meaningful to the individual and focus on lifetime activities.

THINK BACK

1. How might Terrance's focus on physical activity be the same or different for his elementary students compared to his high school students?

2. How might Terrance use both formal and informal procedures to assess a student? Can you provide an example of each?

3. What might be some of the advantages of the transdisciplinary play-based approach to assessment over other standardized tools for Terrance's preschoolers?

4. Terrance would like to create a rubric for tennis. Can you help him design a rubric for the forehand that he could use with students of all abilities?

Figure 4.17 Adult activities should be meaningful and can focus on improving skills, social interactions, and contact through physical activity to enhance quality of life.

Adults

Physical activity programs for adults can focus on several goals, including maintaining strength and flexibility for activities of daily living, enhancing social interactions and contact through physical activity programs, developing skills for leisure or recreational pursuits, and providing sport opportunities for both recreation and competition (figure 4.17). Assessment at this stage should focus on the skills and exercises that directly relate to and facilitate individual goals and physical activity participation choices.

Assessment is an important aspect of exercise programming for at least three reasons: (1) it establishes the participant's current level or functional ability, (2) it provides the basis for individualized goals and safe and beneficial exercises, and (3) it allows participants and practitioners to gauge progress. Physical fitness or exercise programs should include all aspects of fitness—flexibility, strength, and cardiovascular endurance. Developing and maintaining sufficient levels of muscular strength, flexibility, and endurance are essential in enhancing independent living skills, preventing disuse atrophy, and avoiding acute or chronic injury. As such, assessment is important before starting any training to determine needed adaptations and techniques and appropriate training regimes. Table 4.10 displays some common tests for these fitness components.

Organizations such as the American College of Sports Medicine (ACSM) offer guidelines in exercise testing and evaluation. Some assessment instruments or testing protocols might not be suitable for all individuals with disabilities. Before any fitness testing takes place, the practitioner must review the individual's medical history to determine the safety of conducting any fitness test. Complete understanding of conditions for which exercise testing is contraindicated (e.g., blood pressure problems, heart conditions, diabetes, etc.) is necessary. The practitioner should also be aware and knowledgeable of the signs and symptoms of exercise

Table 4.10 Common Fitness Assessments for Adults

Test name	Description	Age
Passive and active range of motion	Flexibility	Adult
Manual muscle test	Strength	Adult
Hand-held dynamometer	Strength	Elementary to adult
Repetition maximum weights	Strength	High school to adult
Isokinetic testing	Strength	High school to adult
Submaximal and maximal HR tests	Cardiovascular endurance	High school to adult
Arm crank and wheelchair ergometry	Cardiovascular endurance	Middle-school to adult
AAHPERD functional fitness test for older adults		Adult

Table 4.11 Common Tests of Mobility and Balance

Test name	Description	Age
Berg balance scale	Balance evaluation	Adult
Functional reach test	Activities of daily living	Adult
Tinetti balance	Balance evaluation	Adult
Timed get-up-and-go test	Speed and agility	Adult
Gait abnormality rating scale	Walking gait performance	Adult

intolerance and when an exercise test should be terminated. In addition, the practitioner must know the individual's history and current use of medications and the effects of medications on exercise.

Activities that facilitate balance and mobility might also be important for some individuals as they endeavor to maintain independence and competency in functional everyday tasks. Several clinical instruments allow baseline data from which to later assess progress. Table 4.11 includes several tools for measuring balance and mobility.

There are also many scales and instruments that assess functioning in various activities of daily living (e.g., stair climbing, dressing, etc.) that involve balance and coordination components (figure 4.18). Practitioners without experience in administering these specific tools might elect to assess these things through observation. Care must be taken when evaluating results and making decisions based on information that might be unreliable or not measured using set criteria and sensitive measurement scales.

Activity participation of adults might also involve sport-specific or leisure-related experiences (table 4.12). Assessment of the prerequisite skills and performance of these individuals is necessary for programming or training efforts to improve performance. Much of this assessment is conducted within the context of the sport or activity, and practitioners use their experience and observational skills or self-design assessment scales to obtain the needed information. Assessment would include fitness and balance aspects and activity-specific movement skills as well as the use of personal equipment, such as mobility aids and wheelchairs, and activity-specific equipment, such as the monoski or other modified devices.

As is true for younger participants, the goal of any physical activity program for adults and older adults is continued involvement in a physically active lifestyle. Whether the focus is increased independence, skill development for recreational pursuits, or enhanced performance for competitive sport involvement, accurate assessment data must be gathered for optimal programming to ensue. Assessment of progress is also critical to determine if goals have been achieved or if present activity plans or training regimes need to be further modified. This assess-

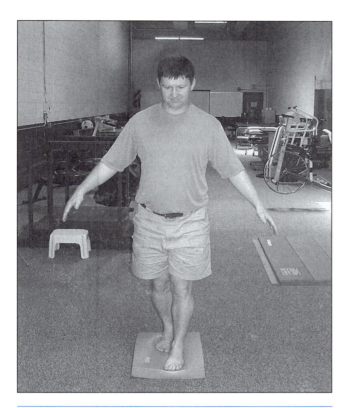

Figure 4.18 Balance is critical to the functional ability of many adults.

Table 4.12 Sport and Leisure Activities

Individual	Dual	Team
Bowling	Table tennis	Basketball
Archery	Tennis	Volleyball
Golf	Badminton	Hockey
Skiing	Fencing	Soccer
Billiards	Dance	Softball
Skating		Quad rugby
Track and field		
Weightlifting		
Aquatics		
Walking		
Aerobics		
Hiking		

*This table represents many of the sport and leisure activities in which adults participate. It is not intended to be comprehensive but rather to offer examples of activities.

ment information—supplemented by continual communication with individual participants and others in the support network—provides the foundation for these decisions.

▶ SUMMARY

Assessment is a multifaceted approach to collecting information about an individual's performance and abilities. It's an ongoing process that is inseparable from programming and critical to any effective program. Several of the functions of assessment include legal obligations, screening, support decisions, planning and instruction, progress, and testing for sport classifications. Assessment is an inherent part of all effective programs and instrumental in planning for individual family service plans, individual education programs, and individual transition plans. However, the selection of the most appropriate tools for data collection is critical to this process, and practitioners must consider specific test characteristics before choosing which tools to use. Both formal and informal procedures are important in the assessment process to gain a complete picture of an individual's abilities. In examination of an individual, the focus of programs and assessment might change across the life span, but it is always important to determine what is most important to and for the individual learner. Not every person needs to be evaluated on every skill; rather, those skills that are functional and appropriate for them in a given setting and in future settings should be tested. In this chapter we have supplied a general overview of assessment and program focus; in chapter 5 we'll expand on this information by providing details on issues related to preparing and planning for inclusive physical activity programs. Then, in chapter 6, we will help you better understand considerations regarding the needs of individuals and how to make appropriate modifications based on individual learners' capabilities.

What Do You Think?

1. Identify two standardized tools available in your profession for assessing individuals' movement abilities.

2. Think of someone you interact with through volunteer hours or your job and design an informal tool to help you understand this person's movement abilities.

3. Using the same individual, what assessment considerations would you need to make based on the individual, the environment, and the tasks?

What Would You Do?

Scenario 4.1

Beth is working with adults in an individualized community-based exercise program. A new participant, Ann, has just joined her program. Ann has a spinal cord injury at T-8. She uses a manual wheelchair for mobility and is very active in sports for individuals with disabilities. She competes in wheelchair basketball and wants to train for a marathon.

1. What are the possible purposes of assessment for Ann?

2. How might Beth go about assessing Ann's abilities?

3. What skills would Beth want to evaluate with Ann?

4. What questions would be important to ask Ann in the assessment process?

Scenario 4.2

Francisco is 11 years old and has just entered Erica's adapted physical education program. He also attends Ms. Franks' fifth-grade class as well as special education services. Francisco was diagnosed at birth with severe cerebral palsy and uses a wheelchair for mobility. His potential intellectual abilities are unknown because his ability to communicate is very limited. He communicates with his facial expressions and has some head control. His chair is manually operated, and his instructional assistant pushes him to his class and other services. The speech-language pathologist is working to find a functional means of communication for Francisco. He also receives regular physical therapy.

1. What types of tests would be appropriate for evaluating Francisco's abilities?

2. How would you go about assessing Francisco? What methods would you use?

3. What would be an appropriate program focus for Francisco?

Preparing and Planning Inclusive Physical Activity Programs

Learning Outcomes

After completing this chapter, you should be able to

» discuss the steps for creating inclusive physical activity programs;

» describe the referral process for an individual who might need physical education support from birth through 21 years of age;

» explain how youth and adults with differences in ability can access physical activity programs involving sports, recreational, and fitness activities;

» provide examples of physical activity goals, objectives, and benchmarks for an individual of any age; and

» apply the steps to planning an inclusive program to your particular field of study.

INCLUDING ALL INDIVIDUALS

Beth and Tom are the parents of Jackson, an 11-year-old who was diagnosed with Down syndrome shortly after birth. The family received early intervention services when Jackson was an infant, which then continued as he went on to an integrated preschool from three to fours years of age. At five he entered the local general education school, where he received support services for full inclusion in physical education. He has lived in the same neighborhood since he was a baby and currently attends Marimont Elementary School and is in the fifth grade. He loves his teacher, and his neighbor and best friend Sean is in physical education class with him. Jackson has been very involved in sports because his parents are avid outdoors people who go camping, hiking, and cycling every weekend that the weather permits. Jackson has recently become involved in Special Olympics and enjoys competing in track and swimming. He has also played in the local community soccer league since he was seven. Tom and Beth are considering moving closer to Tom's mother, who's beginning to need assistance because of arthritis. However, a move would mean going to a neighboring community and changing schools for Jackson. Beth has contacted the school district and is waiting to hear about the possible transfer. She's becoming increasingly concerned because she has heard that Jackson might not be placed in the general sixth-grade physical education class. She wonders what the referral process will be like if they change districts and how long it will take. The idea of this change raises many questions for her about Jackson's education. What will the middle school be like? How will the transition to high school go? Will Jackson be able to make new friends?

The road toward inclusive physical activity is founded on a commitment to the philosophy of inclusion as well as knowledge of how all participants can gain access to and become meaningfully involved in physical activity opportunities. Although Jackson has been involved in physical activity programs from an earlier age, what procedures are in place to ensure his continued involvement in general physical education? If you were his physical education teacher, what steps would you follow to provide Jackson with the best program?

Physical activity professionals need to know the process through which all individuals enter into physical activity, how those involved find support and guidance, and how practitioners responsible for the programs are held accountable. Although legal requirements and the personnel involved might differ across settings and programs, the process of prioritizing goals, ensuring best practice, providing support, and making accommodations is the same for all individuals regardless of age or context. In this chapter we'll begin with an overview of the steps involved in inclusive physical activity programming and will then provide some insight about how these steps are followed for infants and toddlers, school-age children, and both young and older adults.

▶ A PRACTICAL APPROACH TO INCLUSIVE PHYSICAL ACTIVITY PROGRAMMING

Inclusive physical activity involves a sequence of steps that practitioners must take to ensure equal access and optimal programming for everyone. Figure 5.1 shows the process of developing and implementing inclusive and individualized physical activity. The process involves five steps necessary to break down the barriers to inclusive physical activity (as discussed in chapter 2). The process also integrates collaboration and network skills (discussed in chapter 3) and appropriate ecological assessment (described in chapter 4) that lead to appropriate planning and programming.

This process includes two phases. The first is the **preparation phase,** which consists of three steps:

1. Ensuring access
2. Establishing supportive networks
3. Promoting positive physical activity environments

The second phase is the **planning and implementing phase,** which includes two more steps:

4. Planning for individualized instruction
5. Assessing success

Although this process might appear to be a linear one, there's continual reevaluation and flow between the preparation phase and the planning phase. Figure 5.1 illustrates this flow and the need for ongoing reflection involved in the planning process. The process involves the three Rs of reflective practice, as discussed in chapter 1: ready, rethink, and retry (see figure 1.12, p. 18). All good practitioners reflect on every step of the process and make changes throughout each phase.

Ensuring Access

The first step toward offering an inclusive physical activity program is creating and ensuring access for all potential participants. The physical activity practitioner must advocate on behalf of the participants. For some youngsters, this entails determining who qualifies for services and how to obtain increased support. For instance, in a school-based setting, a student might become eligible to receive support and services associated with physical education if, by law, this child is identified as having a disability (figure 5.2). In addition, the student must qualify for these supports and services by meeting appropriate assessment and state-determined performance criteria. For youngsters in non-school-based settings or adults in the community, access means increasing avenues for entry into physical activity programs and assisting them in overcoming barriers to physical activity they might face.

As we discussed in chapter 2, access also involves educating participants regarding the benefits of physical activity, the opportunities available to them, and informing them of their rights related to accessing physical activity programs. A physical education teacher should seek out students with ability differences in the school who might not yet be assigned a physical education class or inquire if all students in the school are indeed receiving physical education. The teacher might need to discuss with students and parents the requirements of physical education and help them understand the benefits of meaningful participation. Likewise, a fitness practitioner might explore programs at the facility that currently include individuals with differing capabilities. If these programs are limited, more programming opportunities must be developed; the public must then be made aware that these new programs exist and that individuals of all abilities are welcome. Spreading the word about new programs might involve open houses or invitations for people to come and tour the facility and hear about the programs available. Presentations could also be provided to particular community groups regarding the benefits of physical activity and how people can become more active. It is also a good idea to tell local organizations or community agencies about the program, emphasizing that everyone is invited to participate.

Of course such efforts might be in vain if administrators, supervisors, and other persons significantly involved with potential participants are not also educated about inclusive programming. School administrators should be supplied information about the legal rights and responsibilities of their school regarding physical education for children with identified disabilities;

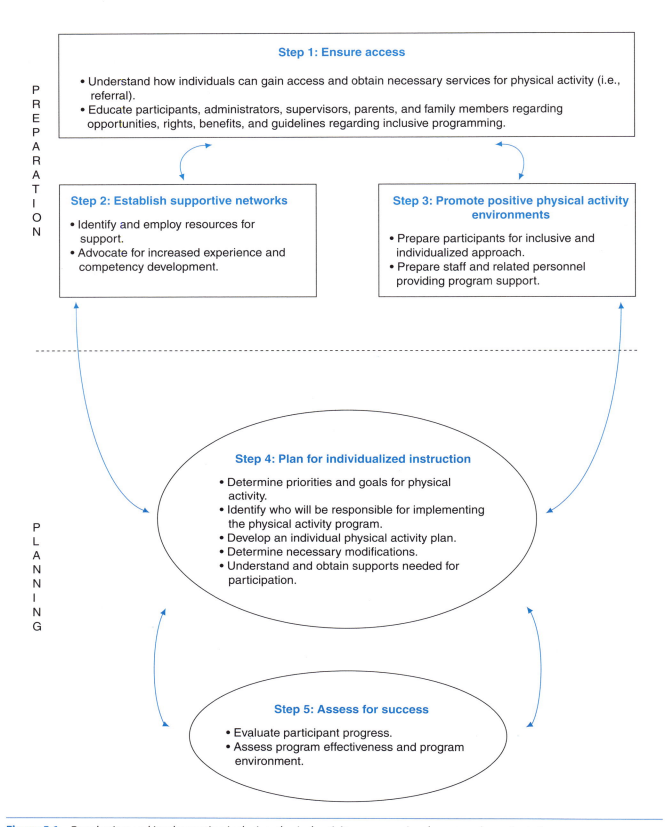

P R E P A R A T I O N

Step 1: Ensure access

- Understand how individuals can gain access and obtain necessary services for physical activity (i.e., referral).
- Educate participants, administrators, supervisors, parents, and family members regarding opportunities, rights, benefits, and guidelines regarding inclusive programming.

Step 2: Establish supportive networks

- Identify and employ resources for support.
- Advocate for increased experience and competency development.

Step 3: Promote positive physical activity environments

- Prepare participants for inclusive and individualized approach.
- Prepare staff and related personnel providing program support.

P L A N N I N G

Step 4: Plan for individualized instruction

- Determine priorities and goals for physical activity.
- Identify who will be responsible for implementing the physical activity program.
- Develop an individual physical activity plan.
- Determine necessary modifications.
- Understand and obtain supports needed for participation.

Step 5: Assess for success

- Evaluate participant progress.
- Assess program effectiveness and program environment.

Figure 5.1 Developing and implementing inclusive physical activity programs involves many important steps.

Figure 5.2 Infants with suspected or documented delays can qualify for early intervention programs that involve movement activities.

they should also understand how children with physical activity needs are referred and supported. Directors of community recreation centers or health clubs and appropriate medical professionals should be informed about the variety of programs available in the community. Whatever the situation, the program facilitator should commit to include all individuals and support them by opening the doors and welcoming them into the program.

Establishing Support Networks

Once a commitment to creating and increasing access is made, the next step is to identify and establish networks of individuals who might offer support or serve as resources for the physical activity practitioner. As we mentioned in chapter 3, collaborative teams are critical to the success of any program. Certain individuals might offer valuable insight and information regarding medical information and physical activity recommendations or contraindications for particular participants. They might also provide information about effective adaptations, instructional strategies, and behavioral practices that have been successful in other contexts.

Support networks are invaluable in that physical activity professionals must advocate not only for participants but for themselves as well. The success of inclusive practices rests with the knowledge and skills professionals have regarding effective strategies and insights for individualized programming. Practitioners must advocate for increased support and training to this end. They might ask to observe other inclusive programs or professionals effective at implementing inclusive activities, to attend conferences and workshops, or to complete other courses focusing on inclusive physical activity. Through collaborative and supportive networks, practitioners can gain the insights, knowledge, and skills to become adept and confident in developing and implementing inclusive physical activity programs for all individuals.

Promoting Positive Physical Activity Environments

Regardless of how committed a practitioner is to including all individuals, the overall success of the program depends largely on the attitudes of all those involved. The next step in the process then is promoting positive physical activity environments by preparing everyone involved for the inclusive and individualized approach. Participants with differences in ability, as well as the staff and related personnel who support them, must be informed of the philosophy underlying the program and understand the capabilities and needs of all participants.

Preparing Participants

Preparing potential participants with diverse abilities involves increasing their knowledge about what the activity setting comprises and their confidence that the program can meet their needs. Raising participants' comfort levels before they begin the program will ease their transition into the program. Here are some suggestions to assist with this process.

- Distribute written material describing the mission statement, philosophy, and program or activity.

- Invite potential participants to visit the program to observe and ask questions.
- Provide a videotape of the program for potential participants to watch at home.
- Provide contact numbers of staff members for obtaining additional information.
- Provide contact numbers of current participants in the program for information sharing.
- Schedule an individual visit with a program staff member or teacher.
- Offer one day of participation as a visitor.

Preparation of participants also involves those individuals who require less direct support or accommodation and are already in the program. Several strategies can help these participants become familiar with the wide range of participants who might join them and the array of methods and materials that might be employed to promote everyone's involvement and success. These individuals too should feel comfortable and confident that their program can only be improved through the diversity of experiences and abilities that new participants can bring.

When the practitioner leads by example, establishes an atmosphere of acceptance and equity, and employs an inclusive style from the start, program participants will be more positive and accepting. In this way, participants become committed to the success of the program or activity and have a vested interest in the success of all those involved. This can only happen if all participants are made aware of the range of abilities existing within the program, provided an explanation regarding why accommodations and modifications are necessary, and given opportunities for ideas and strategies to further promote success and enjoyment of all those involved.

Prepare Support Personnel

The staff that supports individuals within the program must understand the program's philosophy and goals. Support members should know the range of abilities of individuals who might join and the supports necessary for these participants to have success. Such supports might include the use of assistive devices, variations in instruction or activities, or the assistance of another person. Support personnel must be clear about their roles and expectations in supporting participants and knowledgeable about the activities or modifications in which they will be involved. It is important to understand that those providing support must be continually supported themselves. Open lines of communication should be emphasized before the program starts and should continue throughout the support staff's involvement in the program.

Planning for Individualized Instruction

Once participants and support personnel involved in inclusive programs are prepared for the program's onset, the process shifts from program preparation to program planning. At this point, the participants themselves become the primary focus, with the goal being to individualize instruction.

- *Determine priorities and goals.* Now is the time to determine the priorities and goals for participants in the various programs. For example, the emphasis for a toddler might be balance and mobility so that the child can move across a grassy playground to play with his or her peers. A middle school student might be interested in participating in a general physical education cooperative games unit with classmates, whereas an older adult might want to participate in an aerobics or yoga class at the local fitness center. In each case, program priorities are participant-based, and goals are meaningful to the individual. As we discussed in chapter 4, many factors must be considered when developing the focus of an individual's program and assessing skills and capabilities to determine appropriate goals. Most important to consider are the skills the individual needs to participate in physical activities or perform functional tasks in both the present and the future. Of course, the specific activity interests of the individual and his or her family must also be considered when determining goals and priorities.

- *Determine who is responsible for teaching the physical activity program.* The next step of planning focuses on who will teach participants the skills they need to participate in the physical activities that have been identified. In some cases, the program instructor might have the knowledge and skills required to teach all participants, regardless of their ability level. In other cases, practitioners might need the assistance of trained professionals to help modify activities to accommodate individual differences. Although some programs might involve previously organized large groups and prestructured programming, in some cases it might be necessary to offer alternative activities in small group settings. Whether these activities are supervised by the program instructor or by an adapted physical activity practitioner, decisions regarding an individual's activity program must be made with inclusion in mind. The activities need to involve participants with a range of abilities and not only those with low skill levels.

- *Develop an individual physical activity plan.* Once priorities have been determined, an individualized physical activity plan is developed. These plans take into account the priorities and goals identified and also the professional standards or guidelines set forth by the profession. For school-age children, these standards relate to lifelong physical activity participation and might be achieved in many ways. For the fitness professional, guidelines and practices have been established by health and fitness organizations (as provided in appendix C). Some sport organizations have also established rules and regulations to help guide coaches in the training and sport skill development of their athletes.

- *Determine necessary modifications.* We've discussed the "what" and "where" of individualized physical activity programming. Now we turn to the "how." As we touched on in chapter 1, what a person is capable of achieving does not depend solely on his or her abilities but also on the task being attempted and the context. Based on the concept of "capability shifting" discussed in chapter 1, modification strategies can be directed toward the task or the context to promote success. Strategies to modify the context include changes in instruction, organization, or procedures. Modifications in the type of equipment used and the physical setting might further promote inclusive physical activity. For students with differences in ability, curricular or program tasks might be modified as well. In chapter 6 we discuss the breadth of modifications possible when developing inclusive physical activity plans and the key considerations in determining the appropriateness of such changes.

- *Understand and obtain supports needed for participation.* Given the range of abilities and needs of participants in inclusive programs, no one person can be expected to have all the expertise and skills necessary to provide an individualized and effective program for every participant. Thus, it is important to identify who will provide support to the participant if support is necessary, what supports are best to provide, and what degree of support is needed. Remember that the goal is to promote independence and increased competence of each participant regardless of age or ability. Practitioners should be aware that, in some cases, providing unnecessary support might have a negative effect on the participant's interaction with others in the program or could lead to increased dependence and learned helplessness.

Assessing Success of Inclusive Efforts

In inclusive physical activity, program assessment and evaluation are just as important as program planning. Those who organize and implement programs must be accountable for what they do, and evaluation of participant progress is essential to this end. Some of the issues discussed in chapter 4 regarding assessment for individuals with differences in ability must be carefully considered to ensure that evaluation information is accurate and meaningful. However, accountability goes beyond measuring to what extent a particular individual has reached his or her goals. Inclusive programs intend that all participants in the program reach their potential. It also includes continued reevaluation of the program environment, which includes the attitudes of others and the effectiveness of modifications and accommodations being implemented. As discussed in chapter 1, practitioners must continually employ the 3 Rs. They must *ready* their own practice and the influence it has on the people involved. They must *rethink* practices they have just implemented. They must *retry* new methods that include and accommodate all participants in their programs.

THE PLANNING PROCESS IN ACTION

When planning a program for infants and toddlers, school-age children, or adults, the steps in the planning process are similar. In the sections that follow we'll describe how the process works for different age groups.

INCLUSIVE PHYSICAL ACTIVITY FOR INFANTS AND TODDLERS

The benefits of early physical activity for infants and toddlers are well accepted and, in fact, led to the passage of legislation mandating services for infants and toddlers who might be at risk for delays (see appendix D, P.L. 99-457). Physical activity contributes significantly to a child's early development in all aspects of learning, including cognitive, social–emotional, language, and fine and gross motor development. With the proper supports, all infants and toddlers can participate in meaningful physical activity to help them develop into physically active and healthy children.

Ensuring Access

Many infants and toddlers have ample opportunities to be physically active, such as playing with mobiles in their crib or reaching for toys while lying on the floor. Infants might also participate with their mothers or fathers in structured group programs such as infant massage class, "baby and me" swim class, or a parent–infant exercise class. Toddlers often have chances to play with other children through parent-organized playgroups or community programs. Much of this activity occurs in informal or loosely organized settings such as at home, at community parks or recreation centers, or in neighborhood backyards. For some children, opportunities are wide and diverse, but other young children might not have occasions to play with others or to participate in infant and toddler programs because of the barriers they and their parents experience. As we discussed in chapter 2, such barriers as time, transportation, cost, or a parent's own physical activity habits or beliefs can influence how much physical activity infants and toddlers get.

Unfortunately, access issues often surface for infants and toddlers with differences in ability. These children have less impromptu opportunities or invitations to join in play and physical activity. In addition, many infants and toddlers born prematurely or with significant "disabilities" are medically fragile in the early months and might not be ready to participate in physical activity programs. However, research reveals that the earlier a child with suspected delays receives intervention, the less likely he or she will encounter delays later in life (Weiner & Koppelman, 1987). Knowledge of the increased benefits of early intervention coupled with the awareness that decreased opportunities exist for these children have led to legislation promoting physical activity involvement for this age group. Early intervention services are mandated by the Individuals with Disabilities Education Act (IDEA) (NICHCY, National Dissemination Center for Children with Disabilities, 1998). Any infant or toddler from 0 to 36 months of age who has an identifiable disability or is at risk for delays might be eligible for early intervention services (see appendix B for eligibility criteria). School districts, county programs, regional centers, or local public or private agencies might provide supports and services. The services would relate to any areas of suspected delay and might include communication, physical, cognitive, social or emotional development, or adaptive behavior (self-help skills).

Infants who qualify for services are generally identified through the local education area's child-find procedures. These child-find procedures provide information to parents via the following methods:

- Contact through neonatal intensive care units
- Local parent support organizations
- Community health and developmental screening
- Local pediatricians or other public health providers
- Public service announcements

Once a child is identified and referred, the early intervention program is required to contact the family to determine if they'd like an evaluation. If the parents decide they want early intervention services, they give written permission for an early intervention team to begin an assessment of family and child needs.

Establishing Support Networks

Many parents find support and guidance during playgroups or activity sessions. During these times, information about development, observed behavior, and future expectations is freely shared and discussed. But this is often not the case for parents of infants or toddlers with disabilities. Many times these parents aren't yet connected to other parents of children who have ability differences and needs. For these parents, the early intervention team can provide several supports, including infant and toddler parent support groups, parent networks, a resource library for information on development and disabilities, toy lending, and other direct intervention services.

On completion of assessments, the early intervention team meets with the parents to develop a service plan for the family. The early intervention team might include special educators, speech and language pathologists and audiologists, health care providers, therapists, adapted physical educators, social workers or psychologists, and others who might provide services to the infant and family. Generally, a designated service coordinator or case manager coordinates these individuals and all services.

The service coordinator can be any individual on the team and is generally the person the family feels most comfortable with and who has the skills to carry out the plan. This person is responsible for making contact with the family and should be knowledgeable of early intervention regulations, community services, parent support groups, family resource centers, recreational programs, childcare services, respite care, and community medical and financial assistance programs.

Promoting Positive Physical Activity Environments

Infants are naturally active learners, and much of their initial learning comes through movement experiences. For example, infants learn about cause and effect by pushing the buttons on a pop-up toy; they learn about gravity by pushing their bowl off the table; and they begin to roll over while reaching for an intriguing toy. For infants, positive physical activity means setting up an environment that is safe and encourages interaction and exploration through self-initiated and facilitated play. The importance of parent–child interaction to promote development is well documented (McCollum & Hemmeter, 1997), and the safer and more comfortable a child feels, the more likely he or she is to explore and learn. However, for the parent of a child with a significant difference in ability, this interaction might be even more critical because the parent might need to assist the infant in exploring their world. Although most children follow a similar developmental sequence from rolling to creeping to walking, the pace at which these skills develop varies significantly. Some children might even skip a particular skill altogether. Variations in ability and the way in which children participate in play or activity should be accepted and encouraged. For parents of children with ability differences, it is critical to have a supportive environment in which to relax and play with their child. Sharing information with other parents, initiating playgroups, or inviting parents and children over for a visit are all ways to create environments for positive physical activity experiences for infants and toddlers. Professionals can help create positive environments by providing positive support to parents for the great parenting they are doing, helping parents with ideas for homemade toys, demonstrating how to set up a play environment, or showing how to integrate motor development activities into everyday activities (e.g., assisting a toddler to stand while holding onto the coffee table to play with a toy or having the child stand on one foot while the parent removes each shoe).

Planning for Individualized Instruction

For an infant or toddler who might be at risk of a developmental delay or who has an identifiable disability, early intervention is beneficial. The early intervention team, along with the parents, discusses and develops an individualized family service plan (IFSP) as outlined in IDEA. The IFSP is a written document that describes and explains the strengths and needs of the family, which services are to be provided, and when and how these services will be implemented (figure 5.3). For infants and toddlers, the IFSP includes written objectives for the child in each area of need. These goals are called *outcomes*. During the IFSP meeting, the early intervention personnel share the results of their assessments and evaluations and together with the parents determine appropriate outcomes for the child based on child and family needs. The parents' desires are paramount to this process, and outcomes should be written in the words of the parents as much as possible. For example, if parents say they'd like to see their child roll over or crawl, then the outcome is written with that in mind. Figure 5.4 is an example of an IFSP developed for a toddler.

Services for infants and toddlers should be provided "to the maximum extent appropriate" in the natural setting. This might include the home, a childcare facility, or a school program, and should be where the family feels the most comfortable receiving services and where the child naturally interacts with his environment. Ideally, serving

- Statement of the family's resources, priorities, and concerns
- Statement of the infants or toddler's present level of functioning
- Expected outcomes for the infant and family, including criteria, procedures, and time lines
- Statement of services needed to meet the needs of the family and infant including frequency, duration, and method of delivering services
- Date of initiation of services
- Identification of the service coordinator
- Transition plan for preschool when the child turns two years, six months

Figure 5.3 Sample content for the IFSP.

Individuals Who Might Serve on the IFSP Team

- Parent or guardian
- Early intervention teacher
- Physical therapist
- Adapted physical education specialist
- Occupational therapist
- Pediatric nurse
- Psychologist
- Speech pathologist

Northeast Region—Individualized Family Service Plan (IFSP)

Child's name _Francisco Juarez_   DOB _6 – 01 – 03_

IFSP date _5 – 24 – 04_

Child-Related Family Concerns, Priorities and Resources
(To be included only with the concurrence of the family)

Strong family support and extended family. Grandparents live in the home with the family and assist with childcare.

Family Outcome Statement(s)

Family would like to see Francisco walking and standing independently.

Child's Strengths and Present Level of Development

Comments: _Francisco is a wonderful and happy boy. He smiles and engages with others easily. He enjoys music and toys and is starting to babble._

Vision: _Screened by vision specialist. No concerns_   **Hearing:** _Screened by audiologist. No concerns_

Source of Information: _Hawaii Early Learning Profile, observation, parent interview_

Physical (fine & gross motor): _Rolls in either direction. Pushes up on one hand when on stomach. Can pivot on stomach. Can sit unsupported. Protective extension to right but not left._

Cognitive: _Throws and drops objects. Listens to speech attentively. Rolls to get a toy. Looks at pictures in a book when named and turns to find a sound. Likes to play "Peek-a-boo."_

Communication: _Babbles single consonants such as "ba." Says "dada" and "mama" and waves goodbye._

Social or Emotional: _Shows likes and dislikes for people or objects. Prefers mother to meet his needs. Cooperates in play and smiles frequently._

Self-Help Skills (eating, dressing, bathing, and the like): _Enjoys putting toys in his mouth. He can feed himself a cracker with his right hand and drink from a cup with assistance. Takes a nap each day for about an hour and a half._

Health Status: _Francisco is in good health. He was six weeks premature at birth but has made consistent gains in all areas since he has been home from the hospital._

Current Physician: _Dr. Joy_

Medications/Equipment: _No medications or equipment at this time._

Figure 5.4 Sample IFSP outcomes for a toddler with developmental delays involved in an inclusive physical activity program.

Figure 5.5 Serving children at home allows professionals to provide families with intervention ideas and suggestions that match their environment.

children at home allows professionals to provide families with intervention ideas and suggestions that match their environment (e.g., demonstrating for a family in their living room how to assist a toddler with pulling up to standing at the couch). Implementing services at home makes it more likely that parents can help their children practice on a daily basis independent of professionals (figure 5.5).

Although there is no legal requirement of a written document for children without identified disabilities, individualizing activity goals and needed supports is still important. For instance, parents often decide which activities their children should participate in, who should be present to offer support and guidance, and which behaviors or skills they desire for their children to achieve (e.g., social skills, sharing, communication, dressing, motor skills). How each family goes about planning for their child's development varies significantly, but some activities include the following:

- Read infant or toddler books and magazines on development.
- Talk with family members and friends.
- Seek out parent–toddler playgroups.
- Talk with other parents about their experiences.
- Complete background checks on childcare providers and check necessary credentials.
- Interview other parents who have attended a particular facility before placing the child.
- Consult with physician during well-baby check-ups.

Anyone who has grown up with younger brothers and sisters, infant cousins, or nieces and nephews has seen first-hand the natural developmental progression of infants and toddlers. However, for many new parents the first-born child is their first chance to watch the developmental process unfold. Many new parents have common goals for their children, which are often based on a sequence of skills that include rolling over, sitting up, crawling, standing, and taking their first steps. All children, regardless of their ability level, need adult guidance and a supportive environment for optimal physical activity development.

Assessing the Success of Inclusive Efforts

Assessing the success of inclusion for infants and toddlers includes examining the extent to which a child can participate in his or her natural environment. This might be at home with family, in a playgroup with peers, or among other people or objects. For most children, this examination is an informal process, a type of authentic assessment, that takes place through well-baby check-ups, photographs, videos, and baby books containing dates, times, and locations of such events as the first step, first word, or first solid food. Families of children with

← **THINK BACK**

Think back to Beth and Tom as new parents and their experience with Jackson.

1. How might they have been referred for early intervention services?

2. What types of services might they have needed for Jackson?

3. What types of programs or activities would have been appropriate for Jackson as an infant and toddler?

4. What is an IFSP? Based on what you know about Jackson and his family, what kind of information might have been included on Jackson's IFSP?

differences in ability might use these same methods to document growth and development in the natural environment. However, if the child is receiving early intervention services under IDEA, they will also have additional documentation through the IFSP process, as described earlier.

IFSP meetings and documentation are required *every six months* to review progress and determine new outcomes as the previous ones are met. An IFSP meeting can also be held at any time that parents or other team members think it's necessary. Along with an evaluation of skills, parents and professionals can assess a toddler in how well he or she interacts with peers in a play setting.

As a toddler nears school age, many families begin to assess and explore preschool placements. This time is an important transition for many families and children because it's their first "school" experience. Parents and childcare providers often spend time touring the facility as they prepare for this important transition. Some parents visit the school with their children and help them get familiar with the new environment before school officially starts. Children with differences in ability that have an IFSP are required to have a formal transition planning meeting as they get ready for preschool. This meeting is required by the IDEA to occur by the time the child is 2 years and 9 months. The purpose of the transition meeting is to discuss a re-evaluation of the child to determine if he or she will continue to need intervention services. The discussion also involves if and where the child will receive preschool programming and which and how special education services will be implemented. The same multidisciplinary team of individuals who implemented the IFSP completes the transition plan along with the individuals who will be working with the child in his or her next placement (e.g., the preschool teacher and any other new faces). During this transition phase the child is also oriented to the new environment.

Regardless of an infant's or toddler's abilities, keeping records of changes that occur over time is a good idea for parents or caretakers. Families will appreciate looking back at pictures, videos, or notes recording the child's development. Plus, through such documentation professionals can help parents see the incredible growth their child is making.

▶ INCLUSIVE PHYSICAL ACTIVITY FOR SCHOOL-AGE CHILDREN

Many benefits to inclusive physical education environments exist for school-age children. First, inclusive environments allow children to be educated in their home school in their natural environment. Children who go to their neighborhood schools have the opportunity to become friends with their peers and are more likely to be involved in class birthday parties, local field trips, and community events. Second, all students are provided with an opportunity to value and respect individual differences; they grow up appreciating their own skills and valuing the unique skills and abilities of others. The children of today are the future parents of children with differing abilities tomorrow, and mutual respect for one another is critical. In regard to physical activity, research shows that students with ability differences can improve their motor skills in an inclusive setting (St. Clair, 1995) and that the skills of other students are not negatively affected by inclusive programming (Block & Zeman, 1996; Lieberman, 1996; Murata,

1995; Vogler, Van der Mars, Cusimano, & Darst, 1990). Furthermore, the attitudes of students toward their peers with differences in ability were more positive in inclusive programs, and students were more accepting of curricular modifications (Block & Zeman, 1996).

Ensuring Access

As with toddlers, many children of school age have opportunities for unstructured physical activity involvement. Unlike their younger counterparts, however, their involvement tends to be in more organized and structured settings. School-age children typically have physical education classes scheduled for various amounts of time within their school week. In addition, many youngsters have opportunities to participate in after-school physical activity sessions, recess, and sport programs. Although access to physical activity programs such as recreation leagues and physical education classes is usually not a problem for most children, these programs are often less inclusive of children with significantly different abilities. As such, the children who do participate in them have little opportunity to experience and interact with peers of diverse ability. As described earlier, an inclusive program is one in which individualized and accommodating instruction exists for everyone, and the range of individual abilities offers a far richer experience for all those involved.

For children with disabilities, access to inclusive physical activity programs is not easy. Children who previously were involved in an early intervention motor program through an IFSP will either exit out of the program at age three if services are no longer needed or transition into another individualized movement program through their school. Some children who did not receive early intervention services as infants or toddlers might also need support and services as they grow older because many educational concerns and physical needs are not revealed until a child gets older. School districts have procedures and guidelines for public school-age children who might need referral for special education services, including physical education. Most students with variations in ability may be provided instruction within the general physical education class with or without modifications. However, if a child's motor or behavioral concerns are great enough, the general physical education teacher might need additional support services within the class to teach the child effectively. All teachers of physical education programs should feel supported and know that special education services are available in these settings for children who qualify and need additional assistance (figure 5.6).

The referral process for a child who needs assistance in physical education or other educational classes usually begins with a student study team (SST), also known as child study team (CST). The SST is a team of individuals from the school that serves to assist teachers with modification ideas to help a child succeed in the general education program. The make-up of the student study team might vary, but their primary role is to serve as a support team for general education teachers, including physical education. Often a screening form (figure 5.7) can be helpful in the initial data collection process to assist in determining the needs of the learner.

The purpose of the SST is to assist teachers in resolving challenges they might be having with particular students in their teaching and learning environments. The role of the SST is to generate ideas and solutions to create more successful learning experiences

1. Mental retardation
2. Hearing impairment, including deafness
3. Speech or language impairment
4. Visual impairment, including blindness
5. Serious emotional disturbance
6. Orthopedic impairment
7. Autism
8. Traumatic brain injury
9. Other health impairment
10. Learning disability

Figure 5.6 Eligibility categories for services under the IDEA ages 3 to 21 IDEA, Part A, Section 602(3)(i).

Did You Know?

All children with identified disabilities are *required* by the Individuals with Disabilities Education Act to have physical education instruction.

Adapted Physical Education Pre-School Motor Screening Form

Name of child _____   Date _____

DOB _____   Age _____

Evaluator _____

Please indicate with a "Y" for yes or an "N" for no, for each of the following items based on your experience with the child.

General motor skills:

_____ Stand on one foot momentarily.

_____Walk on tiptoes.

_____Walk up stairs alternating feet.

_____Walk down stairs alternating feet with one hand held.

_____Runs well without falling and can change speed.

_____Jump off the floor with both feet.

_____Attempts to hop on one foot.

_____Walk on a balance board on the ground with one hand held.

_____Catch a playground ball that is bounced into arms.

_____Throw a beanbag overhand in a forward direction.

_____Pedal a tricycle.

_____Climb a short ladder to go down a slide.

_____Balance on a swing to be pushed.

Other observations:

_____Child chooses to watch when others are playing.

_____Child bumps into objects and/or others in their environment.

_____Child has a need to touch everything around him/her.

_____Child is able to follow simple directions with others.

_____Child seems over stimulated by sounds, touch, or other sensory stimuli.

Favorite activities include:

Comments or concerns:

Figure 5.7   A sample screening form might include these specific skills appropriate for youngsters at this age.

Individuals Who Might Serve on the SST

- Classroom teachers
- Principal
- Special education teachers
- Counselor or psychologist
- Related service personnel

for the child. These suggestions are then implemented and documented by the physical education teacher. If the SST suggestions were unproductive in creating a more positive learning environment for this student, the child may then be referred to special education services for further assessment and evaluation.

The special education process usually begins with a written referral notice (figure 5.8) (although a referral may be verbal) that describes current concerns and what has been attempted in the past. An assessment plan is then designed to determine what areas need to be tested, which might be any area of suspected concern, such as hearing, vision, motor development, cognitive skills, perceptual motor learning, or behavior. The written plan is then taken to the parents for permission. Consent from the parents or guardians to assess must be obtained before any evaluations are conducted. Once the parents give permission for assessment, the areas of concern are evaluated. However, if the parents do not want their child assessed, this request must be respected and the assessment may not be conducted. Individuals who may assess a child include the psychologist, special education teacher, physical therapist, occupational therapist, adapted physical education teacher, speech pathologist, nurse, or other personnel needed to evaluate the child. Following the assessments, an individualized education program (IEP) meeting is scheduled at a time convenient for the parents. Each individual who completed testing with the child shares a written report with the parents and IEP team members (figure 5.9).

Unlike physical education programs in the public schools, no formal guidelines exist for ensuring children with differences in ability access to community-based recreation programs, intramural programs, or public sports programs. Students, however, may not be denied access based on section 504 of the Rehabilitation Act and the Americans with Disabilities Act legislation (see appendix D).

Physical activity practitioners need to be aware of these laws and provide programs that

- meet the needs and abilities of all individuals within their community,
- offer programs that follow a philosophy of inclusion, and
- provide a diverse offering of activities.

Establishing Supportive Networks

The physical educator can find support and guidance from many other individuals. The parents or guardians of the child are most important to communicate with and can usually provide helpful insight. The family members know the child better than any other individual and have information regarding the child's likes and dislikes, medical history, natural physical activity rhythms, and what the child responds to best. Physical educators might also network with other teachers within the school or district, educators from sessions at professional conferences or workshops, related service personnel (such as physical and occupational therapists and school psychologists), and other professionals within the school.

A physical activity practitioner working to develop and implement inclusive programs in the community needs to establish ongoing communication with the participants themselves, of course, and also with their family members, medical personnel, human service or agency personnel, and even community resource and volunteer organizations. Regardless of whether an individual is planning programs within the public schools or community, no practitioner should function in isolation. Planning for inclusive physical activity programs requires positive collaboration from many professionals. No one should feel alone in the process.

Referral to SST for Adapted P.E. Grades 2 and 3

Each person requesting an assessment or screening for adapted PE should fill out this checklist. If the student does not demonstrate difficulties in many areas and does not really stand out compared to his or her peers, a referral for assessment is not appropriate.

Student observed _____ Age _____ Grade _____ Date _____

School _____ Classroom teacher _____

Person making referral _____

Potential DIS condition _____ Enrolled in special education Y ❑   N ❑

Playground skills
____ Will jump long rope independently
____ Can hit moving tetherball
____ Will walk forward and backward heel, toe 10 ft on playground line

Social-emotional
____ Plays well with peers
____ Follows playground rules
____ Participates in group activities

Object manipulation
____ Bounces ball four times with one hand (dribble)
____ Catches playground ball from 15 ft with hands only (no trapping)
____ Kicks playground ball rolled from 15 ft
____ Can throw bean bag overhand approximately 15 ft

Physical fitness
____ Performs standing long jump for approximately 30 inches (Forward arm swing and balance on landing)
____ Can do 8 curl-ups in 30 seconds
____ Can touch toes with legs extended while sitting on floor

Other observations or reasons for referral:

Recommendations of SST:
____ Refer to APE teacher for assessment
____ Classroom or PE teacher to provide minimal modifications in general PE and return to SST if problems continue

_____   _____
SST chairperson   Date

Figure 5.8   Sample referral form.

Members of the IEP Team As Required by the IDEA 97 [Part B, Section, 614(d)(1)(B)]

Parents of the child with a disability

At least one general education teacher

At least one special education teacher or at least one special education provider

A representative of the local education agency

An individual to interpret the instructional implications of evaluation results who might be a member of the team described previously

At the discretion of the parent or agency, other individuals who have knowledge or special expertise regarding the child, including related services personnel, as appropriate

The child (when appropriate)

Figure 5.9 Although these are the required members of the team as defined under IDEA, the parents may also invite any other individuals they would like to attend the meeting on their behalf.

Promoting Positive Physical Activity Environments

Preparing peers and support personnel for inclusion of children with different abilities results in a positive physical activity environment.

Preparing Peers

Successful efforts to include children with differing abilities in physical activity programs depends heavily on peer acceptance (Block, 2000). If a child's ability differences are not understood and accepted by classmates, peers might view the child negatively and be reluctant to accept any accommodations he or she might need (Wilson & Lieberman, 2000). Several awareness strategies can be used to help peers increase their awareness of the wide range of abilities existing within a program (Lieberman & Houston-Wilson, 2002). Figure 5.10 provides some examples of ability awareness activities (figure 5.11). Remember that in any awareness activity or simulation, the focus should be on the new skills that are to be learned and how the environment can support this learning through modification rather than focusing on deficits and difficulties of individual learners.

In any learning activity, especially ability awareness activities, time should be spent at the close of the lesson discussing what occurred. This can be done in many ways, including group discussion, individual journals, or role-playing experiences. Whatever method is selected, the instructor must promote and model positive communication skills and effective listening and assist students in processing their learning and encourage them to talk about any difficulties they might have experienced. Again, the physical activity instructor should focus on what changes need to be made to increase access during the activity or what skills need to be learned to foster enjoyment and

1. Invite guest athletes with ability differences to speak in class.

2. Watch videos on disability sports.

3. Explore the Internet for disability sport information and competitions.

4. Participate in an activity while simulating a difference in ability, such as using a wheelchair while playing basketball or doing parachute activities.

5. Participate in a specific disability sport such as goalball or beep baseball.

6. Play a game without talking and using only hand signs to communicate. (Teams create their own communication system.)

7. Hold a class discussion about modifications for individual differences.

8. Discuss ways that students can work with each other in the class.

Figure 5.10 Ability awareness activities.

Figure 5.11 Inviting speakers with differences in ability to visit and speak with youngsters about their physical activity experiences can pave the way for increased awareness and acceptance of individual differences.

achieve success. The focus should be on the new skills an individual would develop and use to participate in a given activity.

Most important, the physical educator can foster increased awareness and acceptance of individual differences through adopting an instructional approach that's individualized for everyone, including those with high ability, right from the start. For example, in a basketball program learners might be given the choice to work at several areas, such as a skill-development station, two-on-two half-court mini games, a full-court modified game, or a traditional competitive game. In this way students can select the practice area that best meets their needs, abilities, and interests. In an inclusive program, modifications are viewed as common practice and used for all individuals in the program, not just for those with low abilities or perceived to be in need of modifications. Enhancing peer awareness of needed modifications also shows how individuals can participate in activities in many ways. Peers can more fully understand the need for activity modifications by experiencing these modifications themselves. For example, peers might take turns using a wheelchair during a game of tag or in a tennis match with minor rule modifications. Regardless of the activity variation, peers must realize and appreciate that modifications don't give individuals an unfair advantage. Emphasize to them that modifications are used instead to allow students increased participation and a chance to achieve success equal to theirs. Students also see that modifications used during activities in fact make a game more challenging and exciting for everyone involved. When the students in the class accept this practice, a positive and accepting environment exists for all. These principles hold true whether planning for a physical education classroom or teaching in a community recreation program.

In school physical education programs, students of all abilities are placed in classes together, but in community sport programs children might be placed based on age and skill level. For example, in Special Olympics students compete based on age and skill classification, as occurs in most competitive recreational sports programs. However, as any coach knows, even when children are classified by age and ability there remains much variation in the skills of particular children and even within an individual child across different skills. By using an inclusive approach within all programs, all children can succeed.

Preparing Support Personnel

In addition to preparing peers for inclusive programming, it is also important to prepare other individuals who might be offering support to children with ability differences participating in the program. This support might be provided by instructional assistants, peer tutors, or community volunteers, many of whom might not have had any formal training or experience in this realm beforehand. As such, it's critical that support personnel be given guidance by those responsible for the child's physical activity program. In physical education, there is sometimes a misunderstanding about who provides support personnel with this guidance. General physical educators might assume that special educators inform support staff about their role and responsibilities, whereas special education teachers might believe that the physical educator is offering this guidance. As a result, support personnel staff members are sometimes at a loss regarding how to facilitate a learner's participation within the class. For learners to benefit from inclusive physical education programming, collaborative communication among all team members must occur. Training of support personnel should involve information pertaining to the individual learner with whom they'll be working as well as methods in which they might assist this individual within the program (Doyle, 1997). This can be achieved through staff in-service trainings, conferences, disability awareness workshops, and site visitations to other inclusive programs. Several resources are available that might further assist support personnel in their roles as facilitators of inclusive physical activity programs (appendices A and C). Block (2000) offers some suggestions about information that can be shared with support personnel:

- Provide information about the philosophy of the physical activity program and general outcomes of physical education for all students (e.g., NASPE standards, program goals).
- Offer general information about the support person's role and the expectations associated with this role.
- Provide detailed information about the learner, the learner's goals, specific concerns, health issues, and safety procedures that might be related.
- Offer continual suggestions and guidance regarding modifications that might be necessary and alternative activities that might be used when activities are deemed inappropriate or unsafe.

Taking the time to prepare individuals who might be supporting learners with ability differences benefits everyone involved in the program. Many times, support personnel not only assist learners with significant differences in ability but also help with the instruction of the class or work with small groups as they interact and learn together. In essence, support personnel offer a second pair of hands, allowing practitioners to teach all learners more effectively and successfully.

Planning for Individualized Instruction

After ensuring access, establishing networks, and promoting a positive environment, it's time to plan for individualized instruction. In an inclusive setting, learners with significant differences in ability might need an individual program plan. In a school setting, this process of planning is required by IDEA for students with identified disabilities and results in the development of an individualized education program (IEP). An IEP documents the What, Where, and How of the child's physical activity plan (figure 5.12). The planning process should also include transition plans and planning for participation in recreation and sport programs.

Developing an Individualized Education Plan

The development process and the foundation for the IEP begins with several questions:

- What skills do individual students need to be successful in present and future physical activity experiences?
- What are the goals, objectives, and benchmarks of the plan?
- Who will teach these skills?
- What modifications will be helpful for individuals of differing abilities?
- What supports will be needed for students within this setting?

What skills do individual students need to be successful in present and future physical activity experiences? For a child with a significant difference in ability, some activities might be more meaningful than others. Priorities for programming should be based on the child's abilities, needs, age, both the child's and parents' interests, as well as future goals for the child outside of school with their family and in the community.

Developmentally appropriate curriculum is generally based on national and state standards for physical education and guidelines for community sports and recreation programs. For the young child, programming generally includes the development of skills themes and movement concepts that will gradually be combined into individual, dual, or team sports, as well as skills

Key Elements of the IEP As Required by IDEA 97 [Part B, Section, 614(d)(1)(A)]

"The term 'individual education program' or 'IEP' means a written statement for each child with a disability that is developed, reviewed, and revised."

The IEP must include

- Present level of educational performance
- Statement of measurable annual goals, including benchmarks or short-term objectives
- A statement of the special education and related services and supplementary aids and services to be provided to the child (or on behalf of the child) and a statement of the program modifications and supports for school personnel provided for the child.
- The extent to which the child will be in the general education class.
- A statement of any modifications in the administration of state- or district-wide assessment of student achievement.
- The projected date for the beginning of services including the frequency, durations, and location of those services.
- Beginning at age 14, an annual update on transition service needs.
- How the child's progress will be measured.
- How the parents will be regularly informed (at least as often as parents of children without disabilities).

Figure 5.12 The IEP serves as a legal and binding document between the family and the school district.

in aquatics, rhythms, and dance. The physical educator must consider which skills are appropriate for a child with significant differences in ability within the program and which skills will lead to appropriate and meaningful participation in the future. At the elementary level, this approach seems to coincide with the skill development considered appropriate for other children the same age and the kinds of activities they participate in to develop these skills. As students grow older and enter secondary school, their program needs to begin to shift focus to lifetime activities. What will the individual participate in outside of school and after graduation? What kinds of activities does the community provide? What does the environment support? Are there recreational programs such as dance, martial arts, teams sports, or swimming? Are there health clubs? If so, what programs do they offer? Is the environment conducive to cycling, mountain biking, rock climbing, or hiking? As a student grows older, it's critical that the physical activity program support development of skills that support lifelong physical activity. At this level, there might be a greater divergence between the routinely offered curriculum and the nature of the activities that might be more meaningful for students with significant differences in ability. Although the physical education program might involve units in team sports such as soccer or flag football, these activities might not be appropriate for every student based again on individual preferences, likelihood of future participation in the community or post graduation, and the like. It's necessary to consider those skills and activities most important for the individual student rather than considering involvement in all the activities available in that program. This decision is made by the general physical educator, adapted physical educator, parents, and other team members, all of whom contribute information and work together to decide the most meaningful focus of the child's physical activity program.

What are the goals, objectives, and benchmarks of the plan? Practitioners should have goals and objectives for individuals within their programs. These can be written in a variety of ways; in physical activity programs they're written in three areas or domains of behavior: the cognitive, affective, and psychomotor domains. According to experts in the field, these are the appropriate categories for objectives. The cognitive domain includes thinking skills, memory, analysis, and synthesis of information. For example, remembering the rules of a game, analyzing a movement sequence, or creating an original game are cognitive goals. The affective domain focuses on feelings about oneself, others, and movement. Examples of the affective domain include how someone feels after participation in an activity, how he or she interacts with others during a competitive or cooperative activity, and how he or she internalizes feelings about a movement after performing a task, such as hitting the sweet spot on a tennis racket. Finally, the psychomotor domain relates to the movement itself. The performance of a skill might be based on the process or *how* the skill is performed or the product or *outcome* of the movement.

Goals generally focus on a broad category, such as improved eye–hand coordination, understanding strategies for basketball, or improved positive interactions with peers. The goals written for any student should relate to the general physical education curriculum and to his or her interests and desires for activity and fitness after graduation from high school.

Objectives are very specific and relate to a goal. A well-written objective includes the following elements:

- Behavior: What observable skill or task will be performed?
- Condition: How will this task be performed? Consider the equipment and environment.
- Criteria: How will you determine that the skill is mastered? What are your criteria for success?

Benchmarks, or short-term objectives, are subcomponents of an objective. Recent revisions to IDEA 97 require that special education services report progress to parents at the same frequency as general education programs. This generally means quarterly or triannual

Goal: Bobby will increase his knowledge of the skills for softball.

Objective: Bobby will identify the four critical elements of the overhand throw with 100% accuracy.

Benchmarks:

By _____, Bobby will identify one critical element of the overhand throw with 100% accuracy.
    date

By _____, Bobby will identify two critical elements of the overhand throw with 100% accuracy.
    date

By _____, Bobby will identify three critical elements of the overhand throw with 100% accuracy.
    date

Goal: Maria will develop positive social skills for game play during physical education.

Objective: Maria will demonstrate positive social interaction with peers by giving at least two high fives to peers during game play in four out of five games.

Benchmarks:

By _____, Maria will demonstrate positive social interaction with peers by giving at least one
    date
high five to her peers during game play in one game.

By _____, Maria will demonstrate positive social interaction with peers by giving at least two
    date
high fives to her peers during game play in two out of five games.

By _____, Maria will demonstrate positive social interaction with peers by giving at least two
    date
high fives to her peers during game play in three out of five games.

Goal: Ming will improve her upper-body strength.

Objective: Ming will decrease her time for pushing the length of the basketball court in her sport chair by three seconds in four out of five trials.

Benchmarks:

By _____, Ming will decrease her time for pushing the length of the basketball court in her sport
    date
chair by one second in four out of five trials.

By _____, Ming will decrease her time for pushing the length of the basketball court in her sport
    date
chair by two seconds in four out of five trials.

By _____, Ming will decrease her time for pushing the length of the basketball court in her sport
    date
chair by three seconds in two out of five trials.

Figure 5.13 Sample goals, objectives, and benchmarks.

reporting for grades or IEP objectives. A well-written benchmark includes the same elements as an objective, looking at the behavior, condition, and criteria. Also included is the date that the objective will be accomplished. Figure 5.13 illustrates some sample goals, objectives, and benchmarks. Can you identify the domain for each objective as well as the behavior, condition, and criteria?

Although specific objectives and benchmarks are required to be documented for children who have an IEP, all learners within a program should have goals and objectives. Although the IEP process is more formalized and the multidisciplinary team decides the goals and objectives together with the parent or guardian and child, goals and objectives should be developed for each individual within any program and be documented through such means as journals, portfolios, and student files. These goals should be determined based on curriculum standards and by the student in combination with the teacher and the parents or guardian. Parents can play an important role in helping practitioners identify physical activity goals that support family activities and discover what's available in the community. Figure 5.14 shows a sample

Welcome to Physical Education!

Physical education can be an important part of your life. Being physically active can help you live healthier, avoid disease, participate in fun activities, and even help you feel better about yourself. In physical education this year, we'll provide you with many challenging activities you can do to stay physically active and have fun.

Over our semester together, I want to make sure that you get the opportunity to develop skills and participate in activities that are meaningful to you. To give you input on what we do in physical education this semester, fill out the following survey and review it with a parent or guardian before handing it in. Also, make sure to have your parent or guardian complete and sign the back before handing it in for credit. Thank you!

1. What physical activities do you participate in after school or on weekends (sports, skating, walking, bowling, and so on)?
2. What other physical activities, games, and sports do you enjoy participating in?
3. Can you think of some physical activities, games, or sports that you would like to try but haven't?
4. What games, sports, or physical activities would you like to participate in during your semester in physical education?

• Note to parents and guardians: To help in the development of the activities your child will be participating in, please answer the following questions and sign the bottom of this form. Thank you!

1. As a family, what physical activities do you participate in or encourage your child to participate in?
2. Are there any activities, games, or skills that you'd like to see your child participate in or develop through physical education?
3. Any other comments?

Parent Signature _____

Student Signature _____

• Return this survey by September 15th for full credit.

Figure 5.14 Sample physical activity survey.

Reprinted, by permission, from S. Hanningan-Downs and B. Fitzgerald, 2002.

physical activity survey that can be given to parents to solicit their input on physical activity programming for their child.

Who will teach these skills? The next step in program planning is to consider who will teach the student the predetermined skills and activities. Most students will receive physical education by the general physical educator working within the school. For students with differences in ability, there are several options regarding who will facilitate their physical education. According to IDEA, students with disabilities should be educated to the maximum extent appropriate with students who do not have disability labels or in the least restrictive environment (LRE). This principle allows some children with more mild ability differences to be taught by the general physical educator within the general physical education program, but it also accepts that other students with identified disabilities receive their physical education from a physical activity professional in segregated or more isolated settings. Such practice often translates into noninclusive programs existing within our public system of education.

Although inclusion of students with disabilities into general physical education is not always achieved, for many reasons, an inclusive philosophy should be applied to all situations through which children receive their physical education program. Regardless of who teaches these students, an inclusive approach is paramount. Physical education for public school children can be facilitated by the general physical educator, the general physical education teacher with support from an adapted physical educator, or the adapted physical education specialist alone. Physical education can be offered in many different settings. The ultimate goal, however, is an educational experience that best serves the child within a program that is as inclusive as possible. The decision of where and how a student with a difference in ability is to receive physical education ultimately rests with the IEP team that serves the child. If a child has an identified disability that qualifies him or her for special education services, he or she will have an IEP. In the following section we'll discuss the range of inclusive practices for individualized physical activity programming for school-age children.

- *Full-time general physical educator within general physical education (GPE)*. Ideally, general physical education taught by a GPE teacher would be the most inclusive setting. Students of all ability levels participate with their age-appropriate peers with necessary modifications and support in order to be successful. For instance, a child might use a different piece of equipment or have a slight change in rules while participating in an activity. These more simple modifications might be implemented quite easily with the child not requiring any specialized services. The GPE teacher might ask other personnel (e.g., other physical educators, adapted physical education teacher, physical, occupational, or recreation therapist) for ideas on how to create an inclusive environment for all students. All students, regardless of ability level, should be provided successful experiences and challenged to improve their skills.

- *Full-time general physical educator with adapted physical educator support within general physical education*. Adapted physical education (APE) is a service, not a placement. This means that adapted physical education services can be provided in a range of contexts, one of which is the general physical education class. Adapted physical education is taught by an adapted physical education specialist. In many states, an APE specialist credential or an endorsement in APE is required to teach in this area. These individuals are trained in how to make the curriculum accessible to all individuals, regardless of ability. In this case, the APE teacher works alongside the GPE educator within the general physical education program. The APE professional can either assist the general educator more broadly with the ongoing activity or work directly with an individual child needing support within this program.

- *Part-time general physical educator within GPE and part-time adapted physical educator within specialized PE*. APE services might also be provided within more than one context, or a student might receive more than one type of physical education. For example, a student might be included within the GPE class with modifications two times a week and receive adapted physical education by an APE specialist within a more specialized physical education context three times a week. Within the context of individualized physical education, programming should be inclusive in nature. It's the teacher's responsibility to ensure that a philosophy of inclusion prevails within the context of any physical education setting. Again, all students must have access to physical activity and the opportunity to be valued, respected, and successful members of the class.

One way to promote appreciation for diverse learners in this environment is through the inclusion of students from the GPE program. This involves inviting students from the GPE program to serve as peer tutors or to participate alongside students with differences in ability as team members or player coaches. Regardless of who participates in the specially designed physical education program, it should meet the needs of all learners, regardless of ability.

Although it's not the best practice, specially designed physical education is sometimes taught by a special education teacher. In specially designed physical education, the special education teacher is responsible for the students' academic education plans and teaches the physical

Figure 5.15 Fitness activities can be individualized to meet varying capabilities and needs. One student might perform sit-ups to work on abdominal strength and another might perform sit-backs in his wheelchair to work on back strength.

education curriculum just as he or she would any other subject area. This scenario is analogous to an elementary classroom teacher being responsible for teaching physical education rather than an elementary physical education specialist. If a student is in a separate special education class and doesn't leave the special education class to go to general physical education, then that teacher is responsible for teaching the student's physical education. Even in this situation an inclusive approach should be followed, and students without disabilities may be invited to participate.

What modifications will be helpful for individuals of differing abilities? Practitioners can employ many modifications to individualize activities for students. One way in which programs can be tailored to meet specific needs of children is by modifying the task that's to be completed. For example, in a modified kickball game a student who uses a wheelchair because of limited leg strength might be required to throw the ball rather than kick it. Or this same student might practice sitting up while in his or her wheelchair to strengthen the muscles in his or her back while others in the class do sit-ups on a mat for abdominal strengthening (figure 5.15). In each example, the task is altered to include all participants by allowing them to practice appropriate and meaningful skills or exercises. Another focus for modifications is related to the context. This might involve changes to instructional procedures, such as teaching style, type and amount of feedback, and sequencing of activities. The organization of the activity might also be modified. For some students, the distribution and duration of activities might need to be changed, whereas for others the way in which students are grouped might promote their participation. The physical setting is another strategy for individualizing activity. Equipment modifications are commonly used to include students with differing abilities. For instance, a student with less developed eye–hand coordination might be more successful in a softball game when using a lighter bat and bigger ball. For others, the size of the space they're using might influence their performance and need to be modified. In chapter 6 we look closer at activity modification and strategies effective for including students of differing abilities into physical education.

What supports will be needed for individuals within this setting? One of the guiding principles underlying inclusive physical activity is that individuals with differing abilities should participate together within physical activity programs. Within a school setting, the goal is for students with differences in ability to be taught by the general physical educator within the GPE program. To achieve this end, a range of support strategies might be used. Decisions regarding who will provide support, what type of support will be most effective, and how often support is necessary must be made by the individualized education program team. They base their decisions on several factors, including the expertise of the general physical educator for modifying activities, the nature of the activities in which the student will participate, and the grade level of the class in general. Block and Krebs (1992) proposed a continuum of support that begins with no support needed by the participant to progressively more support provided as necessary (figure 5.16). In each case, remember that support should be provided when necessary with care taken not to oversupport or automatically revert to the maximum level of support possible. Not all students with ability differences need much assistance; giving them more than they need can lead to increased dependence on the part of the student and less interaction with peers. Again, it's likely that many students can benefit from some form of support within the class, even students with increased skill.

Level 1: No support needed

1.1 Student can make necessary modifications on his or her own.

1.2 GPE teacher feels comfortable working with student.

Level 2: APE consultation

2.1 No extra assistance is needed.

2.2 Peer tutor watches out for student.

2.3 Peer tutor assists student.

2.4 Paraprofessional assists student.

Level 3: APE direct service in GPE 1 or 2 times per week

3.1 Peer tutor watches out for student.

3.2 Peer tutor assists student.

3.3 Paraprofessional assists student.

Level 4: Part-time APE and part-time GPE

4.1 Flexible schedule with reverse mainstreaming.

4.2 Fixed schedule with reverse mainstreaming.

Level 5: Reverse mainstreaming in special school

5.1 Students from special school go to general school for GPE.

5.2 Nondisabled students go to special school for GPE.

5.3 Students with and without disabilities meet in community for recreation training.

Figure 5.16 There are many ways to provide support to create successful inclusive learning environments for all individuals.

Reprinted, by permission, from M.E. Block and P.L. Krebs, 1992, "An alternative to least restrictive environments: A continuum of support to regular physical education,: *Adapted Physical Activity Quarterly* 9:97-113.

Transition

In general, transition planning means preparing an individual to make a change from one environment to another. Transitions take place frequently in the lives of children as they move from one grade level to the next and then on to college or into the community. For individuals with ability differences, transition planning meetings are required by federal law during specific times. These times include during the transition from an infant–toddler program into preschool and during the move from high school into college or to the community.

The transition from high school to the community can be challenging for any individual, as this is the transition into adulthood. Many questions related to an individual's physical activity habits and skills must be answered at this time, including the following:

- Will the individual participate in a community college or university physical activity program?
- Where will the individual live and what's available in that community?
- What types of physical activity skills does the individual have, and what skills will he or she need?
- How independent is this person in his or her physical activity?
- What types of programs will be accessible for this individual?
- What type of transportation services will he or she need?
- What type of medical services does the individual have?
- What family or social supports does he or she have for help with physical activity goals?
- What types of recreational and leisure activities does he or she enjoy?

Because there are so many issues and questions that need to be addressed for a successful transition, the law requires that for persons with identified disabilities, this process begin at age 14. This is a good idea for any child, and physical activity instructors should begin thinking about where their students will be when they leave high school. By planning early, the necessary skills can be taught and programs and services identified before students graduate and move on. The transition planning team for students with identified needs is made up of the same individuals as the IEP team. However, as the student gets older and agencies and services are identified outside of the school system that will support the student, representatives from those agencies are invited to be a part of the team. During the initial transition plan is a good time to identify an action plan. The action plan should include what needs to be done, who will address that need, and when it will be accomplished (table 5.1). The action plan helps identify who's responsible for what; the plan should be revisited at each meeting to track progress (along with the IEP documentation).

Whether a student has a formal transition plan or not, practitioners need to think about the kinds of physical activity and recreational programs that will be available to the student after graduation. How will he or she maintain physical fitness for daily living, health, and stress reduction? Programs that students might access include the YMCA, community recreation programs or park districts, fitness clubs, and community college classes. The school's adapted physical educator along with the general physical educator, therapists, and parents can be excellent resources during the transition process and might be able to assist with information, community outreach, and program coordination. The adapted physical education specialist knows what activity programs are available in the community as well as what disability sport organizations might be of interest to the student. Professionals can provide questionnaires to the parents or guardian and the student regarding what the student needs and desires relating to physical activity. Professionals can serve as a community liaison, contacting directors of recreation and physical activity programs in the community. For example, they might contact a local health club to determine how accessible the club is and what types of programs and activities they offer. They might also discuss the club's willingness to provide scholarships for students with physical activity needs during their senior year as an incentive for them to continue to participate in fitness club activities after graduation. Practitioners might begin community programming for physical education during the junior and senior year. In this case, the adapted physical education specialist might take students off campus to participate in aerobics classes, swim class, rock climbing, or other community-based activities,

Table 5.1 *Sample Action Plan*

Outcome or need	Steps to meet the need	Who is responsible?	When will this be done?	Date to be completed	Follow-up
What activities are available in the community?	Visit or call community, recreational, and physical activity programs	Adapted physical educator and regional center worker	September/October	By next IEP meeting in November all information should be gathered	Evaluate all information at the next IEP meeting and set a new action plan with specific community based goals for the following year. Specific goals and objectives will be determined at the IEP meeting and written up as part of the IEP.
What communication skills are needed to participate?	Consult with speech pathologist	Speech pathologist			
How will the individual get there?	Explore public transportation programs. Check on family support	Special education teacher			
What support services are available?	Talk with regional center and family members	Psychologist			
What support services will Joe need to participate in the programs?	Talk with regional center and family members	Psychologist APE			
What skills does Joe already have that will allow him to be successful?	Talk with physical activity teachers/APE/PT and review reports at next meeting.	PT/APE/GPE			
What skills will Joe need to learn to be successful and independent?	This will be identified after the programs are determined	Team discussion following data collection			

depending on the student's interest and abilities and what programs are offered. Again, these experiences should be inclusive and involve students with a range of abilities.

Physical Activity Participation in Recreation and Sport Programs

In the preceding section we focused mainly on inclusive efforts within school-based physical education programs, but the questions that should be asked and decisions that need to be made follow a similar sequence for community-based programs as well. Children interested in participating in a recreation or sport program should first be interested in the activity; the activity should also be meaningful for the child. Although some of these opportunities might be within a general recreation or sport program offered by a general practitioner, others might be more specialized and offered by physical activity practitioners with more experience and knowledge in modifying for individual differences. Similar to specialized school physical education programs, these specialized recreational or sport activities might be less inclusive than general programs. Although this might be common, inclusive specialized sport programs do exist. For instance, Special Olympics offers unified sport skill development and competition in which athletes with and without identified disabilities participate on the same team. Once activity preferences and opportunities have been identified, modifications and supports might be necessary for optimal involvement.

Assessing Success of Inclusive Efforts

Determining the extent to which a program is successful for each individual is critical for program effectiveness and an integral part of inclusive reflective practice. Practitioners must evaluate by the minute, day, week, month, quarter, and year the extent to which their instruction is meeting the needs of their learners. Practitioners accomplish this in several ways, including through the use of

- observations,
- check sheets,
- journals,
- portfolios,
- formal standardized assessments,
- informal teacher-made tests related to physical and cognitive skills,
- group projects,
- reevaluation of goals and objectives,
- videotaping of skills, and
- rubrics.

Refer to chapter 4 for examples of these kinds of assessments.

The documentation process helps students set goals and watch their progress unfold in a meaningful and tangible way. Good records also provide an ongoing feedback loop between the practitioner and learner to see their development and progress. For learners, this feedback lets them know how they're doing and allows them to check their goals against their progress. For the practitioner, documentation provides valuable information about whether specific teaching strategies and methods are working so that modifications can be made if necessary. Good documentation also allows practitioners to evaluate progress toward goals and educational standards. For most learners, the methods of evaluation previously listed are used to determine quarterly and semester grading as well as end-of-the-year reports to parents. Learners with differences in ability might also have their goals and objectives identified on the IEP. For the purpose of meeting federal guidelines as mandated by IDEA 97, these goals and objectives must be evaluated at least annually with progress reporting matching that of any other child within the general education program. Details about assessment methods and techniques were covered in chapter 4.

⬅ THINK BACK

Think back to Jackson once again. Assume you were his high school physical education teacher.

1. Who might also be a part of his multidisciplinary IEP team with you?

2. Why would Jackson be required to have an IEP?

3. What types of goals and objectives would you write for him?

4. How might you prepare your students to foster a supportive inclusive environment for diverse learners in your class?

5. What activities might he be involved in after he graduated from high school? How would you prepare him for these activities?

▶ INCLUSIVE PHYSICAL ACTIVITY FOR ADULTS

It's well documented that physical activity is important for overall health and well-being for all individuals, including younger and older adults (U.S. Department of Health and Human Services, 2000). The many benefits of this involvement include increased energy, greater flexibility and strength, reduced risk of cardiovascular disease, maintenance of general mobility and functional independence, decreased stress and depression, and improved metabolism. Whether an individual is involved in exercise programs, sport participation, or recreational pursuits, the right amount of physical activity can maintain health and improve quality of life. All individuals, regardless of their abilities, need access to and programming for physical activity throughout their life span.

Ensuring Access

Many of the barriers discussed in chapter 2 limit the physical activity involvement of some adults. While some of the strategies presented in that chapter might promote increased adoption of physical activity by some individuals, for others with significant differences in abilities access to physical activity is much more challenging. Access to programs for these adults often depends on what the community has to offer. Some opportunities might include community recreation programs; physical activity clinics or labs within a hospital, university, or community college setting; or events and teams offered through specialized sport organizations. Many such programs exist to benefit adults with significant differences in abilities. These adult programs are entirely voluntary for the participants, who often hear about them through medical professionals, other participants, or resource materials distributed to local or regional agencies and organizations. For instance, individuals with differences in ability interested in exercising might find that the local YMCA offers aquatic exercise classes; those wanting to learn to ski might hear about special ski programs through state organizations geared to adapted physical activity programming. In addition to the exercise or fitness setting, many programs also exist for elite athletes who compete in world-class events, such as goalball, water skiing, or track and field, just to name a few. These elite athletes generally participate via a sport organization or governing body that oversees training and competitions. Some examples include Paralympics, Special Olympics, United States Association for Blind Athletes, United States Cerebral Palsy Athletic Association, and the Les Autres Games (see appendix C for complete list of associations).

Establishing Supportive Networks

A physical activity practitioner working to develop and implement inclusive programs in the community should establish ongoing communication not only with the participants themselves but also with medical personnel, family members, human service or agency personnel, and even community resources such as transportation services or volunteer organizations. In most cases, obtaining a medical history and consent before having participants begin a program can start this process of communication and collaboration and help establish the link between professionals that might support the practitioner when individualizing physical activity programs. (A sample medical history and referral form is provided in appendix F.) Networks could also include individuals who come with participants to a particular program to assist or simply to get more information about participating. For practitioners interested in providing recreational or sport programs, networking with others who might support them in their efforts to promote better programming or training for interested individuals is effective. These practitioners might find that other coaches and recreation leaders have valuable information and strategies to share.

Although a team approach to programming isn't always mandated by law for adults as it is for individuals in the public school system, it's still considered best practice. The more practitioners communicate with participants and others, the more likely the practitioner will have a holistic view of the person and be better able to plan programming to improve daily living, functional skills, enjoyment, and independence.

Promoting Positive Physical Activity Environments

Participants' involvement and continuation in an inclusive program depend largely on their comfort level. Adults interested in joining a physical activity program or facility might first need some questions answered. Informational brochures, visits, and direct communication with staff and other participants help at this stage. The program staff also has an obligation to ensure that new participants are welcomed and accepted into the program by others already involved. This can be accomplished in three ways: (1) by ensuring that adequate equipment and resources are available so that already established programs are not interrupted, (2) by offering similar support and benefits to all members so no one is perceived as getting special treatment or inequitable services, and (3) by giving all participants the opportunity for feedback and suggestions about how the program or activity might run more smoothly and inclusively. Again, education and information sharing are essential to fostering acceptance of individuals with differences in ability, even in community-based fitness programs or recreational or sport activities.

Planning for Individualized Instruction

As with other age groups, program planning for individuals begins with determining priorities and the focus of the program. For an adult in an activity program, priorities are determined by his or her interests, needs, future activity pursuits, and nature of activities of daily living. This information is then used to develop the focus of the program, the goals desired, and the amount of time that needs to be devoted to achieving these outcomes.

Safety and well-being are critical within the context of any activity program. As mentioned earlier, practitioners offering community-based activity programs must have participants obtain medical consent or physician approval before they start in the program. Any limitations or concerns should be documented and kept in the participant's file. Recommendations for specific activities might also be offered. The program file should include a medical history, the participant's priorities and desires within the program, the exercises or activities of the individualized plan, and a daily record of activity and progress notes.

An individualized exercise plan based on personal goals and needs is developed for most adults in community-based exercise programs (figure 5.17). For adults who receive services from regional centers, an individual program plan (IPP) is provided. Although no specific individualized plan is developed for individuals involved in sport programs, training regimes might be tailored to meet individual goals, needs, and functional abilities. Coaches involved with these athletes work together with sport participants to achieve this end.

Assessing Success of Inclusive Efforts

Unlike physical activity programs for children in schools, physical activity programs for adults aren't legally obligated to conduct program or participant evaluation. Nevertheless, assessment of participant success and program effectiveness is just as important for adults as for young people. Daily exercise logs or records can be used to determine if exercise goals are being met or if participants are making progress toward achieving their goals. Program staff might also solicit participant evaluation or feedback regarding program aspects such as facility appropriateness, equipment availability, support, and staff assistance.

Figure 5.17 Individualized exercise programs are developed with the participant's interests, goals, and capabilities in mind.

THINK BACK

Let's consider Jackson once more as he transitions into adulthood.

1. What type of physical activity programs might he be involved in as an adult?

2. How would he find out about these programs?

3. What might be the focus or priority areas in this program?

4. What would you use to assess whether Jackson is making progress in his physical activity program?

▶ SUMMARY

Although team members, settings, and program goals vary across the life span in planning for inclusive programs, the steps to the process remain the same. Physical activity practitioners must carefully and purposefully plan and evaluate the cycle of inclusive physical activity on a regular basis to ensure access, establish supportive networks, promote positive environments, plan for individualized instruction, and assess success. It's through the continued reflective process and implementation of the 3 Rs—Ready, Rethink, Retry—that practitioners can continue to promote success for every individual in the program.

What Do You Think?

1. Think about your future professional career and the setting in which it will take place. How might the "cycle of inclusive physical activity programs" apply to your setting?

2. What kinds of supportive networks are available in your community for infants with diverse abilities? For children? For adults?

3. How might you design a disability-awareness training program for your setting?

4. How might you go about evaluating the success of inclusive programming in your setting?

5. Infant–toddler programs require an IFSP, and school-age children have an IEP. If you were going to write an individualized program for an adult, what would you consider as important information to include in this documentation? How might you go about gathering this information?

What Would You Do?

Scenario 5.1

Judy is a teacher at Little Tikes preschool program. As the coordinator of the program, she has recently met with a family in the community who has twins that will be starting the program the following year. The parents have asked Judy to attend a transition planning meeting for their children, Jason and Julie, who were both born five weeks premature. Jason has some visual problems, and Julie shows some delays in general development. Judy is a little concerned about meeting the needs of Julie and Jason but is committed to making this a positive preschool program for them. Judy is knowledgeable about general development and appropriate curriculum, but she wonders how to make adaptations for the children. She also has never attended an IFSP or IEP before and is curious what's involved in this process.

Imagine you're a member of the IFSP team. Answer the following questions for Judy.

1. Who will be at the meeting for Jason and Julie?

2. What will take place at this meeting?

3. What supports are available for Judy in planning for Julie and Jason?

4. How might she best prepare the environment for Julie and Jason's transition?

Scenario 5.2

You're a personal trainer at your local fitness facility. You've been informed that you will have a new participant next week who has made an appointment for an initial orientation and program design. The following week, you arrive to meet Sam, your new participant. On meeting with him you discover that he's blind because of complications caused by diabetes. As you talk with him, you discuss his fitness goals and needs. You learn he's interested in a spinning class as well as some general weight training.

1. How will you go about finding support networks for yourself in providing appropriate programming for Sam?

2. What strategies might you use to ensure that Sam feels welcome within your facility?

3. What information might you need in planning for Sam's programming?

4. How might you go about determining the success of Sam's program?

CHAPTER

A Functional Approach for Modifying Movement Experiences

6

Learning Outcomes

After completing this chapter, you should be able to

» describe how person-related changes and task and context modifications can facilitate skill and activity performance;

» provide examples of contextual and task modifications for individuals with differing abilities;

» apply modification strategies to activity programs for individuals of varying ages and capabilities; and

» describe the functional components model and its application to inclusive physical activity programming.

INCLUDING ALL INDIVIDUALS

Karen Morgan, a new kindergarten teacher at Marsh Elementary School, has eighteen children in her class, including one child with a cognitive difference, Sara. Sara is generally good natured but often doesn't follow the rules of the class. This has become a problem for Karen, especially when they go outside for physical education because Sara doesn't want to come back inside. Sara also wanders away from the blacktop area where the class is playing and refuses to get off the swings. Karen wants to make sure all the students in her class are successful. She plans on discussing her concerns at Sara's next individualized education program (IEP) meeting, but in the meantime she's determined to find a way to keep Sara involved during physical education. She has tried to plan fun activities for the children and has been working with them on bouncing and catching playground balls with partners. All the children seem to be actively involved except Sara.

In chapter 5, we presented the sequence of steps necessary to include all individuals in physical activity programming. These steps highlighted the need to prioritize goals and secure necessary supports when preparing and planning for inclusive practice. Once the focus of the program has been determined and the program practitioner has been identified, efforts shift to modifying the physical activity program for participants with differing abilities. Effectively involving all individuals in physical activity requires good problem-solving skills on the part of the practitioner. He or she must be able to assess the situation and determine how and what could be changed to foster increased participation and success for each individual involved. In this chapter we'll help guide practitioners through this process and suggest methods to make activities inclusive for everyone through a functional approach for modifying movement experiences (FAMME).

The FAMME model provides the conceptual framework for accommodating all individuals within a physical activity program. The four-step process helps practitioners consider the range of possible modifications to promote success for all participants (figure 6.1). The feature stressed in the FAMME model is matching modifications to ability differences in efforts to provide optimal challenges and task completion for every participant in the program. An optimal challenge is a task goal that allows success while presenting a challenging experience to foster continued skill progress for the participant, regardless of his or her skill level. The purpose of the FAMME model is to achieve this optimal point for every participant by matching an individual's capabilities to the task and the context during movement activities. In doing so, the practitioner considers all factors that contribute to a movement skill or task outcome—what the individual can do, how the setting should be constructed, and which goal or task the individual is attempting to accomplish.

In chapter 5 we also detailed how to individualize the planning process and determine meaningful goals and activities for all participants. In this chapter we'll take this further by looking at individualized activity plans and determining how the skills and activities can be modified for differences in abili-

The FAMME Model

Step 1: Determine underlying components of skills

Step 2: Determine current capabilities of the individual

Step 3: Match modification efforts to capabilities

Step 4: Evaluate modification effectiveness

Figure 6.1 The four steps leading to inclusive physical activity programming.

ties. First we'll describe the process of matching modifications to the capabilities and needs of participants. Then we'll present the range of possible modifications that can be employed as they relate to the individual, the setting, and the task being performed. Last, we'll discuss our insights regarding the process of evaluating the appropriateness and effectiveness of chosen modifications.

▶ STEP 1: DETERMINING UNDERLYING COMPONENTS OF SKILLS

The first step in providing inclusive physical activity is understanding the foundation for performing the skill or activity. Although all skills vary in terms of their intended use as well as in the movements necessary to carry them out, many of them have similar underlying components or requirements (figure 6.2). These components are prerequisites for any individual attempting to perform the movement activity or skill. For instance, kicking a ball to a stationary target involves eye–foot coordination, balance, leg strength, task understanding, and other related factors. Running to catch a disk requires eye–hand coordination, balance, task understanding, speed, leg strength, and flexibility. Many of the same components underlie a variety of tasks, but they have different degrees of importance or influence depending on the goal being achieved. Throwing a ball to a stationary target requires a degree of strength, balance, and coordination. When the target is farther away or moving, a greater degree of these skills is required. Thus, the first step toward providing optimal challenges is to assess the task and identify the underlying components needed to perform the skill.

The figure below identifies several components related to the performance of a skill, but practitioners should also be aware of other performance-related factors that can affect task completion and success, including levels of motivation, fatigue, and energy.

Prerequisite Components Needed for Various Activities

- Strength
- Flexibility/range of motion
- Balance/postural control
- Coordination (eye-hand, eye-foot, body)
- Speed/agility

- Endurance
- Concept understanding
- Self-responsibility/self-control
- Attention
- Sensory perception

Figure 6.2 The performance of different activities or movement skills requires a range of underlying components.

◀ THINK BACK

1. Think back to Karen Morgan's kindergarten class. What are the underlying skill components necessary to participate in the activity she has selected for her students?

2. Based on the list of skill components, what might be some of the challenging areas for Sara given what little information you know about her?

▶ STEP 2: DETERMINING CURRENT CAPABILITIES OF THE INDIVIDUAL

The next step in the process of including all individuals in physical activity programming involves identifying the capabilities of the individuals. When considering which modifications to make, practitioners need to keep in mind the capabilities of the individual rather than the general characteristics associated with a particular label or category (e.g., athlete, learning disabled, autistic). Modifications should be directly related to and based on current capabilities necessary to participate in the activity and perform the task. As indicated in figure 6.3, several person-related factors can influence an individual's capability in the different components underlying physical activities. For example, obvious differences in capabilities exist because of differences in age. A 7-year-old child might be considerably less strong than a high school student. Most adults have a greater capacity to understand complex concepts and strategies than children have. Other factors, such as a specific medical condition, might also influence functional capabilities. An adult with joint pain and swelling caused by an injury or arthritis might have limited range of motion compared to another individual, such as an adult jazz dancer. An athlete with increased muscle tone caused by cerebral palsy might have differences in balance compared to other members on his or her team. Experience, genetics, and motor ability are also factors that influence the functional capabilities of physical activity participants. As we discussed in chapter 1, practitioners must understand that the capabilities of an individual are not permanent but are rather a function of the person, task, and context; a person's capabilities are subject to change with practice and modifications.

Many factors influence an individual's capability in the different skill components underlying performance. Two individuals might have very different factors that contribute to similar movement capabilities. For instance, a ninth-grader might have increased flexibility because stretching is a regular part of her fitness program, whereas another ninth-grader with Down syndrome might have increased flexibility caused by genetics. An adult in an exercise class might demonstrate decreased body awareness because of sensory perception differences caused by multiple sclerosis, whereas another adult in the class might have poor kinesthetic awareness because of limited experience. It's important to realize that many factors can influence the

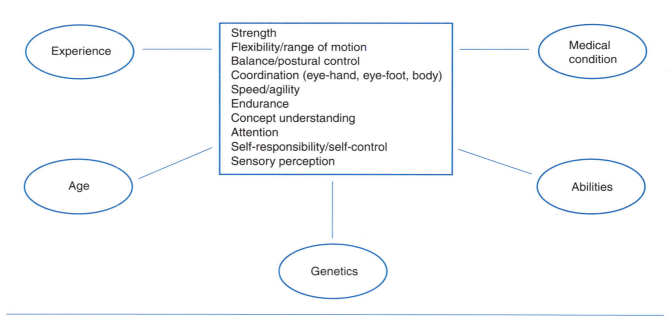

Figure 6.3 Many person-related factors influence the components underlying movement skills.

capabilities that an individual brings to a movement situation and that it's these capabilities that are given priority when making modifications for inclusive participation. For example, the adult who has decreased body awareness due to multiple sclerosis might need to use mirrors for visual feedback on limb position. Likewise, the adult with limited movement experiences might also benefit from instructional strategies that incorporate visual feedback. Regardless of the cause for capability differences, the strategies and modifications to promote success might be the same.

Did You Know?

When we talk about a person's abilities and his or her capabilities, we're talking about two different things.

- Motor abilities—stable, enduring traits that are largely genetically determined and that serve as determinants of a person's *achievement potential* for the performance of specific

skills. These can include perceptual motor abilities and physical proficiency abilities.

- Capabilities—characteristics of individuals that are subject to change as a result of practice and that underlie skilled performance of a task.

Magill, R.A. 2004. *Motor learning and control: concepts and applications.* New York: McGraw-Hill Companies, Inc.

THINK BACK

1. Based on your personal history, which factors have influenced your capabilities in the skill components?

2. Imagine you are Sara in Karen Morgan's kindergarten class. Now which factors do you think

might be influencing your capabilities as a kindergartner? How might you perform in each of the prerequisite components underlying various activities?

STEP 3: MATCHING MODIFICATION EFFORTS TO CAPABILITIES

Once an individual's capabilities have been identified, the next step is to direct modifications specifically to the underlying prerequisite skill components. As we described in chapter 1, the capability of an individual, and thus his or her performance, can change as a result of changes within the person over time, changes to the context within which tasks are performed, and changes to the tasks themselves (figure 6.4). As such, modifications can be made in some or all of these areas. Table 6.1 lists examples of how changes in the person, context, or task can affect performance.

To ensure success for some participants, practitioners might need to incorporate a range of modifications. For the success of others, just a few minor modifications to either the task or the context might be enough to provide an optimal challenge. Table 6.2 shows an example of matching modifications to functional differences in the skill of throwing. In the left column are some of the underlying skill components for throwing. On the right are possible modifications related to the person, context, or task that might be employed to ensure an optimal challenge for all participants.

Figure 6.4 Matching modifications such as body positioning and shot weight to participant capabilities can increase this youngster's performance.

Person-Centered Changes

One way to increase a person's skill performance is to directly influence his or her physical, cognitive, emotional, or behavioral capabilities. For example, as an individual changes in strength or flexibility, his or her capability to perform or complete the same task also changes; a task that was once difficult might now be easier to accomplish. Person-related factors such as alertness, attention, understanding, and motivation can also influence the realization of the task goal. Some of these changes might be more a function of physical training or continued practice and learning. There are also other strategies related to the individual that might directly alter performance. For instance, medication to reduce increased muscle tone might increase range of motion, ultimately improving functional movement and performance. Although these person-related changes are not necessarily considered modifications, they do influence the performance of the individual and are viable strategies for "capability shifting," as described in chapter 1. However, these types of strategies are often guided by the individual and their medical personnel rather than by the physical activity practitioner. The practitioner should be familiar, though, with any individual strategies such as medication that might affect performance. Again, practitioners should remember that performance success doesn't rest solely with the individual but is a function of the interaction among the person, task, and context. The practitioner is responsible for making changes within the task and context to create opportunities for optimal challenge and success that consider person-related factors and promote, when possible, person-related changes.

Table 6.1 Examples of Changes in the Person, Context, or Task and Their Influence on Performance

Factor	Example
Person over time	Increase in strength for older adult after an individualized resistance exercise program
Changes in context	Increase mobility for an individual who uses a wheelchair in a game of flag football by playing on a hard surface rather than on the grass
Changes in task	Increase in success of dribbling a basketball by dribbling with two hands simultaneously rather than with only one

Modifying the Task

Creating modifications to a task is one way to provide inclusive programming for participants with a wide range of capability levels. Modifications can be created through several approaches, including closed to open skill progressions, skill extensions, skill switching, and individualized goal setting.

Closed to Open Skill Progression

Practitioners often employ general guidelines when designing activity sessions and delivering the most effective instruction. One popular practice is to have participants practice closed skills before attempting them in an open environment. Closed skills are skills performed in a stable or predictable environment in which performance demands and the objects don't change during the performance of a skill. The performer determines when to begin the action and doesn't need to make any changes during the performance of the skill. For example, hitting a ball off a batting tee is a closed skill. The ball doesn't move during the time the performer decides to swing and when the swing is taken. On the other end of the continuum are open skills, which are attempted in dynamic, unpredictable contexts. The

Table 6.2 Possible Modifications for Throwing

Capability difference	Person	Context	Task
Strength	Resistance exercises	Increase or decrease target distance Increase or decrease weight of ball	Throw, roll, or push ball off a ramp or table
Range of motion	Specific stretches	Closer or farther target Smaller or larger ball Use of throwing extension	Swinging underhand versus overhand throw
Coordination	Brain integration activities	Larger or smaller target Stationary or moving target	Throw or roll ball
Concept understanding	Preteach concepts or cues Focus on one cue at a time	Visual cue Verbal cue Auditory cue Tactile cue or physical prompt	Break skill down into smaller tasks or increase complexity and strategy use in game
Balance	Balance training activities	Decrease or increase target distance Increase base of support with wall, chair, or walker Decrease base of support	Throw seated in chair Roll ball with two hands Throw off one foot or into the air

The above table provides only examples of capability differences with accompanying person, context, and task modifications.

THINK BACK

1. As a physical activity practitioner, what might be your role in relation to person-centered changes?

2. What are three person-centered changes an individual can make to improve performance?

performer must respond to the action of an object or to the changing environment or both. Batting a pitched ball is an example of an open skill. In this case, the performer responds to when the pitch is delivered and the flight of the ball after it's thrown. Depending on the type of pitch, the batter might need to adjust while the ball is in motion.

Although the progression from closed to open skills is effective in many situations, it might be too quick for some participants and thus not create an optimal challenge at a given capability level. Another important thing to consider in the progression from closed to open skills is whether aspects of the context that determine the movement vary from one attempt to the next (Gentile, 2000). For example, hitting a ball off a batting tee kept at the same height for each swing has no variability across practice trials. However, changing the height of the batting tee so that participants practice swinging at balls placed at different levels more closely simulates pitches coming in at various heights while still keeping the environment stable and the skill closed. With this kind of intertrial variability, the progression from closed to open skills can be expanded. Practitioners can offer increased practice for participants with differences in capabilities by progressing practice more slowly before asking participants to perform skills in more complex and dynamic gamelike settings (figure 6.5).

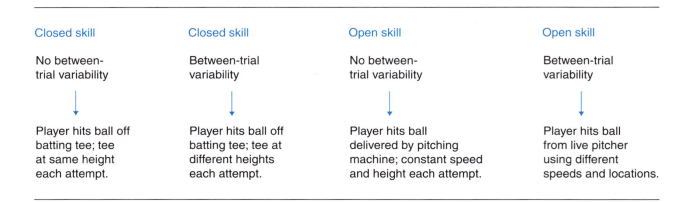

Closed skill

No between-trial variability

↓

Player hits ball off batting tee; tee at same height each attempt.

Closed skill

Between-trial variability

↓

Player hits ball off batting tee; tee at different heights each attempt.

Open skill

No between-trial variability

↓

Player hits ball delivered by pitching machine; constant speed and height each attempt.

Open skill

Between-trial variability

↓

Player hits ball from live pitcher using different speeds and locations.

Figure 6.5 Skill instruction can be progressed from closed to open contexts.

Reprinted, by permission, from R. Magill, 2001, *Motor learning concepts and applications*, 6th edition (New York: McGraw-Hill Companies), 12. © McGraw-Hill Companies, Inc.

The same strategy can be applied to other open skills, such as returning a serve in tennis or catching a pass in football. By increasing the number of steps in the progression and offering increased practice at these stages, tasks are matched to individual capability and readiness levels, thereby achieving more inclusive programming.

Skill Extensions

The ability of practitioners to break a movement task down and sequence it appropriately can significantly influence meaningful activity participation and individual skill improvement. Practitioners often use progressions of tasks to sequentially lead participants from beginning levels to more advanced levels of a skill. Progressions are developed through a series of extension tasks (Rink, 1998). Practitioners start at a less complex point and gradually increase the complexity or difficulty. Many aspects of a movement task can be modified to change its level of difficulty. Figure 6.6 presents common methods for developing task progressions.

Extending traditional progressions or skill hierarchies has been suggested as an effective method for accommodating participants of diverse skill levels (Block, 2000; Block, Provis, & Nelson, 1994). By including more simple tasks in the progression, participants once unable to access the task can now participate. Similarly, extending the progression to include more complex tasks provides others with more developed skill abilities increased challenges and opportunities to develop their skills even further. Figure 6.7 shows an example of an extended skill progression for catching. A student with decreased eye–hand coordination can access the activity by having a ball swung on a rope or rolled to him, as shown in figure 6.8. Another learner proficient at eye–hand coordination activities can participate by catching while both the thrower and receiver are moving.

Similar progressions can be developed for the range of skills used in movement activities. These skill extensions can work for youngsters or participants of any age working individually at stations or playing in games and sport activities. For instance, participants involved in a team handball activity involving throwing and catching to move a ball toward an opponent's goal can use catching from a throw, a bounce, or a roll to achieve the game's objective.

Skill Switching

Another strategy for modifying the task involves the concept of skill switching. With skill switching, skills that have similar functional outcomes can be used interchangeably. For instance, Balan and Davis (1993) offer general task categories that group skills by intended purpose (table 6.3). Throwing, striking, and kicking are grouped together as object propulsion skills because the purpose of each skill is the projection of an object away from the body using a limb or piece of equipment. An

Breaking a skill down into parts

Example: Practice the toss of a ball in the tennis serve.

Changing the goal of practice

Example: Practice batting to connect with the ball and then practice to place the ball in different locations.

Adding or decreasing the number of people

Example: Practice dance steps by yourself, then with a partner.

Changing the conditions of performance

Example: Practice playing basketball without dribbling.

Changing the rules

Example: Practice volleyball allowing for as many hits as needed to get the ball over the net.

Combining two skills

Example: Practice a forward roll and then practice a cartwheel and forward roll in succession.

Expanding the number of different examples of a concept

Example: Demonstrate a balanced position and then demonstrate three different ways to balance.

Adapted, by permission, from J. Rink, *Teaching physical education for learning* (New York: McGraw-Hill Companies). © The McGraw-Hill Companies.

Figure 6.6 Extension strategies help practitioners lead participants from beginning levels to more advanced skill levels.

- Looks at ball placed on lap or tray
- Touches ball placed on lap or tray with one hand or head stick
- Touches ball placed on lap or tray with one or two hands
- Touches ball rolled to optimal position at midline
- Catches ball rolled to optimal position
- Touches ball swung on rope to optimal position
- Catches ball swung on rope to optimal position
- Catches ball swung on rope to side
- Touches with one hand a slowly tossed ball from 5' away to optimal position
- Touches with two hands a slowly tossed ball from 5' away to optimal position
- Catches with two hands a slowly tossed ball from 5' away to optimal position
- Catches with two hands a slowly tossed ball from 10' away to optimal position
- Moves body to optimal position to contact a slowly tossed ball from 10' away to either side
- Moves and touches with one hand a slowly tossed ball from 10' away to either side
- Moves and catches with two hands a slowly tossed ball from 10' away to either side
- Moves and catches with one hand a slowly tossed ball from 10' away to either side
- Moves in a specific pattern to catch a ball thrown from a moving passer 20' away

Figure 6.7 Extended skill progression for catching.

Figure 6.8 This youngster's capability to catch a ball is improved by having the ball rolled rather than thrown to her.

activity requiring participants to propel an object, such as kicking a pitched ball in a kickball game, might allow some players to kick the ball while other participants collect and throw the ball out into the field. Similarly, object-reception skills of catching, trapping, and blocking are grouped together because they all involve stopping and securing a moving object and can be interchanged to increase participation of participants with differing abilities. A youngster with limited arm strength and who uses an electric wheelchair can demonstrate effective pass reception in a flag football game by moving his or her body and wheelchair to the optimal location at the correct time. This player, while wearing a Velcro vest, ensures completion of the pass by moving to allow the pass to contact and stick to the Velcro vest. Others in the game might catch the pass with two hands for a completed play. In each case, skills with a similar functional purpose are performed together. The practitioner must take into account the meaning that task goals or skills have for participants and how skill switching can offer increased participation and benefit.

Individualized Goal Setting

Although the strategies just discussed can increase physical activity participation, practitioners need to remember that the basis for all movement opportunities is the meaning or importance the experience has for each individual. Individuals entering physical activity programs come with widely diverse needs and interests, likes and dislikes, and desires. What's meaningful and appropriate for one person to participate in and achieve must also be individually considered. Individualized goal setting is critical to successful inclusive programming. Thus, the overall focus of the program and reason for participation play important roles in inclusive physical activity. For instance, an adult who regularly uses a wheelchair might participate in aquatic activity to work on range of motion and weight bearing, whereas others in the class may perform aerobic exercise to increase endurance. Practitioners must value the input of individual participants in determining program focus and goal setting. Otherwise, when what's being offered is required of all participants with no regard to individual needs and interests, lack of motivation and effort typically result. The meaningfulness of an activity is the key to motivation, adherence, and continued physical activity.

Particular activity objectives can be modified to emphasize the link between where the participant is currently performing and what he or she is hoping to achieve. Although overall goals and standards might be similar, specific learning or participation objectives will likely need to vary to align individually with the uniqueness of each person. For example, the goal for some participants might be to achieve a more smooth and efficient movement form, whereas for others it might be to achieve a specified number of repetitions. If physical fitness, for instance, is an objective of the physical activity program, developing realistic and individually designed goals and outcomes is critical. While some students might be doing sit-ups on a mat to increase abdominal strength, other learners who use wheelchairs

Table 6.3 *General Task Categories*

Task category	Functional goal	Criteria for success	Skills needed
Locomotion on land	Translating from point A to point B	Efficiency, velocity, distance, spatial accuracy, temporal accuracy, accuracy of movement form	Rolling, crawling, creeping, tumbling, cruising, walking, running, hopping, sliding, galloping, skipping, climbing, jumping
Locomotion in water	Translating from point A to point B	Efficiency, velocity, distance, spatial accuracy, temporal accuracy, accuracy of movement form	Dog-paddle, human stroke, breast stroke, side stroke, butterfly, jumping, diving
Object propulsion	The projection of an object away from the body with the use of a limb or piece of equipment	Velocity, distance, spatial accuracy, temporal accuracy, efficiency	Throwing, kicking, striking, volleying, rolling, heading, shooting, dribbling
Object reception	The act of stopping, securing, or impeding a moving object with the use of the body, body parts, or piece of equipment	Efficiency, spatial accuracy, temporal accuracy	Catching, trapping, tackling, blocking

Reprinted with permission from the November-December 1993 issue of the *Journal of Health, Physical Education, Recreation and Dance,* a publication of the American Alliance for Health, Physical Education, Recreation and Dance, 1900 Association Dr., Reston, VA 20191.

might be doing their sit-ups in their chairs to increase back extensor strength. In both cases, increasing muscular strength of the trunk is the goal, but which muscles are targeted depends on individual needs.

Program focus and activity objectives can be tailored to meet the needs of a range of participants and provide the foundation for inclusive physical activity programming that is important and meaningful.

THINK BACK

1. How might Karen Morgan create both open- and closed-skill challenges in her skill practice for the children on bouncing and catching?

2. Refer back to figure 6.7, the example extended skill progressions for catching. What types of variations could Karen use to make sure all the children in her class are successful?

3. Think of an activity you might be teaching in your future career. How might you use skill switching in a teaching, recreation, fitness, or therapeutic setting? Select one and provide an example.

Modifying the Context

Altering the context is another way to accommodate all individuals. By structuring a physical activity environment that appreciates and respects individual differences and maximizes person-related variables, the practitioner can optimize individual performance. In chapter 5 we discussed the importance of promoting positive attitudes and preparing participants and support personnel. Practitioners involved in physical activity instruction must then go through a series of decision-making steps regarding what participants will do, how participation can be facilitated, and in what ways the setting should be modified. Several critical aspects and considerations must be examined to optimize the learning and performance environment. Rink (1998) identifies three instructional functions as specific responsibilities of the practitioner in the practitioner–participant relationship. These include presenting activities, organizing and managing the instructional setting, and selecting instructional strategies.

Presenting Activities

An important competency practitioners must develop is the ability to present activities and tasks to participants in a manner that motivates them and promotes skill development. Environments that ensure maximum participation through effective instruction more effectively engage participants and increase capabilities. Practitioners can employ several strategies and procedures to meet the needs of their program's participants.

One consideration when presenting task and performance information to participants involves how this information is communicated. Verbal instruction is the most common method of communication with participants and can be modified to meet diverse participant capabilities. For some participants, the length of the instruction might need to be modified. For instance, individuals with shorter attention spans might not be able to sit and listen as lengthy instructions are given. These learners might benefit from shorter instructions and specific performance details shared over time while practicing. Limiting the number of steps given in the instructions and using familiar words might also elicit clearer understanding for some participants. Verbal cues are often effective in conveying critical aspects of the task without overwhelming participants with more lengthy instructions. Good cues are critical to the task, should be brief, and are more effective if organized (Rink, 1998). Cues can also be tailored to participants' capability levels by the language used, number of words used in the cue, and the focus of the cue. For instance, participants with differences in concept understanding might be told to "Keep elbow high! Step opposite! Put hand out and snap wrist!" when learning to throw overhand, whereas others might benefit from a more simple "step and throw" cue.

For some individuals, it's enough to verbally share the details of the activity. For others, demonstrations to supplement verbal cues might be more effective in communicating information. As with verbal instructions, it's important to consider the participant and the content of the information when modifying demonstrations. The proximity of participants to the demonstration can be adapted to ensure its effectiveness. Participants with differences in vision or high levels of distractibility might move closer to the demonstrator for increased focus. Practitioners can also consider whether key points need to be highlighted before the demonstration and whether demonstrations and verbal instructions should be presented simultaneously or not. For some participants with differences in concept understanding and attention, knowing what to selectively look for in the demonstration might be helpful. Or a participant who is deaf, for instance, might not be able to adequately receive all instructions relayed through an interpreter and watch the movements of a demonstration at the same time. For others with differences in cognitive capabilities, repeating the demonstration more than once or twice might be necessary.

Media materials can also help practitioners convey important instructional information. Pictures, charts, video clips, and other visual aids can effectively engage participants for several reasons. These materials can be used to reinforce and repeat details previously shared in

Figure 6.9 Physically guiding this young boy through the draw and release of the arrow might convey important skill information.

verbal instructions or demonstrations. They might also work to motivate participants who enjoy and are reinforced by brightly colored pictures or videos depicting others involved in movement skills. As with other communication strategies, how appropriate media approaches might be for participants should be considered on a case-by-case basis.

For some participants, physical guidance through a desired movement might be necessary to convey information (figure 6.9). For example, a practitioner might stand behind a participant learning to putt a golf ball and help hold the club and strike the ball. By manually guiding the participant through the task, the practitioner can enhance concept understanding and provide important tactile cues for increased sensory perception and body awareness. Although physical guidance might be effective in improving concept understanding and skill capability, practitioners also need to help participants become as independent as possible. With this in mind, the extent and frequency of physical assistance should gradually diminish over time. Physical guidance might be replaced with physical prompts in which the practitioner only helps initiate the movement, and the participant completes the task. Eventually, gestures and verbal cues might be enough to elicit task performance. Through this process, participants don't become dependent on the practitioner and begin to rely on natural cues and less intrusive prompts to participate in the activity.

Organizing and Managing the Instructional Setting

When designing physical activity experiences, practitioners must make decisions about how a setting will be organized and how best to implement activity plans to promote the achievement of identified objectives. There are many organizational and management modifications that help ensure greater inclusion of participants in physical activity programs. Such modifications involve organization of participants, time, space, and equipment.

Group size and grouping techniques. Practitioners must consider the optimal number of participants that can work together and still achieve individual outcomes through practice. In some situations, participants might work individually or in partners, and other times small or large groups might be best. Ideal group size depends on several factors, including the nature of the activity, length of down time for participants, and the attentional focus and capacity of participants. Some participants who are more easily distracted might need to work in smaller groups with increased guidance for their skills to improve. Larger groups might also increase waiting and not provide enough active involvement to maintain attention and on-task behavior.

Another factor to consider when working toward more inclusive participation is how participants are grouped. Best practice has moved from participants choosing their own groups in which less-skilled players are often chosen last to practitioners creating groups of mixed ability. In the latter case, groups or teams are devised so that each team has a continuum of ability levels, thereby equalizing competition or practice. The rationale behind this strategy is that less-skilled players will learn from the more-skilled ones and can be matched or paired against each other in the game. Although less-skilled players might sometimes learn from higher-skilled peers, often there is unequal active participation in the game, and skill development occurs less for those who need it the most. Rink (1998) suggests that heterogeneous or mixed ability grouping might work well for peer teaching or collaborative learning situations but that grouping by ability level might offer individualized and optimal challenge for all involved. Practitioners can offer a continuum of options or different levels of play. One group might have a high level of competitiveness, another a more recreational level, and another an instructional level geared more toward skill development. With guidance from the practitioner, participants can then choose the level of participation they prefer.

Time considerations.   Time is another important management consideration that can be modified to create more inclusive and dynamic capability shifting of participants. Time management relates to scheduling physical activity sessions as well as monitoring the duration and pace of practice. The time of day that participants engage in physical activity might significantly influence their performance and learning process. Practitioners should consider when the best time is for participants to be active and try arranging activities around this time. For individuals who fatigue more easily than others, physical activity sessions might be offered early in the day. On the other hand, some participants, such as those with specific medication schedules, might gain more from sessions offered later in the day, when medication effects have peaked. Participants and others from the support network or IEP team should offer input to help practitioners make scheduling decisions.

How long participants practice a task can also be modified to help optimize skill development. Some individuals might need additional sessions to achieve a desired physical activity outcome, whereas others might attain personal goals in fewer sessions. Within a particular session, some participants can remain engaged in an activity and continue practicing for longer periods of time. Others might tire or become off task within a relatively short time. Practitioners must continually observe and assess whether participants are engaged and ensure that the practice is still productive. The length of the activity session can be shortened or lengthened, depending on how engaged participants are. There should also be enough options available for those participants who might need to change activities more quickly to remain active and on task. It's important, however, to ensure that participants have enough time to practice for skill improvement before transitioning from the task. Clear participation expectations and reinforcements, as well as prompts, might be useful for some individuals with differences in attention and self-responsibility. Regardless of the duration of the task practice, transitions between activities are also critical to effective management. The length of time between tasks and expectations during this time can be modified to meet individual needs. Some participants might need time to rest or receive additional instruction, whereas others might need to quickly begin the next activity to remain involved and less distracted. Also, some participants might need a signal that a transition is about to occur. This pretransition cue can prompt them to finish their last practice attempt and prepare themselves for a change rather than being surprised by sudden shifts in expectations. Again, decisions regarding the length and type of transition should be individualized, based on each participant's capabilities.

Physical activity space.   How physical activity space is used and organized can contribute to the inclusion of all individuals. Defining the practice area is an important first step in accommodating individual needs and differences. The type of surface on which practice occurs might affect some participants' capabilities. For instance, a flat surface might allow for increased performance for those with balance or mobility differences. Although the size of an activity area is often dictated by the nature of the activity or skill, specifically defining the area in which participants practice can also help keep learners on task and close by for further instruction and feedback. Cones or brightly colored markers can accentuate boundaries for individuals with differences in vision, attention, or understanding. Dividing the practice area is another avenue for accommodating individual differences. By breaking up the practice space, practitioners can adjust the amount of total space available, thereby altering task demands for participants. For instance, reducing space for some participants engaged in group activity might result in reducing the force or speed needed and lead to greater success. On the other hand, allowing more space for activity might require greater movement and lead to increased fitness levels. Some participants who are more easily distracted might also need a smaller space partitioned off to stay focused. Mats, markers, poly spots, or hoops can help define an individual's personal space or practice area.

The size of the practice area can also be manipulated to suit participants' needs. Some individuals might require reduced space or boundaries in some activities so that force or speed is modified. For example, reducing the boundaries in a tag game for a participant with a difference in speed might increase the player's success at tagging others. Conversely, other participants with differences in balance, for instance, might need a larger space in which to move during certain movement games. Decreasing or increasing the distance to a target or moving players farther from or closer to a net or basket changes the force needed by these players to achieve success. In all cases, if specific learning outcomes are to be achieved, modifying spaces to match the type of activity and the needs of participants must be thought through before activity begins.

Class format and individual positioning. The organization or formation of participants within the physical activity space also needs to be considered. Many different group formations have been used in physical activity settings, including squads, lines, circles, and scattered formations. Scattered formations are preferred by those who don't like wasting time getting into set formations. However, scattered formations allow less observation of others, including those with less developed skills. Lines and circle formations can place participants with ability differences in the spotlight and can showcase their differences in skill. Regardless of which group formation is used in program activities, each individual's position within the formation should be considered. If squads or lines are used, practitioners should ensure that all participants can see and hear instruction. This might require some individuals being moved in closer to the practitioner, again with consideration for showcasing differences in skill. Some participants, especially those with differences in attention, might need to face away from others and away from equipment to prevent becoming distracted. Some participants with differences in self-control might also need to be in closer proximity to the practitioner for increased guidance and instruction. Positioning participants in the best place to obtain needed instructions, observe demonstrations, and avoid distractions contributes to an inclusive and effective learning environment.

Equipment. The type and arrangement of equipment can promote inclusion of participants with diverse abilities within physical activity programs. Practitioners should consider each piece of equipment and how it's used to support a participant's current functional level and help him or her achieve desired goals (figure 6.10). By establishing a task goal and providing equipment choices for learners, practitioners can more easily accommodate differing capabilities within the same activity (Balan & Davis, 1993). One choice might include changing a characteristic of a piece of equipment. For example, a student with differences in coordination might choose a larger ball when involved in a catching activity with a peer, whereas others in the class might use smaller balls as they practice, and learners with increased capability in eye–hand coordination might elect to throw and catch irregular shaped balls to remain challenged. Targets can also be raised or lowered and distances to targets increased or decreased to provide optimal challenges for participants with different levels of skill. Table 6.4 presents a list of equipment characteristics that can be modified for differences in capabilities.

Another modification strategy to consider is using a different piece of equipment for the intended task goal than what's typically used. For example, someone with differing eye–hand coordination involved in a modified softball game might choose to use a large-headed racket rather than a bat to strike the pitched ball. Beyond changing some characteristic about the

Figure 6.10 Throwing a club rather than a ball and adding stability to this young girl's wheelchair increases her activity participation and chance of success.

equipment or substituting one piece of equipment for another, possible modifications might include adding equipment to assist in task completion. For instance, an adult with decreased range of motion and strength involved in a bowling league might elect to use a bowling ramp instead of a two-handed approach. Increasing the amount of equipment used in an activity can also provide increased opportunities to respond and allow for faster improvement. For example, adding additional balls in a target throwing activity for young children allows for increased contact with the balls and prevents dominant players from controlling the activity. Remember, though, that increasing the amount of equipment likely also increases the attentional demands on participants. Practitioners must determine if participants can handle this increased level of difficulty and ensure the safety of all participants involved in the activity.

Decisions about equipment are not only contextual modifications; they are an integral part of task progressions, as presented earlier in this chapter. Changes in the type or piece of equipment used might allow participants to achieve additional steps in the sequence that they otherwise would not achieve. For instance, a student might be able to kick a small stationary ball to a stationary classmate quite accurately. However, this individual might not be as successful with this same size ball if the task were more complex. He or she might need a larger ball to pass accurately from a dribble to a peer who is also moving down the field.

Practitioners also need to assess how equipment choices affect participant behavior and performance. Although some participants might benefit from colored markers and cones, others might be easily distracted by these visual cues. Practitioners should have the equipment they intend to use ready and attempt to reduce or eliminate distractions caused by equipment when modifying for inclusive programming.

Selecting Instructional Strategies

Effective practitioners develop appropriate content and skill progressions and carefully think about how to organize physical activity sessions. They are also actively engaged in how practice and learning proceed. They are continually deciding what instructional style is best, how skills should be taught, what activity procedures need modification, and how feedback should be provided to best meet individual needs and capabilities.

Instructional styles. One decision practitioners need to make is how to best deliver instructional content for a particular group of individuals. They want to select an instructional style that is most appropriate for the content being taught, the objectives of the lesson, and the abilities of the participants. This decision-making process determines the responsibilities of the practitioner and participants. Table 6.5 depicts the spectrum of instructional styles as developed by Mosston and Ashworth (2002). The instructional style can be considered on a continuum from more practitioner-directed styles to more participant-discovery approaches. The strategy chosen for a group or individual can be selected based on how much practitioner

Table 6.4 Equipment Characteristics

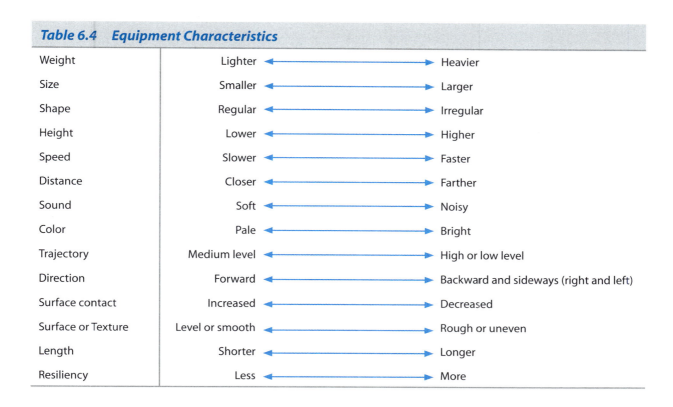

Weight	Lighter ←————→	Heavier
Size	Smaller ←————→	Larger
Shape	Regular ←————→	Irregular
Height	Lower ←————→	Higher
Speed	Slower ←————→	Faster
Distance	Closer ←————→	Farther
Sound	Soft ←————→	Noisy
Color	Pale ←————→	Bright
Trajectory	Medium level ←————→	High or low level
Direction	Forward ←————→	Backward and sideways (right and left)
Surface contact	Increased ←————→	Decreased
Surface or Texture	Level or smooth ←————→	Rough or uneven
Length	Shorter ←————→	Longer
Resiliency	Less ←————→	More

Table 6.5 Continuum of Teaching Styles

	Instructional style	Description
Teacher directed	Command	Purpose: To learn the task accurately and within a short period of time. Teacher makes all the decisions and directs all learning.
	Practice	Purpose: To provide the learner with time to work individually and privately. Teacher provides individual feedback.
	Reciprocal	Purpose: To work with a partner. Partners provide feedback to each other based on criteria set by the teacher or practitioner.
	Self-check	Purpose: To learn to do a task and check one's own work. Criteria for self-check is determined by the teacher or practitioner.
	Inclusion	Purpose: To learn to select one's own level of a task to perform and check one's own work.
	Guided discovery	Purpose: To discover a concept or answer through a sequence of questions presented by the teacher.
	Convergent discovery	Purpose: To discover a solution to a problem, clarify an issue, or arrive at a conclusion by using logical procedures and critical thinking skills.
	Divergent production	Purpose: To discover multiple answers to a single question.
	Individual program-Learner's design	Purpose: To provide the learner with the opportunity to design, develop, and perform a series of tasks organized into a personal program.
	Learner-initiated	Purpose: To provide the learner with the opportunity to self-initiate the design, implementation, and evaluation of their own learning.
Participant directed	Self-teaching	Purpose: To engage in lifelong learning based on complete self-direction. No teacher or practitioner involved.

Adapted from "Teaching Physical Education" (Mosston, M. & Ashworth, S., 2002).

direction is necessary to ensure participant learning. A participant who has more difficulty with concept understanding or self-responsibility might benefit from the command style, in which the task and all performance decisions are made by the practitioner. The role of the participant, in this case, is to follow and perform the task as described. Conversely, a guided discovery style invites participants to engage in problem solving and critical thinking as they seek to meet desired outcomes; this method might work best for participants who are more independent and responsible.

Although instructional methods might be employed to accommodate differences in participant abilities and needs, practitioners working with groups might find it difficult to use multiple styles that are effective for everyone involved. They might need to switch styles throughout an activity session or use a style that's most appropriate for the group and then employ different approaches selectively with individuals during practice. For instance, a practitioner might determine that the self-check style is best for a group of fourth graders involved in a tumbling lesson. As the learners are practicing, he or she might find a command style most effective when working with a child who needs additional support for concept understanding.

When working with individuals of differing abilities, the inclusion style in particular might facilitate the most appropriate programming. The inclusion style involves an approach that incorporates multiple levels of performance within the same task. Instead of a single standard that some will achieve and others won't, the task design allows for all participants to be included by offering choices regarding the degree of difficulty and individual goals. Figure 6.11 shows how changing the task design can foster inclusion rather than exclusion. Instead of holding the rope parallel to the floor for all individuals to jump over, the rope is slanted, thereby allowing participants to access the activity and succeed at different levels. Participants decide at which level they would like to enter the task and how the task will be subsequently attempted. For example, they can repeat the same level of difficulty or choose a more difficult or less difficult level. This same approach can be applied to many activities such as those involving nets, targets, and goals. This style has important implications for inclusive programming. It implies that the practitioner philosophically embraces the concept of inclusion and the idea that legitimate

Figure 6.11 A horizontal rope allows youngsters only one choice in where to jump over a rope. The slanted rope (pictured here) allows the youngsters many choices in where they might jump over the rope.

options must be created for successful programming. The practitioner acknowledges the range of capabilities participants bring to any physical activity setting and is creative in ensuring that each individual is offered meaningful and beneficial experiences.

Whole–part practice. For some participants, it works well to practice a skill in its entirety. For other participants, task complexity can be reduced by having them practice and develop competency in parts of the task before practicing the whole movement skill together. For instance, a participant with coordination differences might begin practicing a delivery of a bowling ball from the line before combining the two-step approach with the delivery. This instructional strategy can also be used to teach participants with differences in concept understanding more complex dance routines in which small sequences of steps are taught before other steps or movements are added and the routine is performed as a whole. Even when breaking a skill into parts, participants should have an idea of what the whole skill looks and feels like before practicing its parts. This whole–part approach is not recommended when tasks are relatively easy or have a natural flow or continuous motion to them, such as the golf swing. In these cases, the entire skill should be practiced and other modification strategies employed.

Activity procedures. The level of involvement and degree of success experienced by participants in an activity can be manipulated by modifying the rules of play. Rules are designed to facilitate the way in which skills are performed and participants interact. By changing the rules, practitioners can increase or decrease the challenge for participants. For instance, a child who moves more slowly than his or her peers in a tag game can be allowed two tags instead of one before being "caught." An adult with proficient eye–hand coordination and accuracy might be allowed to shoot only from outside the key, whereas others can shoot from inside or outside.

More inclusive programming can also be achieved by modifying the roles and responsibilities a participant has in an activity. Individuals can choose specific positions in which they might experience greater success than in other roles. For example, a player with limited mobility might perform very successfully as a pitcher in a softball game compared to how he or she might perform as an outfielder (figure 6.12). A player with less developed balance and speed might choose to serve as the team's goalie in a soccer game rather than play offense. While matching roles to participant capabilities might be effective, practitioners need to take care not to narrow participant options. Some participants might prefer to participate in several positions on the team and need additional skill development and modification in order to succeed in these roles. Responsibilities in an activity can further facilitate inclusive programming. Although some players in a basketball game might play person-to-person defense, others might be more successful in a zone defense in

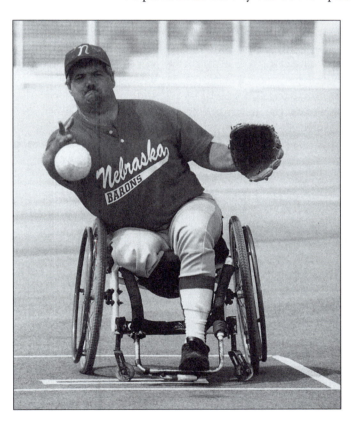

Figure 6.12 Certain responsibilities within a game or activity might provide greater activity involvement and yield more success than other positions.

which they can guard a particular area of the court. Roles and responsibilities can be individualized for each participant, even when involved in the same activity, and these roles can change throughout play as needed to ensure meaningful involvement and success.

Providing feedback. An essential aspect of instruction is providing participants with meaningful information about their performance. Feedback helps participants focus on the task at hand and stay motivated to continue practicing. Although reinforcers such as music, free time, and other rewards might help externally motivate some participants, specific and contingent feedback can be modified to increase motivation and promote skill improvement. Individuals can benefit from feedback that considers the task goal, the abilities of the participant, and the context in which the skill is performed. The type of feedback offered might be tailored to accommodate individual differences. For instance, beginners with differences in concept understanding might be given more corrective feedback or information on how to correct errors rather than just evaluative or descriptive information on what they did. Here are some examples of different kinds of feedback:

- On your next throw, point to the target when you let go of the ball. (corrective)
- I like the way you stepped with your opposite foot on that throw. (evaluative)
- You snapped your wrist on that forehand shot. (descriptive)

The amount of feedback also plays a key role in performer improvement. Too much information might overwhelm participants with differences in attentional capacity, whereas for others greater detail and feedback might be useful. Prioritizing the feedback information given and connecting feedback to cues used during task presentation might help reduce the amount of information and more effectively focus participants on more critical aspects of the skill. Using consistent feedback-related cues might also benefit participants with differences in cognitive understanding or attention. The timing of feedback given participants can further affect their learning. Feedback given immediately after performance might be best for participants with shorter attention spans or decreased on-task behavior, whereas some participants might engage in self-assessment and receive instructor feedback a bit later. The schedule of feedback can also differ to accommodate individual differences. Participants who seem initially less motivated can receive more feedback early on in practice sessions and less information as they progress in skill and desire. Regardless of what feedback decisions are made, practitioners should keep in mind that too much feedback given often results in dependence on the feedback by participants. To foster increased independence, feedback should be given only when needed and be gradually reduced over time.

STEP 4: EVALUATING MODIFICATION EFFECTIVENESS

The last step in the FAMME model encourages practitioners to evaluate the appropriateness and potential effectiveness of modifications being considered. We discussed the specifics of assessing success in chapter 4. In this section, we'll provide further guidelines for determining if modifications are appropriate.

Modifications should be chosen that have a positive effect on all involved—the participants for whom modifications are made, other participants in the program, and the practitioner facilitating the activity. The main objective of reflecting on and selectively choosing the most effective modifications is to promote optimal challenges, positive attitudes, and acceptance. Modifications that are too hard or too easy, or that create negative feelings and resentment toward the individualization process, should be reassessed. The following questions provide practitioners guidance when considering and deciding on modifications. If the practitioner can answer "yes" to each of these questions, then the modifications are most likely appropriate and effective in promoting a positive environment for all involved.

1. Is the modification age-appropriate?

   When making changes to activities, make sure the activities are age-appropriate. For example, a junior high school student with less developed eye–hand coordination might need a lighter and slower piece of equipment when practicing striking to be successful. Having the learner hit a beach ball as many times in the air as possible is less age-appropriate then using the ball within the context of a modified volleyball game. This activity is more likely to be valued by peers and looked on as a similar age activity. In fact, many other learners might want to use this same modification to increase their success rate. This same principle holds true for participants of all ages. The modification should allow for greater success and still be viewed as appropriate for all participants of a similar age.

2. Is the modification functionally appropriate?

   Modifications should be chosen that have the potential for increasing physical activity participation now *and* in the future. For example, promoting a participant's success while bowling by having him or her move closer to the pins might not be as effective as using bumpers or a bowling ramp, which are available and allowed in community bowling facilities. Or, having someone practice serving a volleyball over a lowered net might provide success but fail to promote the participant's involvement in a recreation league or community-based game of volleyball, which requires a specific net height. Instead, having the participant move closer and practice serving over a higher net might lead to more inclusive involvement later on.

3. Does the modification allow the participant to be as independent as possible?

   Modifications should increase success but not at the expense of active involvement of the participant. In the past, a participant using a wheelchair in a recreational or school softball game might have been pushed by a teammate to reach first base before the throw. However, this modification doesn't provide for independence and individual accomplishment. Alternative modifications that would allow for greater independence and skill development for all involved might include changing the distance needed to travel to first base or requiring the outfield to throw two or more times before making a play on the batter. Modifications should always allow the participant the greatest possible amount of independence. However, changing rules for some participants might or might not be appropriate given the activity or context. More competitive leagues, for instance, might not allow such rule changes, whereas schoolyard play might. The level of independent participation must be considered in light of these varying contexts.

4. Does the modification ensure maximum participation of the participant?

   Sometimes it's necessary to identify particular positions on a team that might be a better match for a participant's functional capabilities. For instance, a softball player might find more success pitching rather than playing shortstop. However, in such a case, the practitioner must ensure that the game is designed to provide the pitcher with ample skill development, opportunities to interact in the game, and reasonable success in that position. This would be true for any individual playing in this position.

5. Does the modification avoid singling out or spotlighting high- or low-ability participants?

   Design activities to allow for a variety of ability levels. For example, if participants are running in class for cardiovascular development, have them start at different places in the gym and run in a circle. In this way no one will be in the front or back of the group, and runners can go at their own pace without being spotlighted. In another example, having students throw to targets lined up on the same wall and then move back as they successfully hit the target eventually results in the most skilled participant being farthest away and the lowest skilled learner being closest to the wall for all others to notice. An easy way to prevent this is to have learners throw at targets placed at varying distances in several locations. Students might be required to move around to three or four targets of their choice, allowing for more movement and challenge for all involved without spotlighting any one individual. Relays and obstacle courses are also organizational strategies that don't always lend themselves to inclusive practice and equal opportunity. Organizational decisions are critical in making sure that specific learners aren't put on display for others to view.

6. Does the modification allow for optimal challenge for everyone in the activity?

   Most important, practitioners need to be cognizant of the level of participation of all individuals in the activity. Modifications should be focused on bringing up the skill performance of those for whom modifications were necessary. Equality is not achieved by reducing the skill level of others in the activity. For example, in a game of tag, a student who has difficulty tagging classmates can be provided with a reaching implement, such as a foam tube, or boundaries can be reduced for runners rather than having peers walk so they can be more easily tagged. Having students walk so they can be more easily tagged may lead to resentment by peers or boredom from lack of an optimal challenge.

7. Is safe participation ensured for all participants once the modification is implemented?

   No matter which modification strategy he or she chooses, the practitioner must ensure the safety of all participants. Adapted equipment should be stored away when it's not in use, and practitioners should teach and practice rules and safety procedures for any program.

Practitioners must take the time to ask these questions and decide which modification might be best; as the activity unfolds, they must also determine whether additional modifications or changes are necessary. As we mentioned in chapter 1, the process of Ready, Rethink, Retry can promote success and enjoyment for all participants. This process is no less important when it comes to modifying for inclusive physical activity programming.

◁ **THINK BACK**

1. What are four methods of presenting information discussed in this chapter?

2. What are four of the organizational management considerations when presenting an activity? How might Karen Morgan alter some of these to help Sara achieve more success in her physical education class?

3. Based on Karen's class, think of some modifications for the activities she's doing. Apply each of the seven questions to your modifications to determine if they're appropriate.

▶ **APPLYING THE FAMME MODEL**

Once the four steps of the FAMME model are understood, the process can be applied to any individual in any physical activity context. Tables 6.6 and 6.7 provide an in-depth look at how the model can be used to support the involvement of individuals in two different activities. In the examples presented, notice how modifications are connected directly to the capability differences of the individual in relation to the underlying components necessary to achieve the task goal. Again, it's important for the practitioner to realize that there are many possible modifications that might be used to achieve the desired outcome and that he or she should give careful consideration to those most effective in meeting the evaluation criteria earlier discussed.

Case Study of Jason

Jason is an eight-year-old boy who enjoys physical education. He's at age level in his academics and has very good social and communication skills. He also gets along well with his peers. His balance and agility are less developed because of his cerebral palsy. The class is involved in a tag game, and Jason is chosen to be the player who tags others. Following is an example of the FAMME model applied to Jason's capabilities and the underlying components required to play the game of tag.

Table 6.6 Applying the FAMME Model: Jason

Underlying components of tagging	Jason's functional differences	Modifications
Concept understanding	X	None needed
Balance	Balance	Ensure surface is flat Choose to gallop (Jason) Decrease speed and use reaching extension
Coordination	X	None needed
Agility/speed	Agility/speed	Decrease size of area Use reaching extension
Sensory perception	X	None needed
Strength (legs)	X	None needed
Endurance	X	None needed
Flexibility	X	None needed
Attention	X	None needed
Self-control	X	None needed

Case Study of Laura

Laura is a 35-year-old woman beginning a fitness program involving resistance exercise. She is very articulate and insightful. Although her range of motion is good, she has muscular weakness in her legs and some difficulty with balance and body awareness caused by symptoms associated with multiple sclerosis. Following is an example of the FAMME model applied to Laura's capabilities and the underlying components required for resistance exercises.

Table 6.7 Applying the FAMME Model—Laura

Underlying components of weightlifting	Laura's functional differences	Modifications
Concept understanding	X	None needed

(continued)

Table 6.7 *(continued)*

Balance	Balance	Ensure surface is flat Use hand-held weights bilaterally Perform sitting versus standing
Coordination	X	None needed
Sensory perception	Body awareness	Use mirror for visual feedback Provide tactile cues or manual guidance Offer verbal cues and metaphors
Strength (legs)	Strength	Move limb horizontally in antigravity plane Use elastic bands versus weights
Range of motion	X	None needed
Agility and speed	X	None needed
Endurance	X	None needed
Flexibility	X	None needed
Self-control	X	None needed

▶ SUMMARY

Modifying activities to meet the needs of individuals with differing abilities is critical to the success of any program. The FAMME model provides logical steps to the process of making modifications, including determining the underlying components of a skill or activity; determining the capabilities of the individual; matching the modifications to the capabilities of the individual; and evaluating the effectiveness of the modifications selected. In every instructional situation the practitioner must be able to evaluate the dynamic interplay of the person, task, and environment and make a meaningful match that optimizes success and independence among participants.

What Do You Think?

1. Choose a skill that you have performed many times. What underlying components are important when performing this skill?

2. Consider a recent movement experience you've had. What types of modifications could be made within that experience for another participant with differences in balance? How about differences in eye–hand coordination?

3. In your view, are any of the ways to assess the effectiveness of modifications more important than others? Why or why not?

What Would You Do?

Now that you've seen the FAMME model applied in two situations, see if you can use the model for the following individuals.

Scenario 6.1

Joanne is a sophomore in high school. She loves shopping and socializing with her friends and is trying out to be a song leader for next year. She's a good student and has recently won an award for her artwork at the county fair. She likes physical education well enough, but she despises team sports. Recently, her class finished a unit on dance that she enjoyed very much, but her class will be entering a unit on soccer starting next week. Joanne has asthma that can be aggravated by exercise, and many team sports and fitness activities stress her out. She doesn't like activities in which others depend on her or in which her performance will be spotlighted. She prefers individual activities and doesn't like most ball games.

Underlying components of soccer	Joanne's functional differences	Modifications of soccer

Scenario 6.2

Francis is a physical activity director at his local YMCA and has an adult participant, Jack, in one of his programs who is having some behavior problems. Jack can't seem to stand still during basketball sessions and is often "out of control," as Francis puts it. If things don't go his way, Jack yells at other participants in the group, and several times he has thrown the ball in anger. Francis is afraid Jack is going to accidentally hurt someone if he doesn't get his behavior under control. Francis is frustrated with Jack and has tried talking with him and has also written notes to the staff of the group home where Jack lives. Unfortunately, these strategies haven't panned out yet. Complete the FAMME model for Jack.

Underlying components of basketball	Jack's functional differences	Modifications of basketball

Application of Inclusive Practices

Part III includes four chapters that provide direct application of the programming strategies and FAMME model presented in part II. Each chapter describes various movement skills or physical activities for individuals across the life span and shows how differences in capacity can be matched with specific modifications to increase skill performance and success of all participants. Examples are given for movement skills (chapter 7), games and sports (chapter 8), health-related fitness activities (chapter 9), and outdoor and adventure programming (chapter 10).

Movement Skills and Concepts

Learning Outcomes

After completing this chapter, you should be able to

» explain that skills can be considered as a sequence of critical elements;

» discuss the link between critical elements of a task and functional components; and

» apply the FAMME model to movement skills and concepts when modifying for individual differences.

INCLUDING ALL INDIVIDUALS

Janet is a second grader in Tony Gallant's physical education class at Homer Elementary School. She is a friendly child who enjoys physical activity and participating with her peers. Her academic skills are at age level in all subjects except for math, but these skills are emerging. Janet uses a wheelchair because of paralysis of her legs from spina bifida but has good wheelchair mobility and control. Her class is just about to begin a unit on throwing and catching. Tony understands from the supportive network he has established that Janet will need some modifications to activities because of her functional capabilities and present level of performance. Tony is a new instructor and hasn't had much experience teaching children with disabilities. He very much wants Janet to succeed and hopes to see her progress in performing the fundamental movement skills and concepts covered in his second-grade class.

Tony is clearly interested in ensuring that Janet is provided with a meaningful and optimal physical education program. If you were Tony, what's the first thing you would need to know about the skill of catching before making modifications for Janet? What modifications to this skill might help her the most?

In chapter 6, we presented the process for modifying tasks to meet individual capabilities. In this chapter we'll take the next step by practically applying the functional approach for modifying movement experiences (FAMME) model to fundamental motor skills and concepts. We'll also deal with prioritizing modification efforts by connecting aspects of tasks to functional capabilities of individuals when performing a skill. All practitioners should strive to create variations for fundamental movement skills and concepts that set a foundation for competence and enjoyment in lifelong physical activity.

▶ OVERVIEW OF MOVEMENT SKILLS AND CONCEPTS

Individuals of all abilities require early movement experiences in which they practice and refine basic skills and concepts. Instruction that accommodates individual differences in capabilities results in well-learned basic skills that prepare participants for acquiring more advanced skills.

Did You Know?

Qualitative analysis is the systematic observation and appraisal of movement quality in order to provide effective solutions to improve performance. The qualitative analysis process involves four steps: preparation, observation, evaluation and diagnosis, and intervention.

Many participants who lack fundamental skills exhibit ineffective movements when they try to progress to more advanced play and sport activities.

Fundamental movement skills include locomotor and nonlocomotor movements as well as manipulative skills (table 7.1). These skills are the precursors for many advanced activities and mastering them promotes successful participation in sports and other leisure activities. For example, playing offense in a game of basketball involves dodging and running skills as well as catching and dribbling skills. Golf involves striking, walking, and twisting. Participants should understand how to use their bodies to perform these skills effectively and how to adjust the skill to changing contexts and situations in a variety of activities.

Table 7.1 *Skill Themes and Movement Concepts*

Skill Themes

Locomotor skills	Object control skills	Nonmanipulative skills
Walking	Throwing	Turning
Running	Catching and collecting	Twisting
Hopping	Kicking	Rolling
Skipping	Punting	Balancing
Sliding	Dribbling	Jumping and landing
Galloping	Volleying	Stretching
Chasing, fleeing, dodging	Striking with rackets	Curling
	Striking with long-handled implements	Transferring weight

Movement Concepts

Spatial awareness	Effort	Relationships

Location:
  Personal space
  General space
	Time:
	  Fast or slow
	  Sudden or sustained
		Of body parts
		  Round (curved), narrow, wide,
		  symmetrical, nonsymmetrical

Directions:
  Up or down, forward or backward,
  right or left, clockwise, or
  counterclockwise
	Force:
	  Strong or light
		With objects or people
		  Over or under, near or far, in front or
		  behind, along or through, meeting
		  or parting, surrounding, around,
		  alongside

Levels:
  High, medium, or low
	Flow:
	  Bound or free
		With people:
		  Leading or following, mirroring or
		  matching, in unison or contrasting,
		  alone, in a mass, solo, partners, groups,
		  between groups

Pathways: Straight or curved or zigzag		

Extensions:
  Large or small
  Far or near		

Reprinted, by permission, from G. Graham, S. Holt-Hale, & M. Parker, 2001, *Children moving: A reflective approach to teaching physical education,* 5th edition (New York: McGraw-Hill Companies), 26-27. © McGraw-Hill Companies.

▶ PREREQUISITE KNOWLEDGE OF TASK ELEMENTS

Before practitioners can successfully modify tasks for individual differences in capability, they need to know their participants' abilities and have a good understanding of the task they need to modify. They should know the task's purpose, the movement patterns and techniques involved, and the common sources of error. For example, a practitioner that knows kicking a ball for distance involves weight shifting onto the opposite foot, forward trunk movement, and eyes maintained on ball throughout contact, can more effectively teach cues, make modifications, and provide appropriate feedback for error correction.

A good understanding of a task includes knowing the task's critical elements or features, which are the aspects of a task necessary for effective results (Knudson & Morrison, 2002).

Table 7.2 Critical Features and Sample Cues for the Overhand Throw

Critical feature	Sample cue
Target location	Keep your eyes on the target.
Angle of release	Throw flat or throw up an incline.
Relaxation	Relax your upper body.
Leg drive and opposition	Step with the opposite foot.
Body orientation	Turn your side toward the target.
Strong throwing position	Align the arm with your shoulders.
Sequential coordination	Uncoil the body.
Inward rotation of the arm (follow-through)	Roll the arm and wrist at release.

Reprinted with permission from the August 1996 issue of the Journal of Physical Education, Recreation & Dance, a publication of the American Alliance for Health, Physical Education, Recreation and Dance, 1900 Association Dr., Reston, VA 20191.

Figure 7.1 Practitioners can provide effective modifications to a task once critical elements and associated cues have been identified.

These aspects are the observable features of performance that practitioners often use to offer meaningful instructional cues or points of emphasis to their participants. They are also the basis of analysis and assessment of the participant's performance. Table 7.2 offers an example of the critical elements for the overhand throw and illustrates the instructional cues associated with each element. According to Knudson and Morrison (1996), critical features of skills are identified based on the effectiveness in achieving the movement goal, the efficiency of effort, and safety to the performer. Practitioners' abilities to identify and understand the critical features of skills comes from experience through observation as well as through professional development via the literature in the field. For individuals with differences in capability, these task elements can also provide direction for modification efforts. Through understanding the sequence of critical elements for a given task and acknowledging that a range of effective movement exists across individuals with differences in movement capabilities, practitioners can begin to prioritize which elements are most crucial to successful performance as well as which elements need to be modified (figure 7.1). For instance, a student with differing ability in coordination might perform the critical elements of striking quite well except for optimal contact of the ball. By focusing on this element, the practitioner might be better able to determine necessary modifications and thus provide a successful experience. Given the movement form and outcome observed, the height of the ball or the learner's orientation to the batting tee might need to be changed to allow more accurate contact.

THINK BACK

Think back to Tony Gallant's class.

1. What are the critical elements for catching?

2. How might these elements for catching be the same or different for Janet or one of her peers?

CRITICAL ELEMENTS AND DIFFERENCES IN MOVEMENT CAPABILITIES

Even when the critical elements for a task have been identified, some of the task's features might not be readily observed in individuals with differences in movement capabilities. For example, a participant who uses a wheelchair might be unable to step with his or her opposite foot when throwing overhand, or someone with increased muscle tone in his or her legs who uses crutches for balance might have difficulty demonstrating rhythmic movement while galloping. While practitioners need to understand the critical elements of a skill, they must also know how individual differences affect these critical elements. Only then can they have realistic expectations of movement skill performance for individual participants. Also, the practitioner should be sure to understand the influence of specific elements on skill outcome. For example, a participant using a wheelchair who's unable to step with the opposite foot during a throw can be instructed to move his or her trunk in a forward motion and use trunk rotation to increase force. In this way, the critical element of stepping with the opposite foot is replaced with trunk motion to achieve a similar performance outcome (figure 7.2).

After identifying critical features and variations of tasks for individual participants, the next step is making modifications that promote success of the key elements. Variations based on the task and context, as described in chapter 6,

Figure 7.2 Teaching an athlete who uses a wheelchair to shift his weight and move his trunk forward during throwing leads to skill improvement and success.

can be employed to meet the needs of participants with functional differences in movement capabilities. Here are the considerations for practitioners when modifying a task:

1. How can instruction be modified to provide successful opportunities for all participants involved in the activity? Can concepts such as flow, force, time, or levels be altered to provide optimal challenges? How will the size of the object used, the number of people involved in the task, and the organization of space affect the participants?

2. Does the modified task elicit a participant's best performance? How does the practitioner's understanding of the functional capabilities of learners and the critical elements of a task lead to successful performance?

3. Does the modified task assess the psychomotor, cognitive, or affective content it was designed to assess? Are the goals and meaningful involvement of participants still being realized?

THINK BACK

Think back to Janet's involvement in Tony Gallant's catching unit.

1. Which critical elements might need modifications?

2. From what you learned in chapter 6, which modifications might you want to try?

▶ MODIFICATION OF FUNDAMENTAL MOVEMENT SKILLS AND CONCEPTS

Most often, teaching fundamental movements and concepts involves individual skill practice leading toward partner and small-group activity. For example, students in a physical education class might be working on skipping within a general space or practicing their dribbling and kicking with a partner in a designated space. Regardless of the task, teachers should provide choices and modifications to meet individual needs and provide optimal challenges.

As we discussed in chapter 6, modifications can be made to the task or the context that might include instructional, organizational, or equipment variations. Because of the focus on skill practice and refinement typical of teaching fundamental skills and concepts, these modifications can be implemented more easily than might be possible when teaching more advanced games and sport skills. For instance, a task can be presented in such a way to give choices regarding movement form. A practitioner might ask students to balance on three parts of their body. Because the learners' actions don't directly relate or depend on others in the group, they can choose which body parts they want to use. In another case, an instructor could use task cards to foster skill development. He or she might ask participants to kick a ball toward a target a set number of times. Although the task of kicking the ball to the target remains the same for all participants, changes to the directions could involve an increase or decrease in the number of times players are asked to hit the target or the distance they kick from. Again, practice incorporates multiple targets with learners working independently within the group, thereby allowing individualized goals. The nature of practice at this level also allows more choice in the equipment participants use. Through making a range of different equipment available, practitioners help participants get more comfortable and achieve more success in performance outcomes. For instance, students involved in volleying activities could choose from balloons, beach balls, volleyball trainers, or regulation volleyballs when practicing the skill.

As we discussed earlier, individualizing fundamental movements and skills requires an understanding of the critical elements of the skill as well as an awareness of task sequences that progress participants toward more advanced skills. There are many ways in which participants can practice activities. Table 7.3 identifies several aspects that can be manipulated to present a range of task practice conditions from simple to more complex.

A task can by be modified by controlling the environment in which the task takes place. As we discussed in chapter 6, one way to modify a task is to make it either a closed or open skill. For example, someone shooting a basketball from the free throw line is at the simpler end of the continuum because of the fixed nature of the environment in which the skill is performed

Table 7.3 Common Progressions or Fundamental Movement Skills and Concept Practice

Simple	Complex
Closed skill	Open skill
Individual	Partner to small group
Single skill or concept	Combined skill or concept
Cooperative	Competitive
Offense	Defense

Figure 7.3 Practice in a closed context is an effective strategy for skill development. Eventually, the context can be shifted to an open environment by adding more participants and gamelike play.

(figure 7.3). Someone shooting a jump shot in basketball while being defended is an open skill and thus more difficult.

You can also modify a task by controlling how many individuals are involved at one time. It's typically easier to perform a task alone than with a partner, and partner activities are usually easier than small-group activities. Once a learner can perform a task alone, you can increase the complexity of the task by adding a partner to the activity. For example, when a youngster is first learning to overhand strike, it's easier to practice striking a balloon alone. The task's difficulty is increased when two peers practice striking the balloon back and forth.

Another way to modify tasks is to have individuals participate in cooperative environments before competitive ones. In a cooperative activity, players work together toward a common goal. Such activities can encourage participants to be more accepting of others with abilities different from theirs. Cooperative activities also allow players to practice skills without the threat of being embarrassed or pressured if they do it less skillfully. Cooperative learning activities work best when the groups are small. For example, an instructor could have individuals participate in an activity in which groups of three work on their throwing and catching skills.

In competitive activities, a good way to modify a task is by teaching offense movements before adding defense movements. In general, players need to feel comfortable with their offensive techniques before they're ready to perform with defensive opponents. Adding a defender to a task adds a new level of complexity for them, so instructors must time this choice well. Participant frustration is almost a given if a defender is added to an activity too early in skill practice. In such cases, their progress toward gaining the skill abruptly halts and performance diminishes. Once a player is being defended, he or she may stop attending to proper mechanics and focus on the defender instead.

Finally, tasks can also be modified through a combination of movement concepts (figure 7.4). Movement concepts can be manipulated to help participants with fundamental movement patterns or sport-specific movements. Movement concepts encompass three areas: spatial awareness (where the body moves), effort (how the body moves), and relationships (moving with people or objects). *Spatial awareness* involves location (personal space, general space), direction (up or down, forward or backward, right or left, clockwise or counterclockwise), levels (low, middle, high), pathways (straight, curved, zigzag), and extensions (large or small, far or near). *Effort* involves time (fast or slow), force (strong or light), and flow (bound or free).

Figure 7.4 Movement concepts can be combined by having children moving in general space and in different pathways.

Relationships involve body parts (round, narrow, wide, twisted), other objects or people (over or under, near or far, along or through, meeting or partnering) and interaction with others (leading or following, mirroring or matching, solo, partners, groups). For example, someone learning to slide could also be taught directions. The instructor could have learners slide while moving in a pathway. The participant could then choose to slide in a zigzag, curved, or straight pathway.

THINK BACK

Think back to Janet in Tony Gallant's class.

1. Tony needs some variations for his class to progress their catching skills. Can you give Tony 10 ideas for progression in catching skills using closed to open variations?

2. Using the movement concepts, how many variations for the skill of catching can you think of?

EXAMPLES OF PRACTICE

By understanding task elements and considering simple to complex progressions in movement skills and concepts, practitioners can modify any activity to create optimal challenges for their participants with diverse abilities. Another way to examine skills and their possible modifications is by looking at the general task categories as described by Balan and Davis (1993). This classification system (first touched on in chapter 6) provides a meaningful framework for looking at modifications across skills.

Locomotion on Land

To move successfully on land, individuals need to acquire several locomotor and nonlocomotor skills, including walking, running, hopping, skipping, galloping, turning, twisting, rolling, balancing, and stretching. For example, skipping is a difficult skill that involves balance and rhythm. If a learner is having difficulty with balance, he or she can hold onto an object (e.g., hand or bar) to maintain balance while performing the skipping movement. An instructor can then observe if he or she is skipping correctly. The student might have the rhythm necessary to perform the skill but might lack the necessary balance. If the instructor is attempting to assess the ability of this learner to skip, it's important for the performance context to measure what was intended. Through having the learner perform the skipping skill while holding a hand, the balance element is reduced, and the instructor can observe if the child can indeed skip. Table 7.4 provides an example of modifications for jumping based on variations in capabilities. Table 7.5 lists modifications to locomotor activities to help participants succeed in locomotor skills on land.

Table 7.4 Modifications for Jumping

Capability difference	Modification
Balance	Hold peer's hand during jump
	Perform jump next to wall and touch wall during jump
Coordination	Slow jumping down
	Practice without arm action at first
Strength	Jump down incline mat or off slight rise
Flexibility	Shorten distance or height required to jump
Endurance	Allow rest in between multiple or sequential jumps
	Alternate jumping with walking or slow locomotor movement
Concept understanding	Use visual cues (such as footprints or poly spots)
	Employ counting sequence or verbal cues for critical features
Speed and agility	Increase distance between landing spots
	Reduce angles or need to change directions if jumping sequentially
Attention	Perform jump in direction away from others
	Reduce equipment students are jumping over and around
Self-responsibility	Require limited number of jumps before providing reinforcers or choices
Sensory perception	Use tactile demonstration
	Provide sound cue for jump direction or landing

Object Propulsion

Object propulsion involves an object moving away from the body after contact with a body part or with another object or implement. To propel objects successfully, participants must be able to perform such skills as throwing, kicking, punting, dribbling, volleying, striking, or rolling.

There are many ways to modify skills that involve object propulsion.

Table 7.5 lists modifications for individuals with diverse abilities when performing these skills. For example, in a rolling task, practitioners must understand the factors that affect the outcome of the roll. Factors such as the size, weight, and shape of the ball as well as the size and angle of the roll toward a target or goal line can be manipulated to promote success for participants of all ability levels (figure 7.5). For example, to increase the complexity of a throwing task, practitioners might reduce the size of the target and increase the distance to the target. Table 7.5 also lists possible equipment modifications. That can be used for other object propulsion skills.

Object Reception

Object reception involves taking in an object coming toward the body. Participants need to acquire several skills (e.g., timing, catching, trapping, blocking) before they can successfully receive a variety of objects.

Table 7.5 lists modifications to accommodate individuals with diverse abilities when performing object reception tasks, such as catching skills. For instance, changing the angle of a tossed ball can help someone successfully catch. Also, using a glove may improve his or her success at catching. The glove reduces the need of the grasping component when catching. (Table 7.5 identifies other types of equipment to modify when helping learners practice receiving objects.) Table 7.6 provides an example of modificaitons for catching based on capability differences.

Table 7.5 Modifications for Capability Differences in Locomotor, Object Propulsion, and Object-Reception Skills

	Easy ←		→ Difficult
Locomotor			
Space and speed	Slowly within large space and individually	Slowly within large space with others moving slowly	Fast within small space with others moving fast
Surface	Decline surface Smooth and flat	Horizontal surface Smooth and uneven	Incline surface Uneven and hilly
Object propulsion			
Distance	Very close	Near	Far
Ball size	Large	Medium	Small
Ball color and background color	Yellow and black	Blue and white	Yellow and white
Ball shape	Round	Oblong	Irregular
Ball movement	Stationary	Moving slowly	Moving rapidly
Angle of trajectory	Horizontal	30-35 degree arc	45 degree arc
Net	Lowered net	Slanted net	Regulation net
Weight of implement or object	Light	Medium	Heavy
Object reception			
Reception location	Body midline	Preferred side	Nonpreferred side
Ball type	Balloons or beach balls	Oversize trainers	Regulation ball
Contact area	Large	Medium	Small

Adapted, with permission, from G. Morris, and J. Stiehl, 1999, *Changing kids' games* (Champaign, IL: Human Kinetics), 37.

Table 7.6 Modifications for Catching

Capability difference	Modification
Balance	Catch while seated in chair
	Tossed ball comes to midline of body
Coordination	Use larger ball
	Use balloon or light foam ball that moves slowly
	Tossed ball comes to or near midline of body
Strength	Use light weight ball
Flexibility	Tossed ball comes to midline of body
	Use light weight or foam ball
	Use larger ball to limit joint movement
Concept understanding	Use physical guidance or verbal cues
Attention	Limit number of balls being thrown in area
Self-responsibility	Require limited number of catches before providing reinforcers or choices
Sensory perception	Use tactile demonstration or physical guidance
	Provide sound cue in ball and timing of catch

Note: Difference in speed and agility and endurance are not critical to successful catching.

Figure 7.5 The skill of rolling in a game of goalball can be modified by charging the size and weight of the ball or varying the distance to the opponent's goal line.

THINK BACK

Think back to Janet in Tony Gallant's class.

1. Referring to table 7.4, what types of modifications in equipment might Tony use for catching tasks?

2. What variations to the locomotor skills might Tony make for Janet in his class when he's teaching, galloping, skipping, sliding, and jumping?

SUMMARY

Accommodating for individual differences in the performance of fundamental movement skills requires a thorough knowledge of the critical elements of the task coupled with an understanding of the skill progressions necessary to foster skill development. Practitioners can become more insightful about what aspects of tasks participants might have difficulty with and what modifications would be most effective for increasing ability. Modifications to the critical elements of a skill can also increase the challenge for participants once they've gained competence in a skill. The ability of a practitioner to use modifications wisely and to accommodate for individual differences helps individuals develop and refine the basic skills and concepts they need to build the foundation for continued involvement and success in physical activity.

What Do You Think?

1. How might you vary the movement skills for learners with differences in strength, endurance, or attention?

2. Identify the critical features and sample cues for a skill. How might these be modified?

3. What are the four ways that skills can be modified as discussed in this chapter? Using the same skill you used in question 2, modify the skill in each of the four ways.

What Would You Do?

Scenario 7.1

Frank works for the local basketball league coaching 7- and 8-year-old boys. Frank has been coaching for three years, and in his program he tries to provide all the boys with many minutes of game time as he develops their basic skills for the game: dribbling, passing, catching, shooting, and establishing court position. In his first practice Frank started with introductions and a name game to help the boys get to know each other. Then he ran the boys through a few activities to assess their skill levels. During the activities, one particular boy (a 7-year-old named Devon) seemed to be frequently off task and had a hard time paying attention during the discussion of expectations of the boys and the practice schedules. After the practice, Devon's mom came up to Frank and said how happy she was to see Devon getting involved in basketball. She shared that Devon loved the sport and frequently spent time at home in the driveway shooting baskets, "…just shooting, and shooting, and shooting." She also shared that he'd been diagnosed with attention deficit and hyperactivity disorder (ADHD) and that he took medication to help him focus. However, at times he still had difficulty. Devon's mom felt that the benefits and skill development learned through participation on a team sport would be excellent for Devon. She hoped that Frank would accommodate Devon's learning ability and help him succeed.

1. What questions might Frank want to ask Devon's mom before working with him?

2. Dribbling is one of the basic skills of basketball. How might Frank make variations in dribbling to simplify or increase the complexity of the skill for Devon and others?

3. What modifications might Frank want to consider for Devon when planning his practices?

Scenario 7.2

Shanna Jones, an elementary physical education teacher, has been teaching for six years and loves her job. This year her new fifth-grade class has 25 students with diverse abilities. One girl, Sarah, has muscular dystrophy and uses a power wheelchair. In her six years as a teacher, Shanna hasn't had many students who used wheelchairs. She has heard of muscular dystrophy but doesn't know much about it. She recently received a notice for an IEP meeting regarding Sarah. She saw on the notice that the nurse, physical therapist, occupational therapist, adapted physical education teacher, and classroom teacher would all be there. Shanna was looking forward to the meeting and knew from previous experience that the team of individuals would provide lots of helpful information. She was about to start a unit on balance activities and pyramids and was wondering what types of modifications she might make.

1. What functional capabilities might Sarah have?

2. How might these influence her ability to perform the skill themes and movement concepts in Shanna's class?

3. What are the functional components required for balance and pyramid activities?

4. What types of modifications might Shanna make in her units to ensure success for Sarah?

Play, Games, and Sport

Learning Outcomes

After completing this chapter, you should be able to

» describe the benefits and purpose of play;

» explain the difference between play and games;

» diagram a game or sport's elements and apply the principles of the FAMME model to make variations in games to meet the needs of all individuals; and

» define sport and its relation to play and games.

INCLUDING ALL INDIVIDUALS

Jim Nasium teaches six periods a day of physical education at Blair High School in Vermont and also coaches basketball. During the fall semester he'll be presenting new units to several of his classes, including cooperative games, badminton, basketball, paddleball, volleyball, and team handball. In addition, he teaches an elective physical education class in lifetime and leisure activities that includes cross-country skiing, in-line skating, bowling, and golf. This semester he'll be working with several students transitioning from the junior high school who have been receiving special education services. Blair High has no adapted physical education sections, so these students will be integrated into Jim's program. Jim has been teaching traditional games and sports for five years and is trying to come up with some new ideas for changing his activities to meet the needs of the increasingly diverse students in his classes. In addition to the possible needs of the students from special education, his lifetime leisure class has students with extremely diverse abilities and far-different sport participation backgrounds.

How will Jim include the new students in his existing program? How might he change the current activities and games within his program so that all participants have an equal opportunity for optimal challenge and success? Jim is thinking about the functional approach for modifying movement experiences (FAMME) model (discussed in chapter 6) and wondering how he might apply it to the games, sports, and lifetime activities within his program. He knows that play, games, and sport have critical roles in learning and the retention of skills and knowledge as well as in promoting quality of life. In this chapter we'll discuss the relations between play, game, and sport and how to understand the components of games and sport. We'll follow this by applying the FAMME model to the game components to illustrate how to create optimal challenges and success for individuals of all abilities.

▶ PLAY

In an often-cited definition, Dutch historian, Johann Huizinga (1955) calls play a free activity that is different from ordinary work-a-day life. Although characterized as not serious, and unrelated to material gain, play involves the participant "intensely and utterly." Huizinga also identified social groupings and order, make-believe, disguise, and secrecy as qualities of the play world.

The outcome of all playful interaction is uncertain and contains social, personal, and physical risks. Play is tacitly goal directed without requiring formal or technical rules. Rules in this sense are probabilistic and involve social consensus. Play is pleasurable, done for its own sake, with little thought about consequences. Why this is so, and how play can be beneficially incorporated into our lives, specifically within instructional settings, is the focus of this chapter.

Play is a fascinating and universal human phenomenon described and defined in many ways. Play has been called a means of exploration, assimilation, imagination, symbolism, relaxation, recreation, stress reduction, affect regulation, intrinsic motivation, recapitulation, proximal development, autotelia and paratelia, catharsis, expressing positive emotion, exhausting surplus energy, performing, practicing, and learning. Play has been characterized as paradoxical, reversive, transgressive, both orderly and disorderly, containing contradictions between the real and unreal. Amidst so many differing views, what can we make of this behavior that's so often taken for granted (D.E. Lytle, 1999)?

Figure 8.1 Play is critical to the learning and development of all individuals. How is this child experiencing the world through his senses and play?

Did You Know?

In Latin, *homo* means man and *ludens* means player.

Did You Know?

The somatic–cognitive system is the interaction between the mind and body and their influence on each other.

In this case, definitions are not very helpful in understanding the power and potential of play. With over 50 dictionary definitions of this ubiquitous word, its complexity, importance, and benefits for humans is only hinted at (figure 8.1). One way to understand what play entails is through recognition of the natural human characteristics of playfulness.

Human action–oriented playfulness involves cognitive, social, and physical spontaneity, humor, personal empowerment, and manifest joy (D.E. Lytle, 1999). Of all the primates, humans are the most creative and playful. *Homo ludens* is the term that describes human players with this enduring characterization embedded in our genetic structure. The reason for this has baffled social and behavioral scientists for centuries, and theories—often contradictory—have been proposed dating back to the ancient Greek philosophers. What's obvious is that play is important for all humans, regardless of their age or abilities.

As we've seen already, many questions remain regarding the role of play in human life. Investigators are only recently realizing the intricate, complex, and reciprocal connections among human neurology, emotions, play, reasoning, and learning. The individual's somatic–cognitive system relies on the innate union of play and emotions and feelings. This is important because it's now known that emotions, through their significant impact, are necessary for meaningful retention in learning. For example, cognitive and somatic images from a person's life experiences are the groundwork for learning, deciding, and reasoning. These images can come from the external sensory apparatus for touch, taste, sight, hearing, and smelling and also through the "hidden" senses of the kinesthetic (e.g., muscle and joint awareness) and vestibular systems (e.g., balance). Through playful manipulation of these current and remembered images, play aids in the learning process and is critical for beneficial development and health. For example, if someone moves rhythmically, and the beat and graceful motion feels good, then that individual will retain the movement pattern better than if the movement was ordinary and less emotionally engaging. Through its spontaneity, novelty, and absorbing qualities, play allows for change, creativity, and cognitive flexibility, as well as personal, social, and physical skill development. This is true for infants exploring their stimulus-rich world, adolescents giggling and moving freely, and older men and women who employ more cerebral playfulness through language, joking, and creative thinking.

◄ THINK BACK

1. How are play and learning connected?

2. What's the importance of play in the acquisition of cognitive, social, and motor development?

3. Why are emotions and play important within Jim Nasium's classes? Why might emotions and play be important as he begins to think of ways to modify his current games and sports?

▶ GAMES AND SPORT

Games and sport involve players and foundational elements of play, yet they differ from play in that they have rules and predictable outcomes based on the goal to win. Thus, games and sport, sometimes called "contests," require playful competition and involve a game structure built around physical skill, strategy, or chance either singularly or in combination, as seen in figure 8.2. Moving from the spontaneous nature of play to the competitive elements found in games and sport, an important point must be emphasized. Although games mix the natural and beneficial qualities of playfulness with the learning and personal growth potential of competition, competition can be beneficial only if participants have a chance of succeeding.

Figure 8.2 Sport or contests involve competition. Competition can be beneficial only if participants have a chance of succeeding.

Sport derives from the playful but competitive character of the human being. Although all sports are games, sport is more than just a competitive game. Sport is a microcosm of societal beliefs and values joined with cultural and community ritual, celebration, and festival. One of the important roles of games and sports is to provide an enjoyable, meaningful challenge and the possibility of success for all participants.

Sport games can be categorized in several ways based on how they're played and their basic game structure. The most common categories are invasion games, court games, field–run scoring games, and target games (Almond, 1986).

- *Invasion games.* Invasion games, such as soccer, basketball, or lacrosse, involve such skills as running, chasing, fleeing, dodging, catching, and throwing. They include both offensive and defensive elements and off-the-ball and on-the-ball movements. Players must invade the other team's territory to score.

- *Court games.* Court games such as tennis, volleyball, and badminton involve skills including striking with an implement, running, turning, twisting, balancing, jumping, and volleying. Court games also involve both off-the-ball and on-the-ball movements and offensive or defensive maneuvers, such as setting up to attack and defending or creating space. Court games can be either divided (tennis) or shared (racquetball).

- *Field–run scoring games.* Field–run scoring games such as baseball, softball, and cricket involve many of the same sport-specific skills found in invasion and net games. These skills include striking with an implement, running, throwing, catching, turning, twisting, and fleeing. Field–run scoring games also involve offensive strategies such as getting on base and advancing to the next base, as well as defensive strategies such as preventing scoring.

- *Target games.* Target games include activities such as golf, bowling, darts, and croquet. The sport-specific skills involved in these games include striking with an implement, walking, rolling, twisting, turning, throwing, and transferring weight. Target games require propelling an object with accuracy. They involve strategies such as ways to reduce the number of strokes or hits, knocking an opponent away, and hitting or rolling a ball with spin.

Regardless of how a game is categorized, every game has core elements in common: equipment, players, movement patterns, organization, and rules. By looking at the core elements of games and the purpose for playing a game we can begin to determine how to make modifications based on the functional capabilities of participants. Of primary importance in all games or sports is for all participants to be fully engaged in the process and attain a degree of success. Figure 8.3 lists general guidelines for creating success. In the rest of this chapter we'll describe game elements and how to apply them to a game or sport activity.

Educational Purpose of Games

Games are played for many reasons. Too often teachers and practitioners select games based on what "seems like fun" or what they're familiar with from their past experience, which is often institutionalized, highly publicized versions of sports. These reasons for game choices run counter to a specific learning purpose. Although all learning should be fun and engaging, enjoyment shouldn't be the sole purpose for playing a game. Before beginning any game activity, practitioners should determine the educational purpose(s), also called the activity's goals or objectives (figure 8.4). There are many purposes and associated benefits for games; table 8.1 provides several examples.

Once a practitioner has determined the educational purpose for playing a game, he or she then selects an appropriate activity. For example, if he or she wants to develop communication skills, a cooperative game that requires groups to problem-solve an activity might be a good choice. Because most activities, games, or sports can be modified to meet a desired purpose, one is limited only by the imagination. However, to change games and sports, it

General Guidelines for Successful Activities and Games

- Everyone is active all the time *(no waiting!)*
- Everyone has an opportunity to be successful.
- Avoid elimination games. If there's an element of elimination, rotate players back into the game or into another activity or have them complete a task or skill practice and then rotate back in. This activity should be fun and allow for skill development with no down time for anyone.
- Use creative ways to get into groups. The following are some examples:
  - Birthdays or birth months
  - Names, letters, numbers
  - Playing a game such as Hug, Hug, People to People, or Secret Hand Shake
  - Shoe types, shoelace style, and number of eyelets
  - Favorite TV show, TV character, candy bar, season, and vacation spot
  - Each person is given a card. If a deck of cards is used, groups can then be formed by suits, color, or numbers. Stickers can also be used in this way.
  - Don't be afraid to change the rules.

Figure 8.3 These guidelines provide some simple suggestions that will help in planning and facilitating games and activities.

Figure 8.4 What do you think the purpose of this activity is?

Table 8.1 **Purposes of Games**

Purpose	Benefits
Physical skills	Increased select skills or combination of skills such as throwing, catching, kicking, volleying, skipping, galloping, jumping
Social and psychological dynamics	Improved peer interactions, communication skills, cooperation, self-concept and body image; increased self-esteem and self-worth; stress reduction
Fitness	Increased muscular strength and endurance, cardiovascular development, flexibility, body composition
Cognitive skills	Increased problem-solving skills, content knowledge, etiquette; history of game and sport; strategy development; appreciation of lifetime activity

helps to know and understand the elements of games and how they can be manipulated to meet set objectives.

Elements of Games and Sport

All games and sports have elements that shape the nature of the game. These elements include, equipment, players, movement patterns, organization, and rules (D. Lytle, 1989).

• *Equipment.* Not all games require equipment, but many do. The equipment for any game includes the size, type, number, and locations of items apart from the participant. For example, the equipment required for a tennis match includes rackets, tennis balls, and a net. To play tag one might use no equipment or use cones to mark the playing area or an object for tagging such as a beanbag, yarn ball, or foam noodle.

• *Players.* The participants of a game are generally specified, including the number of players and whether the game is played individually, with another person, or in a small group or large group. Specifications also include who these players are (e.g., men, women, children, individuals who use wheelchairs). In soccer, 10 players form each team, and two teams play against each other to make up a match. Competitive or professional players are often classified by gender, age, and ability. Such is the case with the Special Olympics, Paralympics, Olympic Games, and many professional organized sports. However, in most classroom and community programs individuals of mixed abilities participate in the same programs based on a designated curriculum or on their interest in the activity.

• *Movement patterns.* Movement patterns include all of the skills required for a particular game or sport as well as the movement concepts related to those skills. For example, the game of baseball requires throwing, catching, striking, running, sliding, and walking. In addition, these skills might be performed in different ways, including variations in direction, level, or pathway. In baseball, examples include running straight to the bases, moving sideways to field a grounder, or running backward and jumping up high to catch a fly ball. The movement skills and concepts are listed in chapter 7. All physical activities, from walking down the street to playing ice hockey, are made up of combinations of movements.

• *Organization.* The organization of a game or sport refers to the parameters and dynamics of the playing space. For example, volleyball is played on a court 59 feet (18 m) by 29.6 feet (9 m) and divided in half by a net 7 feet 11 5/8 inches for men and 7 feet 4 1/8 inches for women. However, in sitting volleyball the court is 32.8 feet (10 m) by 19.6 feet (6 m), and the net is 3.8 feet (1.15 m) (for men's division). Each game or sport has traditional guidelines for the playing area, but nothing precludes a practitioner from combining traditional spaces or dynamically changing areas during the game, depending on the game's rules.

◀ **THINK BACK**

1. What's the difference between play and games or sport?

2. Before beginning the activity, why is determining the purpose of playing a game the most important decision? What are some of the purposes Jim Nasium might have for playing games in his programs?

3. Can you explain to Jim the game elements as a possible framework for making modifications?

- *Rules.* The rules structure the game and set the parameters for play. Over the years, games have been modified in many ways using similar elements. For example, the game of golf has been modified to be played with a disc, turning the activity into a game of disc golf.

The rules, followed by the game organization, movement patterns, and then players and equipment, follow an order and relative hierarchy of importance so that any given element could affect a preceding element. This is most clearly seen when rules, game organization, or movement patterns are altered, because equipment and players would also be changed. For example, if the rules of a traditional game of softball are changed to double-diamond baseball, then the organization, movement patterns, players, and equipment all will change. (Double-diamond baseball uses a large space in which two fields are positioned back to back and batters can choose to hit either toward the field in front or into the field behind them; after hitting the ball, they can run to either field's first base. All the field space is used, and there are no boundaries.)

▶ MODIFYING GAMES AND SPORTS

All activities, games, and sports can be diagrammed into the game elements of purpose, equipment, players, movement patterns, organization, and rules. The purpose of the game and the functional capabilities of the participants dictate how the practitioner sets up the game and the types of rules enforced. We'll use the game of 4-square as an example of how to diagram a game or sport, how the game elements can be changed, and how the functional components can be applied to games. Figure 8.5 shows the diagram of a game of 4-square.

Diagram of the Game of 4-Square

Traditional 4-Square

Purpose: Eye–hand coordination

Equipment: Playground ball

Players: Four with no specific criteria; one person in each square

Movement patterns: Striking, sliding

Organization: 8 × 8 box divided into four squares.

Rules:

1. One person in each square.
2. Players can hit the ball in the air or off one bounce.
3. Players can hit to any square other than their own.
4. A fair hit will bounce in an opponent's square.
5. A ball hitting a line is considered in play.

Note: A determination of "fair hit" will also be declared (e.g., contact time with ball, spins, use of body parts)

Figure 8.5 The game elements of 4-square.

Determining the Functional Components of a Game or Sport

The general elements for a game of 4-square are shown in figure 8.5. As mentioned earlier, any of these elements can be changed to increase success for individuals involved. The variations a practitioner employs should follow the guidelines described in chapter 6. Variations should allow for optimal performance by all participants based on the FAMME model (i.e., matching the functional capabilities of participants with the functional components of the activity). For example, the game of 4-square requires the prerequisite skill components shown in figure 8.6. As you can see by the placement of the X on each continuum, some components

Questions to ask when making variations:

1. Do the modifications meet the purpose for playing the activity?
2. Is the modification age appropriate?
3. Is the modification functionally appropriate?
4. Does the modification allow participants to be as independent as possible?
5. Does the modification allow for maximum participation?
6. Does the activity prevent singling out or spotlighting individuals?
7. Does the variation promote optimal challenges for all individuals?
8. Is the variation safe?

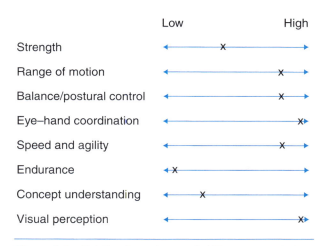

Figure 8.6 Relative importance of skill components in a traditional game of 4-square.

are more important in a traditional game of 4-square than others. However, the degree of importance of each component relative to 4-square might change as game modifications are made. This allows the practitioner to match the activity to the capabilities of the performers to create optimal challenges.

Functional Components Game Wheel

Based on what they know about the relative concentration of functional skills for a given game, practitioners can make variations in game elements to allow for individual differences in abilities, thereby creating optimal challenges for all involved. Figure 8.7 illustrates the functional components game wheel, which includes the five game elements and the functional skill components. The wheel can be turned and the various game elements can align with different skill components to indicate a possible game modification. Once the skill components for an activity and the current functional capabilities of the individuals have been identified, modifications can be made to match the individual and the activity successfully.

A more detailed look at the application of the functional components game wheel is shown in table 8.2 for the game of 4-square. Included are the functional components needed to play the game, sample game elements to be modified, and examples of possible variations. This illustrates how select game elements relate best to given functional components.

As you can see in table 8.2, a game element can be changed to influence several functional components. This is true for any game or sport. For example, in the 4-square game just described, changing the equipment might be beneficial for variations in strength, range of motion, balance, eye–hand coordination, speed, agility, and visual perception. As discussed earlier under organizational elements, the volleyball court size or net height is changed in competitive volleyball depending on gender and if players are standing or sitting. In goalball (figure 8.8), all players must wear blindfolds to equalize the playing field and allow for fair competition. Players are provided with blindfolds regardless of their visual acuity. Competitions may be divided by men, women, adults, or children to create equitable teams for meets. However, in recreational play teams are often mixed. Variations, in both games and sports, are designed to create optimal challenges and successful experiences for all.

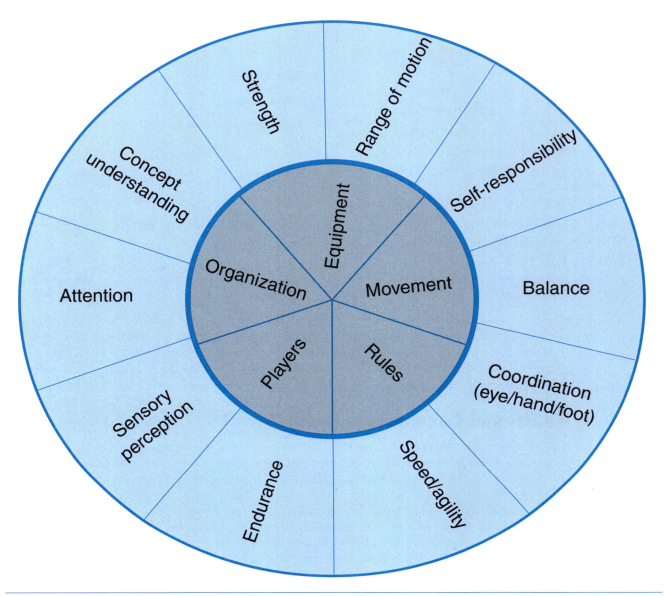

Figure 8.7 The functional components game wheel was created based on the FAMME model. The components on the outside of the wheel are not exhaustive. However, changing the environment might be something you would do because of a particular functional component need. For example, if strength was a concern for an individual in a wheelchair, you might move play to a gym floor instead of grass to allow for ease of movement. This could be considered a change in the rules.

THINK BACK

1. Select any game or sport that Jim Nasium will be teaching and identify for him the functional components required for the activity and their relative importance (similar to the example in figure 8.6).

2. What possible variations based on the games elements might Jim make for this activity?

Table 8.2 Capability Differences, Game Elements, and Variation Possibilities

Capability differences	Game element	Variation possibilities
Strength	Equipment	Use lighter or heavier balls
	Organization	Increase or decrease spaces
	Rules	Catch or hit from rolling to multiple bounces to no bounces
Range of motion	Organization	Increase or decrease space
	Equipment	Increase or decrease size of ball or the use of an extension
	Players	Use partners in square
Balance and posture control	Equipment	Increase or decrease base of support with the use of a chair, walker, or wall.
	Movements	Play sitting on the ground or in a chair.
Eye–hand coordination	Equipment	Increase or decrease size of ball
		Use of extensions (e.g., rackets, hockey sticks, and so on)
	Movement	Touch and push; catch and throw; strike, volley
Speed and agility	Equipment	Increase or decrease size or weight of equipment
	Organization	Increase or decrease size of playing space or change shape of space
	Players	Increase or decrease the number of players
Endurance	Rules	Rotate out for rest if fatigued
	Organization	Team members or partners rotate after each hit
Concept understanding	Organization	Increase or decrease the number of squares
	Rules	Increase or decrease the number of rules
	Players	Use partners or teams
Sensory perception	Equipment	Increase or decrease the size of the equipment
		Use equipment with sound or a bell
	Movements	Rolling, catching, striking, or use of extensions
	Organization	Increase or decrease the playing area
Attention	Organization	Play 2-Square
	Rules	Play for short time period then rotate
	Players	Decrease number of players
Self-responsibility	Rules	Increased time in activity

Figure 8.8 Goalball is designed for individuals who are blind or visually impaired but can be an exciting and dynamic sport played by all.

▶ SUMMARY

Play is important for the well-being of human beings. By extension, playful games and sports can be employed by all individuals to gain knowledge and skills and to reinforce previous learning. However, given the competitive structure of games and sports caution must be used. Only when players have a chance of being successful or winning are games and sports positive experiences. Through analyzing the participants' functional skills, the elements of any game or sport can be modified to meet purposeful educational outcomes. The form of these modifications is limited only by the practitioner's imagination.

What Do You Think?

1. Using the game elements form, diagram a traditional sport you have played. Now examine this sport and create variations based on the functional components (e.g., variations in strength, flexibility, endurance).

2. Go back to table 7.5 in the previous chapter. Examine each of the variations listed in the table. What functional components might each variation support? What game elements could each variation relate to?

3. Determine a purpose for playing a game. Now make up a new game of your own using the below games element model.

Game Elements Model

Game elements	Possible variations
Purpose	
Equipment	
Players	
Movement patterns	
Organization	
Rules	

What Would You Do?

Scenario 8.1

One of the students in Jim's classes next year is Jason, a great kid who loves sports and is an avid football fan. Jason uses a wheelchair and has spina bifida; he also has a shunt in his head. Jason hasn't missed a Monday night football game in five years, a fact he's very proud of. He is also a pretty good student and maintains a B average. During junior high he dealt with a few bouts of depression, as many students do in dealing with puberty, girls, school dances, and social pressures. He gets along well with his peers and has a dog named Hank that is his best friend. Extremely interested in competitive sports and coaching, Jason hopes to help with the school's football team; his dream is to be an assistant coach by his senior year. Jason also attends a wheelchair sports camp every summer and enjoys water skiing, football, and basketball. Jim is looking forward to working with Jason but knows very little about spina bifida and is concerned about Jason's safety in class.

1. Based on what you know about Jason and what you know about spina bifida from appendix A, what might be Jason's functional capabilities?

2. If Jason is enrolled in Jim's general physical education class, what modifications will need to be made for the activities Jim will be teaching?

Scenario 8.2

Valeri Parker, a fourth-grade teacher, loves working with her students in movement experiences and takes her class for physical education three times per week. This year she has two students with disabilities in her class. One young girl, Marta, was diagnosed with fetal alcohol syndrome when she was born. She's a bright young girl but has some general overall delays in her development. She loves to play outside and enjoys the swings most of all. Diego is from Mexico and speaks very little English; he's a bit shy but seems to be getting more comfortable as he gets to know the classroom and other children. There are several other students who speak Spanish in Valeri's class, and she has some conversational skills in Spanish herself. Diego, who was diagnosed with fragile X at birth, loves music and running and enjoys follow-the-leader type games. Valeri is interested in working on cooperation skills in her physical education classes. (She has the following equipment available: 3 playground balls, 5 jump ropes, 4 foam noodles, 20 beanbags, 20 carpet squares, 3 beach balls, 3 foam balls, 2 plastic bats, a large parachute, and several cones.)

1. What functional abilities might Marta and Diego have? How might these abilities relate to other students in the class?

2. Using the game elements model as a guide, create a game (or change a game you're familiar with) for Valeri to use in her physical education class that will teach cooperation and communication skills. Check your activity by answering the "Questions to Ask When Making Modifications." Also, does the activity meet the guidelines for success?

Health-Related Fitness and Conditioning

CHAPTER
9

Learning Outcomes

After completing this chapter, you should be able to

» explain the connection between physical fitness and health for all individuals;

» state the key components of physical fitness and exercise programs;

» describe general modifications to the principles of fitness conditioning; and

» apply exercise prescription strategies to fitness programming for individuals with differences in ability.

INCLUDING ALL INDIVIDUALS

FitnessFirst is the local health and fitness club for the community of Lowden. Sandra Smith has just started as the new director of fitness programming at the club this past June. She has come to the facility with extensive expertise in fitness programming and a desire to increase the number and type of programs offered. This last week, Ricardo has come to the club interested in joining and becoming a member. Ricardo is 43 years old and has some muscular weakness and fatigue caused by multiple sclerosis. Ricardo's physician recommended that he begin exercising to remain healthy and maintain his independence and capabilities. Ricardo and Sandra set up an appointment to begin planning his program. Wanting to set up the most beneficial program for Ricardo, Sandra wonders what his goals should be. What should his fitness program consist of? What will she need to know about modifying exercises given Ricardo's differences in strength and endurance?

Sandra is well aware of the importance and benefits of adopting an active lifestyle. She also understands the link between being physically active and living a quality life. She knows that quality of life is a multidimensional and complex evaluation of life experience that involves general health and functioning. Quality of life also typically includes two other factors: self-esteem and sense of personal well-being.

Convincing evidence supports the idea that exercise is important to overall health and well-being for all individuals. These benefits are varied and include both physical and psychosocial outcomes. According to the Surgeon General's Report (U.S. Department of Health and Human Services (USDHHS), 1996), the physical benefits include increased muscular strength, flexibility, cardiovascular endurance, and weight reduction. Physical activity also reduces the risk of heart disease and such chronic conditions as hypertension, diabetes, osteoporosis, and degenerative joint disease. Physical activity goes beyond these physical benefits to further enhance quality of life, promoting psychological well-being. Exercise enhances general mood, reduces feelings of depression and isolation, and increases self-esteem.

All this considered, it's easy to see that exercise benefits contribute significantly to quality of life and that people of all ages and abilities can benefit from regular physical activity. Unfortunately, despite the known benefits of physical activity, most people in the United States don't exercise regularly in a way that fosters increased health and wellness. Furthermore, compared to people without "disabilities," individuals with significant differences in ability have higher rates of chronic conditions and lower rates of recommended health behaviors, including physical activity (USDHHS, 2000). Involving individuals in appropriate and well-designed physical fitness programs is critical in helping them make physical activity and fitness a regular part of their lives.

Did You Know?

According to Healthy People 2010, 29 percent of people with disabilities and 23 percent of people without disabilities reported no leisure-time physical activity.

▶ PHYSICAL FITNESS GOALS

People have many different reasons for exercising. For some, participation in fitness activities provides the health-related benefits just described. The primary health-related fitness goals are to lower the risk of developing health problems and preventable disease and to avoid pre-

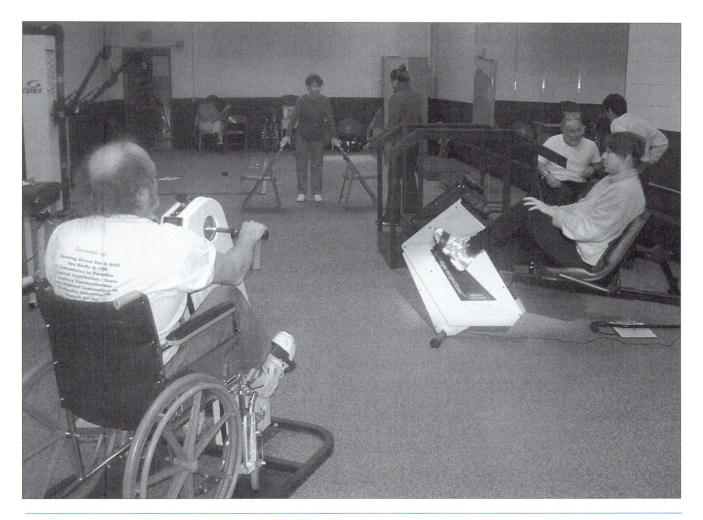

Figure 9.1 Individuals of diverse abilities with different goals for exercising can each benefit from exercising for wellness.

mature death. A person can be well even if he or she has differences in movement capabilities, whether due to experience or because of other person-related factors such as cerebral palsy, injury to the spinal cord and paralysis, or advanced age (figure 9.1). Differences in ability are not considered illnesses or deficiencies. Regardless of ability level, age, or level of experience, exercise benefits can lead to wellness.

For some people with differences in ability, fitness improvement is related more to efficiently conducting and completing activities of daily living. Improvements in strength, flexibility, and balance can increase the functional competence and level of independence in such tasks as cleaning, dressing, and preparing meals. For others, fitness might be based on the desire to achieve greater levels of sport performance and achievement. Athletes who incorporate fitness and conditioning activities into their sport-specific training do so with the hope of increased success. Increases in strength, flexibility, and endurance can result in increased speed, power, and overall performance in sport activities.

▶ IMPLICATIONS FOR PHYSICAL ACTIVITY PRACTITIONERS

Physical activity practitioners agree on the importance and need for physical fitness, but the knowledge and skills needed to include all individuals in fitness activities and programs can be inconsistent. Many physical activity practitioners are quite familiar with developing programs for most people, but including individuals with differences in ability and modifying programs to achieve meaningful fitness outcomes can present significant challenges for some. To include participants of different ability into their fitness or exercise programs, practitioners must consider the type of fitness activity, the capabilities of the person, and the context in which fitness activities take place. We recommend the following guidelines when considering inclusive fitness activities:

1. *Increase your knowledge regarding the foundation of fitness programming.* Practitioners should know the components of fitness and the general training principles associated with fitness development. They should understand the considerations for exercise prescription (how often, how much, which activity best meets the participant's goals) and keep abreast of the evolving recommendations for health and fitness forwarded by professional organizations such as the American College of Sports Medicine (www.acsm.org), the President's Council on Physical Fitness and Sport (www.fitness.gov), and other professional organizations with guiding standards for practice.

2. *Understand exercise implications for individuals with differences in ability.* Practitioners must know which activities and exercises are meaningful and appropriate for participants with differences in abilities considering their present activity status and desired fitness outcomes. In addition to understanding which goals and activities are recommended for their participants, practitioners should also know the exercise implications and activity contraindications for these individuals with differing abilities. For example, although most individuals with differences in abilities display similar physiological responses to exercise, some (e.g., people with spinal cord injuries) might not respond in the same way regarding heart rate response and heat dissipation. General guidelines are available from disability sport organizations and sport programs (appendix C). Other publications, such as Lockette and Keyes (1994) and Miller (1995), are available to educate practitioners and participants with specific differences in ability on exercise implications and considerations.

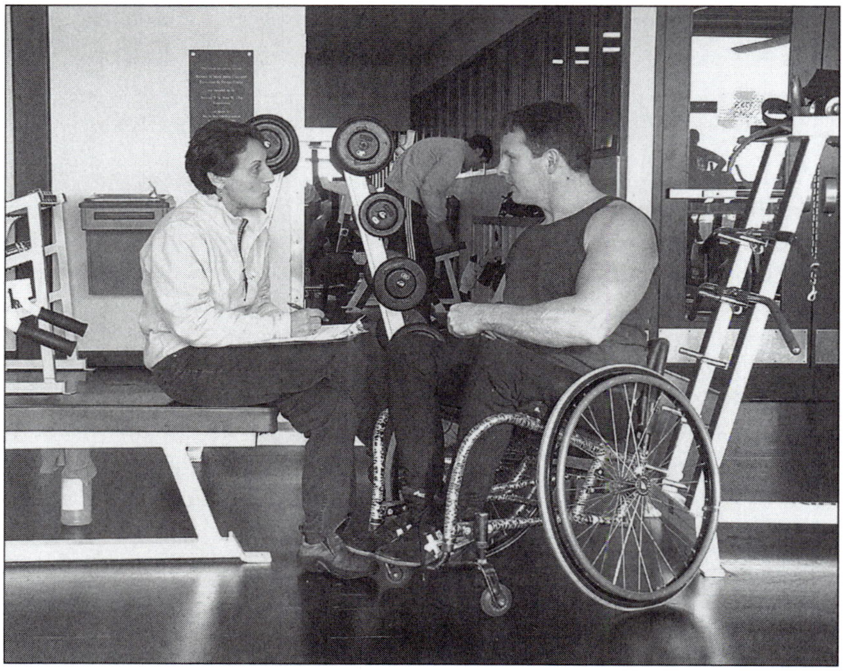

Figure 9.2 Practitioners must obtain important personal and medical information from participants (or others in the participant's support network) to ensure safe and appropriate exercise programming.

3. *Assess participants' readiness to exercise.* Before having participants begin any fitness program, practitioners should complete a health screening or appraisal (figure 9.2). Assessing the exercise readiness of all participants is critical to ensuring a safe program. Participants (and those closely associated with them) should be educated about the nature of fitness development, the specifics of the program, and the implications or inherent risks associated with exercising. It's common practice for practitioners to obtain informed consent from those potential exercisers indicating they're fully aware of the benefits and risks involved and are choosing to engage in the program. Next, practitioners should obtain a medical release form or similar permission from a physician who knows the participant's medical history, current health status, and state of readiness to

exercise. Within this health appraisal, practitioners should then assess the current fitness status of the individual. Baseline fitness data provides information about exercises that might be contraindicated and also lends insight regarding program direction and possible exercise and modifications.

4. *Help participants set realistic and appropriate fitness goals.* Once the practitioner has a basic understanding of fitness programming for individuals with differences in ability and a specific knowledge of a participant's readiness to exercise, identifying realistic and meaningful fitness goals is the next step. For instance, the goal of one participant in a physical education class might be to perform a correct stretch without bouncing; another participant's goal might be to perform a new stretch or exercise. An adult exercising in a fitness center may want to increase the time she spends walking on the treadmill while another participant may want to increase speed and percent grade on the treadmill. Practitioners must know how to assist participants in identifying outcomes that are attainable within the parameters of the exercise program so that participants remain motivated and adhere to their physical activity program. Goals that are unreasonable considering the participant's current exercise level and abilities or that are unattainable in the given period of time designated serve only to frustrate and disappoint participants, sometimes causing them to drop out of the program.

THINK BACK

Think back to Sandra Smith and Ricardo at the FitnessFirst Health Club.

1. Sandra has a strong foundation in fitness and knows her field well. What are the three other implications for programming that she must consider in designing a program for Ricardo?

2. What information might Sandra want to gather?

3. How might she go about setting appropriate goals for Ricardo? What should these goals focus on?

▶ TRAINING PRINCIPLES

For participants in exercise programs to meet their fitness goals, practitioners need to consider training principles known to facilitate fitness improvement. These principles help practitioners guide participants on how the program or exercise sessions should be developed and progressed. An understanding of the concepts of exercise science has served as the foundation for these principles of exercise conditioning. The principles define a range of recommendations regarding the appropriate quantity and mode of exercise that can safely lead individuals toward personal fitness goals. These guidelines define the frequency, intensity, type, and progression of the exercise program.

- *Overload and progression.* Overload refers to the load or amount of resistance placed on the body (or body system). Over time, the body adapts and becomes accustomed to the load and resistance placed on it so that eventually no additional benefit takes place. For continued fitness gains to occur, the load or amount of stress placed on the body or system must increase. The progression of this overload is a critical factor in how effective training regimes are in promoting fitness goals. Practitioners must understand how to progress overload for maximal benefit and safety.

- *The FITT principle.* The FITT (frequency, intensity, time, type) principle is used to describe how exercise training should be planned to promote maximum benefit for participants. For any particular individual involved, practitioners must consider how often the exercise or activity should be performed (frequency) and how hard the exercise should be (intensity). Other factors such as the duration of the activity (time) and the specific mode (type) of activity must be considered in terms of improving a particular component of fitness. The progressive overload of these variables can and does differ depending on which component of fitness is targeted. In the next section we describe these fitness components and how the FITT principle applies to each.

▶ COMPONENTS OF FITNESS AND STRATEGIES FOR INCLUSIVE PROGRAMMING

A comprehensive and well-rounded approach to fitness includes exercises that develop flexibility, muscular strength, muscular endurance, and cardiorespiratory fitness. Although personal fitness goals and individual capabilities will influence which one of these areas is emphasized, each of them is important for overall health and well-being. Inclusive fitness programming involves integrating knowledge of the general principles of exercise training and participant needs with the skills and competency required for modifying exercise plans. To meet the needs of participants with ability differences, individualization of exercise programs must involve decisions about the appropriateness of fitness activities, tailoring of exercise principles, and adaptation of exercise techniques.

Flexibility Training

As we just mentioned, one important component of fitness is flexibility, which involves the ability of a joint, and the muscles and tendons surrounding it, to move freely through a full range of motion (ROM). Optimal flexibility allows a joint to move efficiently. Although some individuals with ability differences might not have full range of motion, they should have enough movement of the joint to perform functional tasks. For instance, someone with increased muscle tone caused by spasticity might not be able to flex fully at the hip, but he or she should do flexibility exercises to maintain functional range of motion and the ability to climb stairs safely. The importance of flexibility can't be overlooked when developing an individualized fitness program; and integration of stretching exercises should become regular practice.

Flexibility and range of motion is affected by several factors. Limitations might be caused by the structure of the joint and properties of the connective tissue (e.g., adhesions, scar tissue, or contractures), or they might derive from neuromuscular influences, such as spasticity. Other influences on flexibility include genetics, age, gender, temperature, pain, and balance of opposing muscle groups (Miller, 1995).

Static stretching, the most common flexibility training method, involves lengthening a muscle group and maintaining a stretched position for a set period of time. Bouncing type movements or ballistic stretching is usually not recommended for general fitness programming. Although flexibility exercises can help maintain or improve range of motion, flexibility can be improved only up to a point. Table 9.1 outlines the training principles applied to flexibility.

Modifications for Flexibility Training

For flexibility training, the frequency of a stretching program might be gradually increased to daily sessions, especially for people with joint limiting conditions such as contractures, spasticity, or arthritis. The intensity of the stretch can be modified by increasing or decreasing the degree of stretch, holding a static stretch for a longer or shorter time, or increasing or decreasing the number of repetitions (figure 9.3). For individuals with differences in coordination or spasticity, a more gentle stretch held for 30 seconds might be most effective for promoting relaxation and more optimal lengthening of the muscle. The number of repetitions might also be gradually increased, especially if the stretch is held for shorter durations. Along with making variations

Table 9.1   Training Principles Applied to Flexibility

Training variable	General recommendation
Frequency	Before and after each exercise session or activity; minimum 3 days per week
Intensity	To subjective sensation of tension—not past point of pain
Time	10-30 seconds for flexibility (not warm-up); 2 or 3 repetitions each
Type	Static stretch of major muscle groups
Overload	Slight increase in intensity and stretch point; increasing number of repetitions and increasing frequency
Progression	Begin slow and easy moving into stretch; major core muscles first, then to extremities and smaller muscle groups

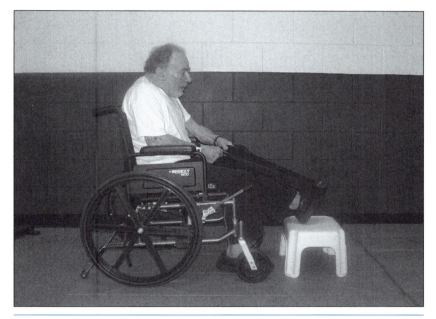

Figure 9.3   The intensity and duration of a stretch can be increased through the use of assistive straps.

to the FITT principles, variations can also be made based on the underlying functional differences, as described in chapter 6. Table 9.2 shows modifications for stretching based on variations in the functional capabilities.

Muscular Strength and Endurance: Resistance Training

Two important aspects of health-related fitness are muscular strength and muscular endurance. Muscular strength is the ability of a muscle or group of muscles to exert maximal force against resistance. Muscular endurance is the ability of a muscle or group of muscles to exert force against submaximal resistance over a period of time. Increases in each of these areas are important to maintain strong and dense bones, prevent chronic back problems, prevent muscle injury, and, for some people, to increase or maintain function and independence.

THINK BACK

Remember Ricardo from Sandra Smith's FitnessFirst program? Using appendix A and what you know about flexibility, answer the following questions.

1. What might be the focus of Ricardo's program related to stretching?

2. Using the FITT principle, how would you develop a stretching program for Ricardo?

3. What special considerations or modifications might you want to make for Ricardo?

Table 9.2 *Modifications for Flexibility Training*

Capability difference	Modification
Balance	Perform stretch sitting or lying down
	Hold wall while standing or use wall for trunk support while sitting on mat
Coordination	Use mirror for visual feedback
	Verbal feedback from others for body or limb position
	Manual guidance for appropriate position or movement
Strength	Self-assist movement of limb or joint with other limb or hand
	Obtain assistance from another participant
Flexibility	Use strap or stable structure to self-assist in stretch
	Position body to allow gravity to assist stretch
	Obtain assistance from another participant for passive stretch
	Use proprioneuromuscular facilitation (PNF) technique if trained and knowledgeable
Endurance	Require fewer repetitions
Concept understanding	Use manual guidance
	Incorporate visuals such as pictures
	Employ peer model and support
Attention	Count to specific number for stretch completion
	Establish stretching routine
Sensory perception	Use verbal feedback for technique
Self-responsibility	Use recording form for monitoring and reinforcing

Note: Differences in speed and agility aren't critical to successful stretching.

An individual's muscular strength and endurance might be influenced by deconditioning, neuromuscular factors such as motor unit recruitment, lack of reciprocal inhibition and spasticity, or progressive muscular conditions (Miller, 1995). Muscular strength and endurance is commonly developed though resistance training involving manual resistance (e.g., push-ups), free weights (using dumbbells or cuff weights), resistance bands or pulleys, and exercise machines. Both practitioners and participants must understand and employ proper safety measures when performing resistance training exercises. Table 9.3 illustrates the application of the FITT principle to resistance training.

Modifications for Resistance Training

Although overload through progressive resistance exercise is often recommended, participants with progressive neuromuscular conditions might have fitness goals geared more toward maintaining strength rather than increasing it. Not only can the FITT principles be modified, increased rest between sets or sessions might further reduce overload and possible fatigue or loss of muscle function. Frequency of resistance exercise sessions can be manipulated based on participant needs and goals. Increasing frequency beyond the two or three days per week typically recommended should involve either alternating muscle groups or high- and low-intensity sessions so muscle groups aren't overfatigued. For most people, two or three days a week are sufficient regardless of capability or condition. Individualization of resistance exercise can be achieved more readily be altering the variables of intensity and duration. By manipulating the number of repetitions, sets, load, and recovery time, the training load can be modified for different individuals. For instance, beginners or individuals with muscular weakness should train

Table 9.3 Training Principles Applied to Muscular Strength and Endurance

Training variable	General recommendation
Frequency	3 or 4 times per week with 1 day of rest between sessions
Intensity	Light to moderate, 40 to 70% projected maximal effort
Time	3-5 sets of 3-7 repetitions for strength; 12-20 for endurance
Type	Body weight, single- to multijoint activities, resistance exercises
Overload	For strength, slowly increase level of resistance to greater level
	For endurance, increase the number of repetitions or time of repetition or decrease rest interval between activities
Progression	Progress slowly to avoid injury

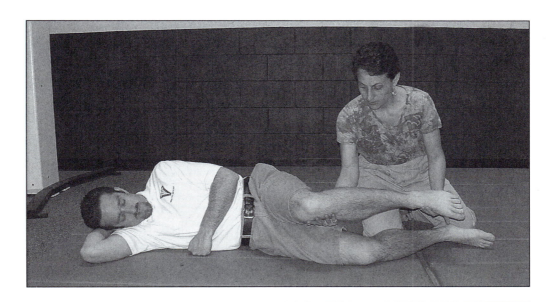

Figure 9.4 Having a participant move a limb in an antigravity plane of motion can reduce the resistance or load and help maintain or improve muscular strength.

with low or easier training loads by decreasing resistance and increasing repetitions (figure 9.4). Typical recovery periods of two to four minutes can also be modified, depending on goals and capabilities. Shorter periods of exercise might be used to promote endurance, whereas longer recovery times might be appropriate for individuals for whom fatigue is an issue. Because the potential for injury increases with increasing workloads, practitioners must always consider ability differences and take care not to progress participants too quickly or overload them inappropriately. See table 9.4 for modifications for muscular strength and endurance training based on functional differences.

Cardiorespiratory Fitness

Cardiorespiratory, or aerobic, fitness, often considered one of the more important aspects of health-related fitness, is a measure of the heart's ability to pump oxygen-rich blood to the rest of the body. Cardiorespiratory fitness also involves the ability to adjust to and recover from physi-

Table 9.4   Modifications for Muscular Strength and Endurance Training

Capability difference	Modification
Balance	Perform exercise sitting Perform exercise bilaterally (free weight in each hand) Use exercise machines
Coordination	Use resistance machines that stabilize and require set movement Use some single-joint exercises to reduce task complexity Perform unilateral exercise Use free weights if appropriate to ease control of movement
Strength	Perform exercise in anti-gravity plane (horizontal movement) Perform in aquatic environment Use different forms of resistance depending on strength level (gravity, band, or free weight) Employ eccentric contractions as well as concentric contractions
Flexibility	Strengthen through available range Strengthen for balance between muscle pairs
Endurance	Do multijoint versus single-joint exercise, fewer repetitions Sequence exercises so muscle group isn't fatigued (alternate between upper- and lower-body exercise, agonist and antagonist)
Concept understanding	Use manual guidance Offer visuals such as pictures Have peer model and support Sequence to perform in set routine and easy order (head to toe)
Attention	Count to guide speed of movement (1-2 for concentric; 1-2-3-4 for eccentric) Establish circuit
Sensory perception	Provide physical guidance, verbal feedback, or mirrors for technique
Self-responsibility	Use recording form for monitoring and reinforcing

Note: Differences in speed and agility are not critical to successful strengthening and endurance.

THINK BACK

Let's return to Ricardo again. Using appendix A and what you know about strength training, answer the following questions regarding Ricardo's strength-training program.

1. What might be the focus of Ricardo's program related to strength training?

2. Using the FITT principle, how would you develop a strength-training program for Ricardo?

3. What special considerations or modifications might you make for Ricardo's strength-training program?

cal activity. Practitioners are well aware that aerobic fitness is crucial for reducing the risk of coronary heart disease, high blood pressure, obesity, diabetes, and other chronic conditions. It also helps maintain functional capabilities, independence, emotional well-being, and life satisfaction.

Practitioners involved in developing fitness programs for individuals with differing abilities must be aware of factors that might influence the physiological systems that support aerobic exercise. For instance, some individuals with paralysis caused by a spinal cord injury or multiple sclerosis might have difficulty with oxygen transport because of dysfunction of the autonomic nervous system (Lockette & Keyes, 1994). Differences in cardiorespiratory fitness might also be due to decreased ability to use large muscle movements during activity because of joint pain, muscle weakness, or difficulty in muscle recruitment. Differences in temperature regulation and muscular fatigue are other factors that might limit aerobic exercise capacity (Miller, 1995).

People develop and improve cardiorespiratory fitness through engaging in a variety of activities that require moving large muscle masses over prolonged periods of time. Swimming, bicycling, jogging, and aerobic dancing are common fitness activities that promote aerobic capacity. The training might involve continuous activity, interval training, or circuit training. Ways to apply the FITT principles to cardiorespiratory fitness are shown in table 9.5.

Table 9.5 *Training Principles Applied to Cardiorespiratory Fitness*

Training variable	General recommendation
Frequency	3-5 times per week
Intensity	55-90% maximal heart rate (dependent on baseline fitness)
Time	15-60 minutes total (can be accumulated over time)
Type	Walking, jogging, running, dancing, or fitness activities
Overload	Increase speed, time, or tempo
Progression	Progress slowly in design

Modifications for Cardiorespiratory Fitness Training

Like the other fitness components, aerobic capacity can be enhanced through gradual overload. To achieve benefit, regardless of capability, people should train three to five days per week. Exercising fewer than three days a week might be meaningful for someone who's extremely deconditioned or unmotivated, but exercise sessions should progress to at least three days for training benefits to occur. Resting between sessions might be necessary for individuals with progressive conditions or fatigue. Lower intensity bouts are also useful to start or for those with excessive fatigue or circulatory problems, heart disease, or history of stroke. Although heart rate and perceived exertion are useful measures for assessing intensity, practitioners should be aware of factors that might render these evaluative methods inappropriate, such as autonomic nervous system differences or certain prescribed medications. Duration of aerobic training can also be manipulated to accommodate individual differences. A participant who is deconditioned might begin with shorter bouts of exercise and gradually increase over time (figure 9.5). Or he or she might begin with an interval training method before progressing to a continuous protocol. Table 9.6 lists additional variations for individual differences in cardiorespiratory fitness based on functional capabilities.

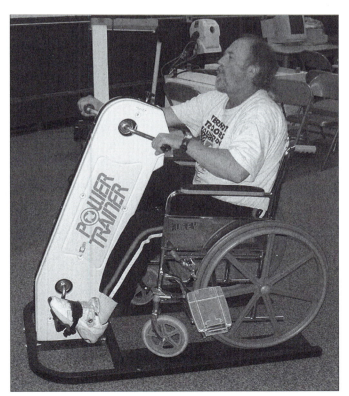

Figure 9.5 Short bouts of aerobic exercise might be appropriate for participants with decreased cardiorespiratory fitness or muscular endurance.

Table 9.6   Modifications for Cardiorespiratory Fitness Training

Capability difference	Modification
Balance	Use stationary or recumbent bike rather than running or use hand supports on treadmill; arm ergometer
Coordination	Move in any manner to music for a continuous period of time
Strength	Use upper body versus lower body or vice versa depending on upper- or lower-extremity strength differences Offer variations in speed, distance, or rest periods
Flexibility	Perform through available range; use less resistance (aquatic versus land)
Endurance	Use interval versus continuous training
Speed	Modify time or distance
Concept understanding	Use peer to serve as pacer, task sheet, or pictures
Attention	Employ intervals Develop aerobic circuit Use fitness stations
Sensory perception	Use step test versus mile run for individual with visual differences; use sighted guide for individuals with low sight
Self-responsibility	Use recording form to monitor progress and reinforce Employ peer support for engagement

THINK BACK

Let's think back once more to Ricardo. Using appendix A and what you know about cardiorespiratory fitness training, answer the following questions:

1. What might be the focus of Ricardo's program related to cardiorespiratory development?

2. Using the FITT principles, how would you develop a cardiovascular training program for Ricardo?

3. What special considerations or modifications might you make for Ricardo's cardiorespiratory program?

Did You Know?

"The first wealth is health."—Ralph Waldo Emerson

▶ HEALTH-RELATED FITNESS ACTIVITIES

So far in this chapter we've focused on components and principles related to traditional fitness programs that routinely involve specific exercises and fitness tasks. Don't take this to mean that

Figure 9.6 Spinning is one option for maintaining health-related fitness.

the only valuable method for fitness improvement is through resistance training, running, or stretching exercises. Individuals of all ability levels have benefited from health-related activities such as swimming, water aerobics, walking, dance, and outdoor activities such as hiking, skiing, and snow shoeing (see chapter 10 for outdoor pursuits). In fact, within the past decade or two widespread interest has developed in alternative forms of fitness enhancement, such as spinning, yoga, and tai chi.

Spinning

Spinning is an indoor aerobic conditioning program using stationary exercise bikes (figure 9.6). It's performed in a group setting and facilitated by an instructor. The benefits of spinning include aerobic conditioning and endurance as well as increased leg strength. There's less potential for injury or trauma to joints in spinning than in other activities, and it might be more motivating for those who appreciate feedback and guidance from others. Spinning also helps people stay in shape during times when cycling outside isn't convenient. See table 9.7 for modifications for spinning.

Table 9.7 *Modifications for Spinning*

Capability difference	Modification
Strength	Reduce resistance on flywheel
Balance and posture control	Use recumbent bike
Concept understanding	Increase verbal cues and feedback
Attention	Have spinning partner close by
Endurance	Use shorter bouts or intermittent bouts
Coordination	Reduce frequency of cadence or pedaling

Note: The table offers examples of modifications for some of the capability differences that might exist. See table 9.6 for other modification possibilities.

Table 9.8 Modifications for Yoga

Capability difference	Modification
Strength	Choose appropriate style
	Practice with one limb or side of body separately
	Reduce intensity or space of pose
Balance and posture control	Widen base of support or open stance more
	Hold on to a chair or wall
Concept understanding	Increase verbal cues and feedback
	Offer physical guidance
Attention	Offer short cues
Endurance	Reduce time pose is held
	Practice few postures
Coordination	Practice components with a single limb

Note: The table offers examples of modifications for some of the differences in capability that might exist. See table 9.6 for other modification possibilities.

Table 9.9 Modifications for Tai Chi

Capability difference	Modification
Strength	Practice with one limb or side of body separately
	Reduce intensity or space of sequence
Balance and posture control	Hold on to partner or chair
	Perform some elements seated
	Increase width of stance
Concept understanding	Provide physical guidance
Attention	Provide simple cues and concurrent demonstration
Endurance	Choose short form
	Practice subsequences
Coordination	Slow sequence further

Note: The table offers examples of modifications for some of the differences in capability that might exist. See table 9.6 for other modification possibilities.

Yoga

Yoga has attracted the attention of people of all ages and ability levels. Nearly all yoga styles are rooted in hatha yoga, a physical discipline that focuses on developing control of the body through various poses. While all yoga styles seek to balance the mind, body, and spirit, they go about it in various ways. They might differ in how poses are performed or where attention is focused (e.g., on mastering and holding a posture, on breathing, or on the flow of movement). For instance, Ashtanga yoga emphasizes power and stamina and can be quite physically demanding, whereas Kripalu yoga emphasizes breathing, relaxation, and inner awareness. There are over eleven popular forms of yoga, and no one style is necessarily better or worse than another. Practitioners thinking of adding yoga to their activity program should find a style that meets participants' needs, focus, and capabilities. See table 9.8 for yoga modifications.

Tai Chi

The origins of tai chi go back many hundreds of years, but just in the last decade or so has the activity seen increased popularity. Many people of all ages, including older adults and individuals with differing abilities, use tai chi as a means of exercise. Tai chi can best be described as a moving form of yoga and meditation combined. Originally derived from martial arts, the slow graceful movements of tai chi are designed to focus the mind and breathing through a complex series of maneuvers.

The benefits of tai chi include relaxation, reduced stress, and improved motor control, balance, and flexibility. There are several styles of tai chi, but the Yang style is the most practiced. This style is made up of two substyles: the long form, which has 128 or so separate postures, and the short form. Both forms consist of a number of moves or postures, each joined by a transition or link. Each movement might be very short or made up of a complex sequence of submoves. Although each is an individual definitive element to the form, they flow continually into each other and are not practiced separately. Table 9.9 lists modifications for tai chi.

► SUMMARY

The principles of fitness conditioning provide the minimum level of exercise necessary for training benefits to occur. Most of the recommendations related to the training principles and guidelines, however, came out of research involving adults without significant differences in abilities and medical status. Exercise programs should be individualized by considering general principles in relation to information about the participant obtained through assessment and screening. Both the participant's personal goals and health status should be taken into account when planning exercise protocols. It's also important to modify the FITT principle based on factors such as age, functional differences, and movement capabilities. Whether the goal is to improve performance in a particular sport or activity or enhance a participant's ability to improve mobility or perform activities of daily living more independently, practitioners can manipulate the frequency, intensity, and duration of exercise programs to assist each participant in achieving personal goals. Recommendations for exercise should be continually monitored to ensure that the program remains appropriate and safe for each participant. Ongoing modifications should be made based on how participants respond to their program and to accommodate any changes in health status or capability.

What Do You Think?

Now that you've learned more about creating inclusive fitness programs, how would you answer these questions about developing Ricardo's exercise program?

1. What might be Ricardo's overall goals related to his personal wellness?

2. How might Sandra Smith create a balanced program of strength, flexibility, and endurance for Ricardo? Try designing a complete exercise program for Ricardo yourself.

3. What barriers might affect Ricardo's progress in his program? How would you help Ricardo overcome these barriers?

What Would You Do?

Scenario 9.1

Marissa is 28 years old and lives with a roommate. During college she studied communications and competed on the volleyball team. Over the winter break of her junior year, she was in a serious car accident when she hit black ice on the road. During the accident she sustained a traumatic brain injury that left her in a coma for a week. After leaving the hospital, Marissa spent five months in rehabilitation, where she relearned how to talk and walk. As a result of her injury, she now has trouble with short-term memory. In addition, her right side is weaker and has some muscle contractures. She can walk with assistance or by using a walker for short distances, but she uses a wheelchair to get around town. She still enjoys physical activity, including water activities and weight training.

1. What kind of program would you design for Marissa?

2. How might Marissa's accident have affected her strength, flexibility, and endurance?

3. What possible modifications might you want to use in designing a program for her?

Scenario 9.2

Jason teaches seventh grade at Johnson Junior High School. As part of the requirements for seventh grade, all students must be given physical fitness testing. These scores are then reported to the state. Jason uses the Fitnessgram, which includes the following tasks:

a. The pacer or one-mile walk–run

b. Percent body fat or body mass index

c. Curl-up test

d. Trunk lift

e. Push-up, modified pull-up, or flexed arm hang

f. Sit-and-reach or shoulder stretch

This year Jason has several students from the junior high sport teams, a few students with limited skill proficiency in most activities, two students with severe obesity, and one with spina bifida who uses a wheelchair.

1. How might Jason develop fitness goals for his students?

2. What types of activities might be appropriate for his class?

3. How might he make adaptations in fitness activities in preparing his students to take the Fitnessgram?

Adventure and Outdoor Programming

Reid Cross

Learning Outcomes

After completing this chapter, you should be able to

» describe the philosophy of adventure-based programming,

» provide examples of activity modifications, and

» apply modification strategies to adventure-based activities.

INCLUDING ALL INDIVIDUALS

Ms. Barb Fox is coordinator for a community recreation program in a medium-sized town in the Rocky Mountains. She administrates several program areas, including fitness and conditioning, aquatics, and competitive sport leagues for people of all ages. Her board has asked that she add outdoor pursuits to the activities the program offers. A significant percentage of the clients at the recreation center are recommended from a physical rehabilitation center. Although Barb has been successful at adapting the recreation center's facilities for diverse populations, she's not sure how to adapt adventure activities to meet the needs of her diverse populations.

Outdoor pursuits are a growing trend nationwide as more people look outdoors for their recreation and leisure activities. Leisure service industries report an increase in participation in adventure and outdoor-related activities. People seek outdoor experiences for many reasons, including spiritual or personal growth, new opportunities to test their limits, and the excitement of taking on extreme physical, emotional, and intellectual challenges (Ellmo & Graser, 1995). Research suggests that the general increase in numbers of people seeking nature as a means of recreational outlet includes individuals with disabilities (Sugarman, 2002). Outdoor activities are also being included more in school and recreation programs that teach skills to promote activities that last a lifetime.

Success in outdoor activities is not measured by the highest score or the fastest time; rather, it's measured by an individual's personal goals. One of the unique aspects of outdoor-related activities is the nature of the competition (or the lack of it). Outdoor activities are perfect for people with diverse abilities. No matter what his or her abilities are, each person has his or her own perception of what's challenging and what constitutes personal success. People experiencing the same event react to the experience in different ways. How each of us interprets an experience is influenced by a myriad of factors. Still, we all have different but related emotional experiences. These emotional experiences are based on our beliefs, ideas, attitudes, and previous experiences in life as well as in physical and outdoor activities. However, regardless of these factors we all experience the same emotional states as humans and can relate to those emotions whether they are fear, excitement, anxiety, elation, or other such emotions.

▶ OUTDOOR ACTIVITIES DEFINED

Outdoor education refers to teaching and learning in the outdoors and stresses relationships among people and their natural environment (Priest & Gass, 1997). Outdoor education is divided into two main branches: environmental education and adventure education. Environmental education typically deals with the ecological aspects of the outdoors, whereas adventure education focuses on interpersonal and intrapersonal relationships. Instructing through adventure education involves teaching the skills necessary to participate in an activity. If these activities are pursued as a means of recreation, then they're commonly referred to as outdoor recreation. When a school or community recreation program implements these types of activities, they're referred to as adventure programming (figure 10.1). In this chapter we'll focus on the component of adventure programming including challenge courses and outdoor pursuits, which includes such activities as hiking, backpacking, canoeing, kayaking, skiing, snowshoeing, bicycling, and many others. Primarily, they are self-propelled activities in outdoor settings that provide personal goals and involve a philosophy of challenge by choice.

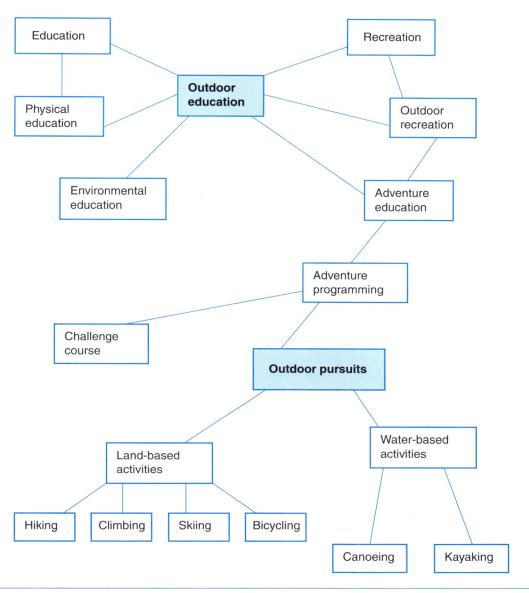

Figure 10.1 Outdoor activities flow chart.

Goals of Adventure Education

A quick look at the common goals of adventure education helps us see why people of all abilities can benefit through participating in adventure activities. These goals have been adapted from those listed in Karl Rohnke's *Cowtails and Cobras II* (1989) and apply equally to people of all ability levels.

1. *To increase the participant's sense of personal confidence.* Personal confidence is a common reason for participation in adventure activities, especially in public schools. Activities can be sequenced in such a way to allow participants to experience risk and the accompanying anxiety through a graduated series of events. Anxiety often accompanies trying something new. When people understand the feeling of anxiety and have success in dealing with situations that carry an emotional and physical risk, they'll be more confident in themselves when they encounter other stressful events in their lives.

2. *To increase mutual support within a group.* Participants in adventure activities learn to support others and to be supported in activities that are emotionally and physically risky. Support and cooperation are essential ingredients in a successful and well-adjusted life. People who interact with others who are genuinely supportive are more likely to overcome obstacles and setbacks in their lives.

3. *To develop and increase agility and physical coordination.* Increased agility and coordination enhances all aspects of life.

4. *To develop an increased joy in one's physical self and in being with others.* Deriving a sense of joy during and following physical activity is incredibly important to life's success and continued participation in physical activity.

5. *To develop an increased familiarity and identification with the natural world.* Adventure recreation takes place in a natural environment that lets people connect with their inner selves and the natural beauty around them.

Philosophy of Adventure Education

Inherent in the philosophy of adventure education is the acknowledgment that it's okay to feel the experience in different ways, which is the basis of the challenge-by-choice philosophy. Using this philosophy, participants set their own goals and decide for themselves how much effort they're willing to put toward achieving them. Challenge by choice puts the responsibility of the challenge on the participant. Adventure is not ruled by arbitrary rules, and success is not measured with a scorecard. With this philosophy, it's impossible to fail; the major barrier for effective programming lies with the teacher or facilitator.

THINK BACK

1. What are some of the goals that Barb Fox might have for her new program in adventure activities?

2. How might outdoor activities be beneficial for individuals of all abilities?

3. What does the term "challenge by choice" mean to you?

▷ MODIFICATIONS FOR ADVENTURE ACTIVITIES

It would be cumbersome to describe every conceivable outdoor pursuit and how well it adapts to the functional approach for modifying movement experiences (FAMME) model. Instead, we've selected some of the most popular activities and divided them into land-based and water-based pursuits. Land-based activities include hiking, backpacking, cross-country skiing, snowshoeing, downhill skiing, rock climbing, and bicycling. Water activities include kayaking and canoeing.

We should note that we've modified the FAMME model slightly for some of the outdoor activities. The biggest difference between outdoor activities and other more traditional sport activities is that outdoor activities can last an entire day or even several days. Such duration could be a challenge for some people who struggle with holding their attention, so to that end, we added the category of Attention to the FAMME model when we deemed appropriate.

Did You Know?

A hummingbird heart beats 70 times per second.

Figure 10.2 The use of animals to assist humans in bearing heavy loads has been a practice for thousands of years.

Table 10.1 *Modifications for Hiking and Backpacking*

Capability difference	Modification
Body strength and endurance	Support animals to carry weight • Goats • Horses • Llamas Shorter trips
Sensory perception	Guide animals Guide people
Balance and postural control	Walking assistance • Walkers • Ski poles
Concept understanding	Verbal cues Visual cues
Attention	Hiking partner Short routes Frequent breaks Break for other activity or game
Self-responsibility	Shorter hikes Increased supervision

Note: Differences in flexibility as well as speed and agility are not critical to successful hiking.

Hiking and Backpacking

Hiking includes activities such as day hikes, multiday backpacking trips, cross-country skiing, snowshoeing, or any type of self-propelled travel (figure 10.2) and allows for individuals to experience, become closer to, and appreciate nature. Through hiking and backpacking individuals realize their connectedness with nature. Adapting these activities is limited by one's ingenuity and imagination. The adaptations (shown in table 10.1) for hiking and backpacking can be generalized to pursuits that involve walking as the main mode of transportation. Backpacking refers to trips during which participants carry food and shelter on their backs in packs; naturally, the longer the trip, the heavier the pack.

Downhill Skiing

Downhill skiing became popular in the United States after World War II, when technological innovations gave more people access to the slopes with greater ease and comfort than before. The skis and boots became more specialized, making skiing accessible to various populations. Some of the primary modifications have been made for people without limbs and with partial or total paralysis of the lower body (figure 10.3). Technological advances have made downhill skiing more accessible to diverse populations than any other outdoor pursuit. Refer to the resource guide in appendix C for more detailed information on this exciting activity. Table 10.2 offers some modifications for downhill skiing.

Cross-Country Skiing and Snowshoeing

We didn't see the same dramatic rise in popularity in cross-country skiing and snowshoeing after World War II. But in the 1970s many people began to seek the solace of a winter environment away from the crowed slopes of downhill ski areas. At first, cross-country skiing and snowshoeing involved only a brave (or crazy) few who had to struggle with equipment that hadn't seen any significant innovations in 75 years. Gradually, the situation changed, and by the 1970s cross-country skiing and snowshoeing became accessible to more people. Because skiing is more of a gliding motion than a jarring motion, moving on skis is less stressful on the joints of the body than hiking. As you can see in table 10.3, many of the modifications for cross-country skiing and snowshoeing are the same as for downhill skiing.

Figure 10.3 All individuals can enjoy the exhiliration of downhill skiing with minimal adaptations.

Table 10.2 Modifications for Downhill Skiing

Capability difference	Modification
Strength	Monoskis
Visual perception	Guide people
Balance and postural control	Outrigger ski poles Monoskis Shorter skis
Speed and agility	Ski length and width
Endurance	Shorter downhill runs More efficient ski lifts
Concept understanding	Verbal cues
Attention	Skiing partner Shorter downhill runs
Self-responsibility	Ski with partner Increased time with appropriate behavior
Flexibility	Adapted equipment Gradual slopes

Note: Differences in eye–hand and eye–foot coordination are not critical to successful downhill skiing.

Table 10.3 Modifications for Cross-Country Skiing and Snowshoeing

Capability difference	Modification
Strength and endurance	Support systems to carry weight • Sleds (designed to be used behind skis) • Snowmobiles • Dog sleds
Visual perception	Guide animals Guide people
Balance and postural control	Outrigger ski poles Wider, shorter skis
Concept understanding	Verbal cues
Attention	Hiking partner Short routes
Flexibility	Sleds Snowmobiles
Self-responsibility	Shorter trips Increase length with appropriate responsibility
Endurance	Shorter trips Use sleds, snowmobiles

Note: Differences in eye–hand and eye–foot coordination as well as speed and agility are not critical to successful cross-country skiing..

Rock Climbing

Today, rock climbing can be done in many different environments and arenas. Rock climbing can be an element of mountain climbing, occurring in remote wilderness environments and involving related skills such as snow and ice climbing, skiing, and back-country travel. Or rock climbing can take place on much less remote vertical walls of rock that take anywhere from a few hours to several days to climb (figure 10.4). Rock climbing can also be understood as a subsport of bouldering, which occurs just a few feet off the ground. Many communities now have indoor walls for rock climbers who don't have the real thing nearby. Such indoor climbing is the easiest to modify because the holds are bolted to a wall and can be moved to accommodate the climber. Table 10.4 lists modifications for rock climbing.

The reasons for modifying rock climbing are the same for outdoor walls as for indoor walls. Modifying outdoor climbing is not as straightforward, but many of the same concepts apply. Instead of making modifications on natural rock, climbers must find rock routes that suit their abilities. A good guidebook is very helpful when deciding which routes to attempt.

Figure 10.4 A simple harness allows this individual to participate in rock climbing.

Table 10.4   Modifications for Rock Climbing

Capability difference	Modification
Strength	Choose routes with large holds with positive grip
	Choose routes that have lots of horizontal ledges for resting
	Low-angle climbs (wall angle less than 90 degrees)
	Pulley-assisted climbing
Eye-hand and eye-foot coordination	Climbs with large holds
	Low-angle wall
Balance and postural control	Climbs with large holds
	Physical support from rope system
Concept understanding	Verbal cues
Attention	Partner climbing
	Short routes
Range of motion	Climbs with large holds
	Holds placed progressively farther apart
Sensory perception	Feel for holds
	Verbal cues
Endurance	Stop for rests
	Shorter climbs
	Bouldering
Self-responsibility	Extra preparation regarding safety
	Must pass safety competencies to participate
	May not spot others until skills are mastered consistently

Note: Differences in speed and agility are not critical for participation in rock climbing.

Figure 10.5 Tandem bicycles are a great way for individuals with limited strength or sight to get out and enjoy cycling, recreationally or competitively with friends or other athletes.

Bicycling

Bicycling saw a big upswing in popularity during the 1970s. With the increased popularity came a corresponding increase in the technological advances of bicycles, one of which was a more efficient design of tandem bicycles (figure 10.5). At one time tandems were considered a novelty, but they quickly became very dependable and efficient machines. Another innovation was the recumbent bicycle, in which the rider sits as in a chair with his or her legs stretched out to the pedals. This lower center of gravity allows the cyclist much easier balance and reduces the strain on the lower back that can accompany traditional bicycles. With modern bicycles, people can find many ways to enjoy the freedom of movement away from crowds, noise, and pollution. Table 10.5 lists modifications for bicycling.

Kayaking and Canoeing

Traveling on water is a great way to participate in outdoor activities. Be it a tranquil and relaxing glide over a flat lake in the early morning mists or a thrilling whitewater ride down the rapids in a raft, water travel allows a perspective of the natural world you can't get on dry land. Canoes are generally used on flat, slow-

Table 10.5   Modifications for Bicycling

Capability difference	Modification
Strength and endurance	Trailers
	Tandem bicycles
	Recumbent bicycles
	Hand-cranked bicycles
Visual perception	Tandem bicycles
	Guide people
Balance	Outrigger wheels
	Three-wheeled bicycles
Concept understanding	Verbal cues
Attention	Cycling partner
	Short routes
	Tandem bicycles
Flexibility	Recumbent bike
	Hand cycles
Self-responsibility	Ride with a partner
	Use tandem bike
	Provide choices

Note: Eye–hand and eye–foot coordination as well as speed and agility are not required for successful cycling.

Figure 10.6 Inflatable kayaks add buoyancy and greater stability.

moving water; they are very stable, can be paddled with a partner, and can carry equipment. They have an even keel, and it's easier to keep canoes traveling in a straight line. Kayaks are designed for easy maneuverability in fast-moving water. They react quickly to the paddle and to the snap of the hips, but they turn over easily, and it takes some skill to roll a kayak back upright without getting out of the boat. Inflatable kayaks can handle rougher water, but they do it with an increase in buoyancy instead of maneuverability (figure 10.6). It's difficult, though not impossible, to turn over in an inflatable kayak. Table 10.6 lists modifications for kayaking and canoeing.

Table 10.6   Modifications for Kayaking and Canoeing

Capability difference	Modification	Capability difference	Modification
Upper-body strength	Slower moving water Feathered paddles Lighter paddles Ergonomically designed paddles Inflatable kayaks More flotation in canoe or kayak	Concept understanding	Verbal cues Slower water
		Attention	Partner paddling Short sections of whiter water Tandem kayaks Inflatable kayaks
Eye–hand coordination	Changing paddle lengths Indexed paddles	Range of motion	Slow-moving water
		Speed and agility	Slower water
Balance and postural control	Kayaks with less rocker Kayaks with more chine Kayaks with more volume Increased deck height and width Canoes Inflatable kayaks	Endurance	Slower water Shorter trips Work with partner
		Sensory perception	Sighted guide Verbal cues Partners
		Self-responsibility	Shorter trips Positive reinforcement Choices

▶ CHALLENGE COURSES

Challenge courses are unique in outdoor education; their development was an offshoot of the Outward Bound experience, attempting to bring the insights, values, and objectives gained in a wilderness-based program to the traditional school experience. Although challenge courses are not considered lifetime activities, the philosophy and goals are in line with other pursuits of physical education; it's an activity that can be successfully implemented in a physical education or therapeutic recreation setting. The main objectives of challenge courses are (adapted from Proudly 1999):

1. To provide a sense of adventure with a high amount of perceived risk
2. To provide an element of uncertainty and drama
3. To create a high level of expectations through intrinsic and extrinsic motivation
4. To promote an atmosphere of mutual support, emphasizing cooperation, encouragement, and interpersonal concerns
5. To encourage a group problem-solving approach, allowing for a variety of personal contributions
6. To combine moments of active involvement with personal reflection

It's beyond the scope of this book to list the types of games and activities used in challenge course programs; a resource list is included in appendix C. However, the sequencing of the events is very important. The following sections are an adaptation of Christian Bisson's (1999) work on sequencing adventure activities.

Group Formation

In this introductory phase of the progression, the focus of activities is on goal setting, awareness of others, cooperation, beginning trust building, and general socialization. The group is getting acquainted; the foundation for the rest of the experience is being built. The activities are designed so the participants can have a fun experience in a safe setting, which includes both emotional safety and physical safety. The activities are designed for group members to get better acquainted. The objectives are normally achieved by playing games and activities that get people to laugh. Toward the end of this phase, the facilitator begins to add activities that incorporate trust and communication skills. The objective at the end of this phase is to have a group that's friendly toward each other and comfortable working together.

Did You Know?

The accident rate in challenge courses is lower than the accident rate in the real estate industry.

Group Challenge

This is the second phase of the process and blends almost seamlessly with the first. The goals in this phase are intended to challenge the group in the area of decision making and problem solving. The activities center on group initiative tasks, group problem solving, and team activities designed to encourage and enhance decision making and leadership. To reach a successful level, leadership and followership must develop around a variety of group-oriented tasks. The objective at the end of this phase is to have a group that has established a working relationship that capitalizes on each other's strengths and supports new ideas and perspectives on solving problems.

Group Support

During this third phase, the activities move away from group tasks and toward individual tasks (figure 10.7). At first glance, this appears to be a step backward; however, although the

activities are individual in nature, they depend on group support for success. The activities in this stage of the progression tend to have a high degree of perceived risk. The participants are placed in situations that are normally high in the air, suspended from cables and ropes. Though there are several safety systems in place and the actual risk to the participant is low, it feels as if the danger is high. In these situations, the group acts as a source for emotional support, and in many cases actual physical support. Christian Bisson describes the focus of these activities nicely: "... these activities ... require not only self-confidence and determination from the participant, but also psychological support and compassion on the group's part" (1999, p. 210). The goal for this final stage is empowerment. The participants feel that they have accomplished something important and moved beyond their preconceived boundaries.

Figure 10.7 The person is mastering their fear as they reach for the trapeze in the "Leap of Faith."

THINK BACK

1. Select any land activity that Barb Fox will be offering. Identify for her the functional components required for the activity. Identify ways she can adapt some of her programs for people with differing abilities.

2. Select any water activity that Barb Fox will be offering and identify for her the functional components required for the activity. Identify ways she can adapt some of her programs for people with differing abilities.

▶ SUMMARY

Adventure education focuses on interpersonal and intrapersonal relationships. The primary goals are to increase personal self-confidence, create mutual support, improve agility and physical coordination, promote a sense of joy in oneself and with others, and increase familiarity and identification with the natural world. Teaching through adventure education involves teaching the skills necessary to participate in an activity. When a school or community recreation program implements these types of activities, they're referred to as adventure programming. One of the unique aspects of outdoor-related activities is the nature of the competition or the lack of it—success is measured by the individual's personal goals. Outdoor activities are a perfect venue for people of all ability levels. In planning and implementing adventure programming it's important to understand the philosophy of challenge by choice, which puts the responsibility of the challenge on the participant. With this philosophy, it's impossible to fail; the major barrier for effective programming lies in the facilitator's ability to plan appropriate programs using the FAMME model to create successful experiences for everyone. The application of the FAMME model has been presented for land activities, water activities, and challenge courses to illustrate the ease with which this model can be used successfully.

What Do You Think?

1. How might adventure programming be relevant to your future professional role or your personal life? Reflect on your personal experiences with outdoor pursuits.

2. Describe how your experiences with outdoor pursuits relate to the goals described in this chapter.

3. How does the philosophy of "challenge by choice" fit with your personal philosophy of programming for individuals of differing abilities?

What Would You Do?

Scenario 10.1

Reid, a new recreation leader for an outdoor adventure program, will be taking a group on a weekend kayaking trip. One of the participants in his group is Joe, who had a head injury in a car accident three years ago. Before the accident, Joe spent many weekends rafting, camping, hiking, and enjoying the outdoors. He continues to enjoy the relaxation, challenge, and enjoyment of outdoor pursuits. Joe currently has some difficulty with balance and is stronger on his left side. He walks independently but finds it helpful to use a walking stick when hiking over uneven terrain. He has limited range of motion in his right side and continues to stretch on a daily basis to help prevent contractures in his right arm and shoulder. Reid has just collected all the release forms, health history, and medical information for the trip's participants. He's wondering if he'll need to make any adaptations for Joe.

1. What are the functional requirements for kayaking?

2. What types of modifications, if any, might Reid need to make for Joe?

Scenario 10.2

Sue's an instructor at the local university and teaches a climbing class. In one of her new sections this semester is a student named Kerri, who is an athlete with differing abilities. Kerry competes in water skiing, downhill skiing, and wheelchair basketball. She's majoring in therapeutic recreation and plans on working with individuals with disabilities in the future. Sue has met with her class once and reviewed the syllabus and course requirements and introduced the concept of challenge by choice; the class has also done some stretching and warm-up exercises, introductory icebreaker activities, and cooperative games.

1. What are the functional skills needed for indoor climbing?

2. What type of adaptations might be helpful for Kerri when climbing?

Person-Related Factors Influencing Capability

This appendix serves as supplementary information to the text regarding individual factors that might influence capability in movement experiences. Although classifications such as these can be helpful in providing general information, they do not provide deep insight into any one person's capability to perform. The task demands and nature of the context significantly affect performance outcomes and benefit. This information is provided so that practitioners are aware of the possible influences on performance and, more important, to give them insight into the implications for physical activity participation, potential safety concerns, and activity recommendations and contraindications. It is important that practitioners do not generalize specific factors to all individuals nor make assumptions about capability should any given factor exist. Individuals will differ in terms of their functional capabilities regardless of any specific factor, thus assumptions about individuals based on categorical labels must be avoided.

Note: The information provided in this appendix has been compiled from the Web sites referenced for each section.

Amputee

Definition

Amputation refers to removal or loss of an entire limb or particular limb segment. Amputation can be congenital or acquired resulting from disease, tumor, complications of frostbite, injury, diabetes, arteriosclerosis (hardening of the arteries), or any other illness that impairs blood circulation.

Selected Facts

- Problems with thermoregulation could be present as a consequence of decreased skin surface.
- Prosthetic devices are typically used to increase functional use of the limb or body part.

Tips and Techniques

- Participants should be encouraged to increase fluids during physical activity to prevent overheating.
- Allow time for participants with new prostheses to become familiar with them as necessary for performing an activity or task.

Informative Web Sites

www.amputee-coalition.org

Amyotrophic Lateral Sclerosis (ALS)

Definition

Amyotrophic lateral sclerosis (ALS) is a progressive neurodegenerative disease that attacks nerve cells in the brain and spinal cord. The progressive degeneration of the motor neurons in ALS eventually leads to their death. When the motor neurons die, the ability of the brain to initiate and control muscle movement is lost. With all voluntary muscle action affected, individuals in later stages of ALS become totally paralyzed.

Selected Facts

- Often referred to as Lou Gehrig's disease.
- At the onset of ALS the symptoms can be so slight that they are overlooked.
- As motor neurons degenerate, functional differences might include muscle weakness in one of the hands, arms, legs; weakness in the muscles involving speaking, swallowing, or breathing; cramping of muscles; difficulty in projecting the voice; shortness of breath; and difficulty in breathing and swallowing.
- Because ALS attacks motor neurons only, the sense of sight, touch, hearing, taste, and smell are not affected.
- For the vast majority of people, their mind and thoughts are not affected by ALS, and they remain sharp despite the progressive degenerating condition of the body.

Tips and Techniques

- Range of motion and stretching exercises can help prevent painful spasticity and shortening (contracture) of muscles.
- Gentle, low-impact aerobic exercise (e.g., walking, swimming, stationary bicycling) can strengthen unaffected muscles and improve cardiovascular health.

Informative Web Site

www.lougehrigsdisease.net/

Arthritis

Definition

Arthritis is a rheumatic disease that causes pain in the joint or the muscle. The word "arthritis" is derived from the roots *arth* (joint) and *itis* (inflammation). The two most prevalent forms of arthritis are osteoarthritis, a degenerative joint disease that leads to deterioration of cartilage and formation of bone in the joint, and rheumatoid arthritis, a chronic and systemic inflammatory disease.

Selected Facts

- Many people report that regular exercise reduces the experience of pain and weakness from arthritis and provides a general feeling of well-being.
- Some arthritis medications might affect the cardiopulmonary systems and inhibit performance levels.

Tips and Techniques

- Heat or ice treatments (e.g., shower, ice, massage, whirlpool) before and after exercise can reduce pain and discomfort.
- It is best to do a variety of aerobic activities to avoid overstressing joints.
- Choose activities that expend less stress on joints, such as aquatherapy, biking, rowing, cross-country skiing, walking on soft surfaces, or low-impact aerobics. Choose activities depending on which joints are arthritic.

- Individuals with rheumatoid arthritis who experience morning stiffness should exercise later in the day.
- Strength training should focus on increasing number of repetitions rather than amount of weight.
- A complete warm-up and cool-down stretching program should be done before and after each exercise program.

Informative Web Sites

www.arthritis.org

Arthrogryposis

Definition

Arthrogryposis (arthrogryposis multiplex congenita) involves the presence of multiple joint contractures at birth. A contracture is a limitation in the range of motion of a joint.

Selected Facts

- In some cases, few joints are affected, and full range of motion might exist. In other cases, the hands, wrists, elbows, shoulders, hips, feet, and knees are affected. In the most severe cases, nearly every body joint is involved, including the jaw and back.
- Frequently, the joint contractures are accompanied by muscle weakness that further limits movement.

Tips and Techniques

- Physical and occupational therapy as well as exercise have proven very beneficial in improving muscle strength and function and increasing the range of motion of affected joints.
- Stretching exercises are extremely important to increase range of motion. Emphasize achieving as much joint mobility as possible.

Informative Web Site

http://sonnet1.sonnet.com/avenues/

Asthma

Definition

Asthma is a lung disorder characterized by wheezing, coughing, breathing difficulty, and lengthened expiration (prolonged exhaling).

Selected Facts

- Wheezing, coughing, tightness in the chest, and general fatigue are signs of an impending asthma attack.

Tips and Techniques

- When individuals with asthma exercise (particularly in cold weather), they can become short of breath and have an attack.
- Remind individuals with asthma to use their medication before exercising.

Informative Web Sites

www.asthma.org.uk

www.aaaai.org/

Attention Deficit/Hyperactivity Disorder (ADHD)

Definition

Attention deficit/hyperactivity disorder (ADHD) is a condition in which individual differences include inattentiveness or distractibility, impulsivity, or hyperactive behavior, or a combination of the three. These difficulties usually begin before the person is seven years old but in some cases are not noticed until the child is older.

Selected Facts

- The behavioral differences of ADHD can be managed through helping the individual manage his or her behavior; creating a structured physical activity program that fits the learner's individual needs; and providing medication, if necessary.
- One effective strategy for people with ADHD is exercise, preferably vigorous exercise. Exercise helps work off excess energy, focuses attention, and stimulates beneficial hormones and neurochemicals.

Tips and Techniques

- Practitioners must be clear, consistent, and positive. Set clear rules and expectations.
- Have a reinforcement program for good behavior.
- Employ effective strategies for managing behavior, such as charting, starting a reward program, ignoring behaviors, and using consistent consequences related to the behavior.
- Help individuals stay focused by making activities fun and rewarding.

Informative Web Sites

www.add.org/

www.chadd.org/

Autism and Pervasive Developmental Disorder (PDD)

Definition

Autism and PDD are developmental disabilities that share many similar functional differences. Usually evident by age three, autism and PDD are neurological disorders that affect a child's ability to communicate, understand language, play, and relate to others. Other functional differences often associated with autism are engagement in repetitive activities and stereotyped movements, resistance to environmental change or disruption in daily routines, and unusual responses to sensory experiences, such as loud noises, lights, or certain textures. This description may also include individuals with high functioning autism and Asperger's syndrome.

Selected Facts

- Children with autism or PDD vary widely in abilities, intelligence, and behaviors.
- Autism is no longer considered a form of emotional disturbance but is now considered under "other health impaired" according to IDEA. "Other health impaired" means having limited strength, vitality, or alertness, or a heightened alertness to environmental stimuli that limits alertness within the educational environment and is caused by chronic or acute health problems.
- Children with autism might also experience seizures or display differences in intellectual capabilities.

Tips and Techniques

- When teaching children with autism, try using physical guidance as the children learn movement skills; also try verbal and visual cues and prompts.

- Physical activity helps children with autism reduce self-stimulatory behavior and increase play behavior.
- Use behavior-management techniques to promote on-task and safe behavior.
- Hypersensitivity to touch can be desensitized through firmly but gently stroking a child with different cloth textures.
- Teach with gentle methods, such as whispering softly to the child.
- Provide a stable, structured environment for the child. Limit the amount of relevant stimuli or activity focus initially.
- Teach to the preferred learning mode.
- Minimize unnecessary external stimuli or distractions.
- Sensory stimulation through activities such as music, dance, and aquatic activities might be successful for on-task and attentive behavior.

Informative Web Site

www.autism.org/

Blindness and Low Vision

Definition

Individuals who are legally blind have less than 20/200 vision in the better eye or a very limited field of vision (20 degrees at its widest point). Those who have low vision generally have a severe visual impairment, not necessarily limited to distance vision. Low vision applies to all individuals with sight who are unable to read a newspaper at a normal viewing distance, even with the aid of eyeglasses or contact lenses. They use a combination of vision and other senses to learn, although they might require adaptations in lighting or the size of print, and, sometimes, Braille.

Selected Facts

- A young child with vision loss might have little reason to explore interesting objects in the environment and thus might miss opportunities to experience and learn about interaction with other people and other things. They might also miss opportunities to learn how to move in a variety of ways.
- Because the child cannot see parents or peers, he or she might be unable to imitate social behavior or understand nonverbal cues.

Tips and Techniques

- A sighted guide (peer tutor) can help an individual who is blind in any physical activity for positive learning.
- Make sure individuals know the size, shape, and boundaries of an activity area before they use it for sport or physical activity. Allow them to explore the area without others present.
- Arrange mats around the out-of-bounds area so participants know when they go out of bounds.
- Use beeper cones or music to mark boundaries. Use different surfaces to mark various playing areas.

Informative Web Sites

www.nfb.org

www.afb.org

Cerebral Palsy (CP)

Definition

Cerebral palsy is a nonprogressive but chronic disorder of movement and posture caused by a defect or lesion to the brain occurring before, during, or within two years after birth. The condition might be accompanied by associated differences in intellectual functioning, vision, hearing, communication, and seizures.

Selected Facts

- Movement differences might involve lower extremities (diplegia), one side of the body (hemiplegia), all four extremities (quadriplegia), or three extremities (triplegia).
- Motor differences might involve spasticity or increased muscle tone and tightness, athetosis or fluctuating muscle tone, or ataxia or low muscle tone and balance and coordination differences. Postural reactions and reflexive activity can influence movement efficiency and outcomes.

Tips and Techniques

- Flexibility is one of the important fitness goals for individuals with CP.
- Aquatic activity is often a preferred physical activity experience for movement, balance, and fitness development.
- Weight-bearing activity is important for bone density and reduced risk of osteoporosis.

Informative Web Sites

www.ucpa.org

www.nichcy.org

Deafness and Hearing Loss

Definition

Deafness is defined as a hearing difference so severe that the individual cannot process linguistic information through hearing, with or without amplification. Deafness might be viewed as a condition that prevents an individual from receiving sound in all or most of its forms. In contrast, a person with a hearing loss can generally respond to auditory stimuli, including speech.

Selected Facts

- Loss in hearing can occur in loudness or intensity or in both areas; the condition might exist in one ear or both ears.
- Hearing loss is generally described as slight, mild, moderate, severe, or profound, depending on how well a person can hear the intensities or frequencies associated with speech.
- There are four types of hearing loss: conductive hearing loss caused by diseases or obstructions in the outer or middle ear; sensorineural hearing loss resulting from damage to the delicate sensory hair cells of the inner ear or the nerves that supply it; a mixed hearing loss or a combination of conductive and sensorineural loss; and a central hearing loss resulting from damage or impairment to the nerves or nuclei of the central nervous system.
- Hearing loss or deafness does not affect a person's intellectual capacity or ability to learn. However, children who are either hard of hearing or deaf generally require some form of support in order to receive an adequate education.

Tips and Techniques

- When planning a lesson, use visual cues, fewer rules, and less equipment. Creating peer tutor programs for the individuals helps keep individuals from isolating themselves from social gatherings. Teach your younger deaf students neighborhood games such as jump rope and hop scotch. Knowing how to play these games helps them interact better with their peers.

- For those who are deaf or have severe hearing losses, early, consistent, and conscious use of visible communication modes (such as sign language, fingerspelling, and cued speech) or amplification and aural/oral training can help facilitate language development and communication.

- People with hearing loss use oral or manual means of communication or a combination of the two. Oral communication includes speech, lip reading, and the use of residual hearing. Manual communication involves signs and fingerspelling.

- Practitioners should attempt to learn some sign language in order to communicate directly with participants. If interpreters are used, be sure to speak to the participant and not to the interpreter.

Informative Web sites

www.nad.org/

www.deafchildren.org

www.asha.org

http://clerccenter.gallaudet.edu/infotogo/index.html

www.nidcd.nih.gov

Deaf-Blindness

Definition

Deaf-blindness is a combination of vision and hearing loss, not necessarily complete deafness and complete blindness.

Selected Facts

- Individuals who are deaf-blind sign tactually on the hand of the person with whom they are communicating.

Tips and Techniques

- Introduce an individual to roller-skating, swimming, biking, skiing, and gymnastics that allow for increased physical activity without the unpredictability of other players and equipment required in team activities.

- Modifications need to be made, such as changing the rules, equipment, or environment. For example, allow choices of activity and equipment. Link movement to language; teach the word for each skill learned.

Informative Web Sites

www.tr.wou.edu/dblink/aadb.htm

www.deafblind.com

Diabetes

Definition

Diabetes is a disease in which the body does not produce or use insulin. Insulin is a hormone that converts sugar, starches, and other food into energy required for daily life. The condition results in too much glucose (sugar) in the blood.

Selected Facts

- When blood sugar is elevated or when basal insulin levels are low, exercise generally causes blood sugars to rise further.
- Symptoms of insulin shock are sudden fatigue, weakness, tremors, hunger, sweating, and double vision. If an individual with diabetes exhibits any of these during physical activity, have the person stop exercising immediately and take a quick-acting sugar, such as sugar cubes or a regular soft drink.

Tips and Techniques

- Encourage exercise and participation in sports for individuals with diabetes.
- Be familiar with the signs, symptoms, and treatment of low blood sugar (insulin reaction).
- Make sure participants drink plenty of fluids. Dehydration can adversely affect blood glucose levels.

Informative Web Site

www.diabetes.org

Down Syndrome

Definition

Down syndrome is the most common and readily identifiable chromosomal condition associated with mental retardation. It is caused by having 47 instead of the usual 46 chromosomes, which changes the orderly development of the body and brain. Down syndrome might result in slow physical development and cognitive differences.

Selected Facts

- There is a wide variation in mental abilities, behavior, and developmental progress in individuals with Down syndrome.
- There are over 50 clinical signs of Down syndrome, but it is rare to find all or even most of them in one person. Some common differences include poor muscle tone, hyperflexibility at the joints, and a variety of physical differences.
- Children with Down syndrome frequently have specific health-related problems, such as a lowered resistance to infection, making them more prone to respiratory problems.
- Differences in vision and hearing might exist.
- About 15 percent of people with Down syndrome have atlantoaxial instability, a misalignment of the first two cervical vertebrae. This condition makes these individuals more prone to injury if they participate in activities that overextend or flex the neck.
- Some individuals might have congenital heart defects or cardiac problems.

Tips and Techniques

- Because of individual differences, it is impossible to predict future achievements of children with Down syndrome. It is important for families and practitioners to place few limitations on potential capabilities.
- For some individuals it can be effective to emphasize concrete concepts rather than abstract ideas.
- Teach physical activity tasks in a step-by-step manner with frequent reinforcement and consistent feedback.
- Find out what the individual enjoys most and begin with this activity first to promote increased involvement.

- Avoid activities that place undue pressure on the neck (e.g., gymnastics, diving, the butterfly stroke) unless otherwise informed by the child's physician that these activities are appropriate.
- Be sure to obtain medical information regarding risks associated with cardiac or respiratory difficulties.

Informative Web Site

www.ndss.org

Dwarfism

Definition

Dwarfism is defined as a medical or genetic condition that usually results in an adult height of 4 feet 10 inches or shorter. In some cases a person with dwarfism might be slightly taller than this.

Selected Facts

- Although achondroplasia accounts for the majority of all cases of dwarfism, there are approximately 200 diagnosed types.
- Although such terms as dwarf, little person, and person of short stature are all acceptable, most people would rather be referred to by their name than by a label. The term "midget" is not well-received and considered offensive by most.
- There are three complications sometimes found in infants and toddlers with achondroplasia: compression of the brain stem, hydrocephalus, and obstructive apnea. These conditions do not always occur, but children should be evaluated.

Tips and Techniques

- Individuals are able to participate in physical activity and athletic events within the limits of their individual medical diagnoses. Swimming and bicycling are often recommended for people with skeletal dysplasias because these activities do not put pressure on the spine.
- Long-distance running or even extensive walking can be harmful because of the constant pounding or trauma to joints, although, as a rule, healthy individuals without any unusual orthopedic problems should be allowed to engage in typical activities and running games or sports.

Informative Web Sites

www.lpaonline.org

www.dwarfism.org/

www.nlm.nih.gov/medlineplus/dwarfism.html

Emotional Disturbance

Definition

According to the Individuals with Disabilities Education Act, emotional disturbance is defined as "a condition exhibiting one or more of the following characteristics over a long period of time and to a marked degree that adversely affects a child's educational performance: (A) An inability to learn that cannot be explained by intellectual, sensory, or health factors. (B) An inability to build or maintain satisfactory interpersonal relationships with peers and teachers. (C) Inappropriate types of behavior or feelings under normal circumstances. (D) A general pervasive mood of unhappiness or depression. (E) A tendency to develop physical symptoms or fears associated with personal or school problems." [Code of Federal Regulations, Title 34, Section 300.7(c)(4)(i)].

Selected Facts

- Children who have emotional disturbances might exhibit hyperactivity and a short attention span, might show aggression or self-injurious behavior, might be withdrawn or have excessive fear or anxiety, might have poor coping skills, and might have learning difficulties.
- Children with the most serious emotional disturbances might exhibit distorted thinking, excessive anxiety, bizarre motor acts, and abnormal mood swings. Some are identified as children who have a severe psychosis or schizophrenia.
- Many children who do not have emotional disturbances might display some of these same behaviors at various times during their development, but these behaviors do not continue over long periods of time.

Tips and Techniques

- It is important to provide students with positive behavioral support (PBS) so that problem behaviors are minimized and positive, appropriate behaviors are promoted.
- Physical activity settings should be highly structured with consistent routines and expectations that are frequently shared with participants.
- Repetition and small sequential, progressive steps should be incorporated into activity plans.
- Removal of distractions, reduction of wait time, and consideration of spacing and groupings can help maintain on-task behavior.

Informative Web Sites

www.nichcy.org

www.dbpeds.org

Epilepsy

Definition

Epilepsy is a neurological condition in which nerve cells of the brain occasionally release abnormal electrical impulses. Individuals with epilepsy have seizures that might be related to brain injury or family tendency, but the cause is usually unknown.

Selected Facts

- About 50 percent of people who have one seizure without a clear cause will likely have another one, usually within 6 months. If a person has two seizures, there is about an 80 percent chance he or she will have more.
- Recent research indicates that up to 70 percent of children and adults with newly diagnosed epilepsy can be successfully treated.
- Seizures can vary from mild to severe. Single brief seizures do not cause brain damage.

Tips and Techniques

- There must be a balance between safety and the desire to pursue a full life of activity.
- For persons with rare or fully controlled seizures, most activities can be safely pursued.
- For those with frequent seizures with loss of consciousness or a brief period of confusion afterward, certain activities might need to be restricted. Activities that include aquatics, high speed, or high places should be supervised and carefully monitored. Helmets should be worn when appropriate.
- Practitioners should be aware of safety and first aid procedures for seizures.

www.epilepsy.com

www.epilepsyfoundation.org

Fetal Alcohol Syndrome (FAS)

Definition

FAS is a lifelong set of physical, mental, and neurobehavioral birth differences associated with maternal consumption of alcohol during pregnancy. Alcohol-Related Neurodevelopmental Disorder (ARND) describes the functional or mental impairments linked to prenatal alcohol exposure, and Alcohol-Related Birth Defects (ARBD) describes malformations in the skeletal and major organ systems.

Selected Facts

- Individuals with FAS have evidence of central nervous system dysfunction. In addition to mental retardation, individuals with FAS, ARND, and ARBD might have other neurological deficits, including poor motor skills and poor eye–hand coordination.

- They might also have a complex pattern of behavioral and learning problems, including difficulties with memory, attention, judgment, and problem solving, as well as problems with mental health and social interactions.

Tips and Techniques

- Keys to working successfully with learners who have FAS are structure, consistency, variety, brevity, and persistence.

- It is important to provide external structure and to be consistent in response and routine. Give the learner lots of advance warning of activity changes or transitions.

- Because of attentional difficulties, it is important to give brief explanations and directions. Incorporate different ways to get and keep attention.

- Repetition of learning is critical. Break work down into small pieces so that the learner is not overwhelmed.

- Establish a few simple rules with consistent language.

- Allow the learner choices and encourage decision making.

Informative Web Site

www.nofas.org

Fragile X

Definition

Fragile X syndrome is the most common inherited cause of mental retardation. A person with fragile X syndrome has a mutation in the FMR1 (fragile X mental retardation 1) gene in the DNA that makes up the X chromosome.

Selected Facts

- Individuals with fragile X syndrome might have significant intellectual differences. The spectrum ranges from subtle learning disabilities to severe mental retardation and autism.

- Individuals might have a variety of physical and behavioral differences, including attention deficit disorders, speech disturbances, autistic behaviors, poor eye contact, and aversion to touch and noise.

- Connective tissue problems might lead to ear infections and skeletal problems.

Tips and Techniques

- Multidisciplinary approaches and therapy are helpful in addressing many of the physical, behavioral, and cognitive impacts of fragile X syndrome.
- Sensory integration activities and calming activities are useful when teaching some individuals with fragile X.
- Try to reduce sensory overload when considering the setting or context in which activities will be performed.
- See "Mental Retardation" for additional tips and techniques.

Informative Web Site

www.fragilex.org

Learning Disability

Definition

Learning disability is a neurological condition that causes a difference in one or more psychological processes that presents an individual with difficulty in listening, thinking, speaking, reading, writing, spelling, or doing mathematical calculations.

Selected Facts

- People with learning disabilities generally have average or above average intelligence.
- There are different types of learning disabilities. Each person is unique and might show a different combination and degree of difficulties.
- Learning disabilities might be accompanied by attentional difficulties.
- People with learning disabilities can be successful at school, work, and in the community given appropriate supports.

Tips and Techniques

- Teach using a multisensory approach (visual, auditory, and kinesthetic).
- Establish a routine and incorporate repetition.
- Break learning down into small sequential steps.
- Provide regular prompts and quality feedback.
- Allow sufficient time for processing and ample time for practice.
- Employ various techniques for memory and organization.

Informative Web Sites

www.ldonline.org/
www.ldanatl.org/

Mental Retardation

Definition

Mental retardation is a term used when a person has specific differences in intellectual functioning and adaptive functioning in skills such as communicating, daily living, and social skills manifested during the developmental period.

Selected Facts

- These differences might cause an individual to learn and develop more slowly.
- Individuals with mental retardation will learn, but it takes them longer. There might be some things they cannot learn.

Tips and Techniques

- Divide tasks into small, meaningful steps and present them to the student sequentially. Limit distractions. Keep the activity area clean and well ordered; store equipment not currently in use out of sight.
- Encourage independence. Use reinforcement strategies and motivational techniques.
- Break tasks down into smaller steps.
- Demonstrations, verbal cues, and physical prompts are useful but should gradually fade to encourage increased independence.
- Teach individuals tasks across settings to promote generalization of skills.
- Physical activities and sports can improve fitness, increase confidence, and help build social skills.
- Programs should focus on age-appropriate activities.

Informative Web Site

www.aamr.org/

Multiple Sclerosis

Definition

Multiple sclerosis is a demyelinating disease of the central nervous system. Myelin, the fatty material surrounding the nerves, is destroyed, leading to symptoms such as muscle weakness, paresis, paralysis, spasticity, tremors, impaired balance, discoordination, heat sensitivity, and fatigue.

Selected Facts

- Some individuals with MS have cardiovascular dysautonomia in which irregular function of the autonomic nervous system (ANS) leads to a blunted heart rate and decreased blood pressure in response to exercise.
- Some people with MS have oversensitivity to heat. This might lead to fatigue, loss of balance, and visual changes.
- Balance and coordination difficulties can lead to dangerous falls.
- Be aware of side effects of medication and how this might affect exercise programming. Medication can affect energy level, muscle coordination, and muscle strength.

Tips and Techniques

- If cardiovascular dysautonomia exists, heart rate and blood pressure must be monitored throughout the exercise program; intensity might need to be decreased.
- Choose exercises and equipment that provide maximum support (e.g., swimming, recumbent cycling) and have participants work out in a safe environment (e.g., avoid slippery floors, poor lighting, and throw rugs).
- For those who are heat sensitive, create a cool environment with fans, air temperature between 72 and 76 degrees Fahrenheit, and pool temperature between 80 and 85 degrees Fahrenheit. If exercising outdoors in hot weather, exercise during early morning or evening hours. Wear clothing that "breathes," and use cooling aids as needed (e.g., cool vests, ice packs, cool baths).

Informative Web Sites

www.nationalmssociety.org
www.ncpad.org

Muscular Dystrophy

Definition

Muscular dystrophies are genetic disorders characterized by progressive muscle wasting and weakness that begin with microscopic changes in the muscle. As muscles degenerate over time, the person's muscle strength, power, and endurance decline. There are several types of muscular dystrophy, including Duchenne muscular dystrophy, the most common, Becker muscular dystrophy; facioscapulohumeral dystrophy (FSHD), and myotonic muscular dystrophy.

Selected Facts

- Muscular dystrophies are inherited, progressive disorders that gradually weaken the respiratory muscles as they do the muscles that move the limbs and trunk. The spinal muscular atrophies and many other neuromuscular disorders can also lead to breathing problems and lung complications.
- Contractures and muscle atrophy are common.

Tips and Techniques

- Maintenance and improvement in muscular strength for performing activities of daily living, maintaining ambulation, and preventing contractures are important.
- Maintaining sufficient respiratory capacity is critical. Work with appropriate medical personnel to assess cardiovascular condition and potential complications.
- Strengthening postural muscles, which can slow the formation of scoliosis, should be included in the exercise program.
- Set reasonable goals involving activities that are achievable and enjoyable.
- Avoid overfatigue of muscles.

Informative Web Site

www.mdausa.org

Obesity

Definition

Obesity is an excess of body fat frequently resulting in a significant impairment of health.

Selected Facts

- Obesity is defined as being over 30 percent above ideal body weight.
- Being overweight or obese might cause little or no inconvenience to a person's career, lifestyle, daily activities, and so on. Over time, however, a disability might occur from obesity. When obesity becomes severe, it can inflict bodily pain and affect normal daily activities.
- Obesity is a chronic disease with a strong familial component.
- Obesity increases a person's risk of developing high blood pressure, diabetes (type 2), heart disease, stroke, gallbladder disease, and cancer of the breast, prostate, and colon.
- Health insurance providers rarely pay for treatment of obesity despite the condition's serious effects on health.
- The tendency toward obesity is promoted by an environment that includes lack of physical activity combined with high-calorie, low-cost foods.
- If maintained, even small weight losses (as small as 10 percent of body weight) can improve health significantly.

- People with obesity are often victims of employment and other kinds of discrimination; they are frequently penalized for their condition despite many federal and state laws and policies.

Tips and Techniques

- During physical activity, frequently monitor blood pressure and heart rate of individuals who are obese to ensure appropriate exercise intensity.
- Offer fun, achievable activities that increase a participant's chances of succeeding in an activity program.
- Use the cool-down phase of class to chat about nutritious foods that taste good.

Informative Web Site

www.obesity.org/

Osteogenesis Imperfecta

Definition

Osteogenesis imperfecta (OI) is caused by a genetic defect that affects the body's production of collagen. Collagen is the major protein of the body's connective tissue and can be likened to the framework around which a building is constructed. In OI, a person has either less collagen than normal or a poorer quality of collagen than normal, leading to weak bones that fracture easily.

Selected Facts

- There are at least four recognized forms of OI, making for extreme variation in severity from one individual to another. A person might have just a few or as many as several hundred fractures in a lifetime.
- Individuals might have loose joints and low muscle tone.
- Some individuals might have underdeveloped lungs and respiratory problems.
- Spinal curvature is possible with the more severe types of OI.
- Hearing loss is also possible.

Tips and Techniques

- Treatment for OI is directed toward preventing or controlling the symptoms, maximizing independent mobility, and developing optimal bone mass and muscle strength.
- Use of wheelchairs, braces, and other mobility aids is common, particularly among people with more severe types of OI.
- People with OI are encouraged to exercise as much as possible to promote muscle and bone strength, which can help prevent fractures. Swimming and water therapy are common exercise choices, as water allows independent movement with little risk of fracture.
- Walking (with or without mobility aids) is excellent for those who are able.
- Individuals with OI will also benefit from maintaining a healthy weight, eating a nutritious diet, and avoiding activities such as smoking, excessive alcohol or caffeine consumption, and taking steroid medications—all of which might deplete bone and exacerbate bone fragility.

Informative Web Site

www.oif.org

Parkinson's Disease

Definition

Parkinson's disease is a chronic, progressive neurological disease. In Parkinson's, neurons in a specific region of the brain degenerate and result in the lack of a neurotransmitter responsible for the control of muscle movement. This can lead to tremors, muscle stiffness, and slower movements. Postural instability can also occur.

Selected Facts

- The functional differences of Parkinson's occur mainly between the ages of 50 to 65 years. Young-onset Parkinson's can occur in persons younger than 50.
- Signs and symptoms of Parkinson's change as the disease progresses.
- With Parkinson's, there might be behavioral and psychological changes including cognitive or memory difficulties, depression, anxiety, apathy, and fatigue.
- Medication plays a significant role in the treatment of Parkinson's.

Tips and Techniques

- Exercise and physical activity are strongly recommended to maintain functional ability and psychological well-being.
- Physical activity should be planned with consideration of medication schedules.
- Walking, swimming, and cycling are particularly good activities for maintaining health.
- Tai chi can promote postural control, balance, and smooth movement.
- Stretching exercises are particularly beneficial.
- Use light weights for maintaining as much strength and muscle tone as possible. Strengthening should focus on the extensor and postural control muscles.

Informative Web Site

www.parkinson.org/

Post-Polio Syndrome

Definition

Poliomyelitis (polio), an acute viral disease, affects the lower motor neurons and causes muscle paresis, paralysis, and sometimes death. Post-Polio syndrome, or PPS, is a name that has been adopted to indicate a constellatiom of *new* symptoms that occur between 20 to 40 years after the onset of the initial polio infection and after a period of "recovery" of at least 10 years. These symptoms often include *new* weakness, pain, breathing or swallowing difficulties, a variety of sleep disorders, muscle twitching, gastrointestinal problems, muscle fatigue, or "central" fatigue.

Selected Facts

- Symptoms can occur in previously affected muscles or in what were previously thought to be muscles unaffected at onset.
- Complications of PPS often include neuropathies, nerve entrapments, arthritis, scoliosis, osteoporosis, and, sometimes, additional atrophy.
- Onset of PPS is usually gradual, over a period of years, but sometimes abrupt, with major losses of function suffered over several months or a couple of years. Onset often occurs after a physical or emotional trauma, illness, or accident.

Tips and Techniques

- Physical activity is recommended for improvement in cardiovascular capacity and in performing activities of daily living.
- Energy management is important and achieved by striking a balance between rest and activity.
- Short-term exercise is indicated for affected muscles showing no signs of weakness and a full exercise program for muscles that have not been affected. Exercise is contraindicated for affected, severely weakened muscles.

Informative Web Site

www.ott.zynet.co.uk/polio/lincolnshire/

www.post-polio.org

www.ninds.nih.gov

Prader-Willi Syndrome

Definition

Prader-Willi is a disorder of chromosome 15 that leads to low muscle tone, cognitive impairment, and behavioral differences.

Selected Facts

- There is likely developmental delay before age six and mild to moderate mental retardation or learning problems in older children.
- Children with Prader-Willi might have excessive or rapid weight gain between one and six years of age; central obesity can occur in the absence of intervention.
- Behavioral problems might include temper tantrums, violent outbursts, obsessive or compulsive behavior, and a tendency to be argumentative, oppositional, and rigid.

Tips and Techniques

- Compounding the pressure of excessive appetite is a decreased calorie utilization in those with PWS as a consequence of low muscle mass and inactivity. Daily exercise (at least 30 minutes) is essential for weight control and health.
- Motor milestones are typically delayed one to two years; although hypotonia improves, deficits in strength, coordination, balance, and motor planning might continue. Exercise and sports activities should be encouraged.

Informative Web Sites

www.pwsausa.org

www.ipwso.org/

Rett Syndrome

Definition

Rett Syndrome (RS) is a neurological disorder in which a child usually shows an early period of apparently typical development until 6 to 18 months of life. A period of temporary stagnation or regression follows during which the child loses communication skills and purposeful use of the hands. Stereotyped hand movements, gait difficulties, and slowing of the rate of head growth might then occur.

Selected Facts

- A child with RS might experience seizures and disorganized breathing patterns.
- Apraxia (dyspraxia), the inability to program the body to perform motor movements, and other motor problems are common occurrences and might interfere with ambulation, speech, and gaze.
- RS is most often misdiagnosed as autism, cerebral palsy, or non-specified developmental delay.
- Scoliosis might develop and range from mild to more severe.

Tips and Techniques

- A combination of interventions are recommended to maintain or improve function, prevent deformities, and promote mobility.
- Practitioners should be familiar with possible alternative communication methods, including eye-gaze response; picture, letter and word boards; and touch- or switch-operated voice output devices.
- Physical therapy, exercise, and aquatic therapy are useful for preventing or treating scoliosis.
- Walking, standing, and assistive positioning techniques are also recommended.

Informative Web Site

www.rettsyndrome.org

Spina Bifida

Definition

Spina bifida is an incomplete closure of the spinal column during the first month of fetal development. In general, the three types of spina bifida (from mild to severe) are spina bifida occulta, an opening in one or more of the vertebrae (bones) of the spinal column without apparent damage to the spinal cord; meningocele, in which the meninges, or protective covering around the spinal cord, has pushed out through the opening in the vertebrae but the spinal cord remains intact; and myelomeningocele, in which a portion of the spinal cord itself protrudes through the back. In some cases, sacs are covered with skin; in others, tissue and nerves are exposed. Generally, people use the terms "spina bifida" and "myelomeningocele" interchangeably.

Selected Facts

- Myelomeningocele might include muscle weakness or paralysis below the area of the spine where the incomplete closure occurs, loss of sensation below the cleft, and loss of bowel and bladder control.
- A large percentage (70 to 90 percent) of children born with myelomeningocele have hydrocephalus or a buildup and accumulation of fluid in the brain. Hydrocephalus is controlled by a surgical procedure called "shunting," which relieves the fluid buildup in the brain. If a drain (shunt) is not implanted, the pressure buildup can cause brain damage, seizures, or blindness. Hydrocephalus might occur without spina bifida, but the two conditions often occur together.
- Children with spina bifida who also have a history of hydrocephalus might experience learning problems and difficulty paying attention, expressing or understanding language, and grasping concepts.

Tips and Techniques

- Participants might not have the ability to sweat and thus should take appropriate precautions to prevent overheating.
- Individuals with shunts should avoid activities that might result in physical contact to the head (e.g., soccer heading, boxing, headstands, forward rolls, tackles).
- Be aware of symptoms such as headaches, dizziness, seizures, irritability, swelling, and redness along the shunt tract, which might indicate a blocked shunt.
- Flexibility in scheduling might need to occur to accommodate bowel and bladder management programs.
- Some individuals with spina bifida have latex allergies. If so, latex equipment (e.g., some types of rubber balls and balloons) should be avoided.
- Children with myelomeningocele need to learn mobility skills and often require the aid of crutches, braces, or wheelchairs. Even if the participant can ambulate on long leg braces, a wheelchair might make sport and game participation easier.

Informative Web Sites

www.sbaa.org

www.easter-seals.org

www.modimes.org

www.naric.com

Spinal Cord Injury (SCI)

Definition

Spinal cord injury (SCI) is a complete or partial lesion to the spinal cord that results in functional loss of sensory, motor, and autonomic systems. The extent of functional differences depends on the level and completeness of the lesion. The physical ability of individuals with SCI is classified according to the amount of function retained. Common categories are paraplegia (SCI affecting level T2 and below, trunk and lower extremities involved) and quadriplegia/tetraplegia (SCI affecting level T1 or above, all four extremities and trunk involved).

Selected Facts

- Individuals with lesions above the sacral level experience a loss of control with their bowel or bladder.
- Spasticity or high muscle tone and hyperactive stretch reflexes might occur in the muscles below the site of injury and be exacerbated by exposure to cold air, urinary tract infections, and physical exercise.
- Autonomic dysreflexia or a sudden rise in blood pressure resulting from an exaggerated autonomic nervous system response to noxious stimuli such as bladder or bowel over-distension or a blocked catheter below the level of injury might occur.
- Individuals with SCI often experience irregular body temperatures.
- Pressure sores (decubitis ulcers) or damage to the skin or underlying tissue caused by a lack of blood flow to the area might be problematic for individuals with SCI.

Tips and Techniques

- In extreme heat, individuals with spinal cord injuries at the 6th thoracic level and above have difficulty sweating. Some individuals with spinal cord injuries should avoid exercising in extremely cold or hot environments because of difficulty with thermal regulation.

- In response to autonomic dysreflexia, monitor signs of profuse sweating, sudden elevation in blood pressure, flushing, shivering, headache, and nausea; seek medical attention immediately if these symptoms occur.
- Monitor blood pressure throughout exercise, avoid quick movements, perform orthostatic training (if available), maintain proper hydration, and use compression stockings and an abdominal binder to avoid significant drops in blood pressure.

Informative Web Site

www.spinalcord.org

Stroke

Definition

Stroke, often called cerebrovascular accident (CVA), is a sudden central nervous system impairment in which the flow of oxygen and nutrients to the brain is halted through a blood clot (ischemia) or bleeding (hemorrhage).

Selected Facts

- Risk factors associated with stroke include hypertension, coronary artery disease, hyperlipidemia, diabetes, obesity, and high amounts of alcohol, caffeine, and nicotine.
- Motor ability and control, sensation and perception, communication, and emotions might be influenced. Individuals might have partial or total paralysis on one side of the body.

Tips and Techniques

- Check with the participant's primary physician before starting an exercise program, and conduct exercise screening and assessments to ensure a safe and effective program.
- Know the implications of necessary medications (e.g., hypertension medications, water pills) on the body's ability to exercise or participate in physical activity.
- Monitor blood pressure periodically throughout an exercise program.
- Be aware of occurrences of orthostatic hypotension, which is dizziness, nausea, and lightheadedness from suddenly sitting or standing up.
- To avoid dangerous falls, make sure you have adequate support for balance while using exercise machines.
- If muscle groups are not functional because of spasticity, the opposing muscle groups might be strengthened to help normalize the spasticity. Any muscle groups incapable of being strengthened should be stretched.
- Spasticity can affect the respiratory muscles of the involved side. Cardiovascular exercise and deep rhythmical breathing can help strengthen respiratory muscles.

Informative Web Sites

www.hemikids.org/stroke.htm

www.stroke.org/

Traumatic Brain Injury (TBI)

Definition

Traumatic brain injury is an acquired insult or injury to the brain caused by an external force. TBI might result in a diminished physical and cognitive capacity or psychosocial difficulties. The term applies to open or closed head injuries resulting in changes in one or more areas, such as cognition; language; memory; attention; reasoning; abstract thinking; judgment;

problem-solving; sensory, perceptual, and motor abilities; psychosocial behavior; physical functions; information processing; and speech. The term does not apply to brain injuries that are congenital or degenerative or to brain injuries induced by birth trauma.

Selected Facts

- Traumatic brain injuries often result from motor vehicle, sports, and recreation accidents.
- Brain injuries can range from mild to severe, as can the changes that result from the injury. It is hard to predict how an individual will recover from the injury.
- In the case of children, as a child grows and develops, functional capabilities might change as he or she is expected to use the brain in new and different ways. The damage to the brain from the earlier injury can make it hard for the child to learn new skills that come with getting older. For an adult, brain injury can result in the loss of, or difficulty with, previously learned skills.

Tips and Techniques

- Give the participant more time to finish tasks.
- Break lessons down into small components and give directions one step at a time. For tasks with many steps, give the individual both visual and verbal cues.
- Show the participant how to perform new tasks. Give examples to go with new ideas and concepts.
- Have consistent routines. This helps the participant know what to expect. If the routine is going to change, let him or her know ahead of time.
- Assist the individual with organizational strategies, such as color-coding activities, using an assignment book, and keeping to a daily schedule.
- Realize that the participant might get tired quickly. Because of fatigue levels, avoid "overloading"; let the participant rest as needed.
- Reduce distractions.
- Offer choices, and be flexible about expectations.

Informative Web Sites

www.neuroskills.com/

www.biausa.org

www.headinjury.com

Elgibility Criteria for Infants and Toddlers

This appendix provides information on the criteria used to determine whether individuals from birth through three years of age qualify for early intervention services as required under part C of the Individuals with Disabilities Education Act (IDEA)*. The criteria to qualify for special services for infants and toddlers are much broader than for individuals from 3 to 21. Infants might fall into one of three categories of need: developmentally delayed, established risk for a developmental delay, or high risk for developmental delay based on state determined guidelines. Following are the definitions of each of the terms based on IDEA and California Early Intervention Services, Act SB 1085 Permanent Regulations, Early Start of August 1998.

DEVELOPMENTAL DELAY

A developmental delay is present if a significant difference exists between the infant's or toddler's current level of functioning and the expected level of development for his or her age in one or more of the following developmental levels:

- Cognitive
- Physical—including gross and fine motor, vision, and hearing
- Communication
- Social or emotional
- Adaptive

ESTABLISHED RISK

Infant has a known disability with a high probability of developmental delay. Has a solely low incidence disability (i.e., visual, hearing, or physical disability).

HIGH RISK FOR DEVELOPMENTAL DELAY

A multidisciplinary team determines a high risk for delay based on assessment and a combination of two or more of the following factors:

- Prematurity of less than 32 weeks gestation or low birth weight of less than 1,500 grams

*Early intervention–IDEA under part C, which took effect July 1, 1998.

- Assisted ventilation for more than 48 hours in the first 28 days of life
- Small gestation for age (below the third percentile)
- Asphyxia neonatorum associated with a five-minute Apgar score of 0 to 5
- Severe and persistent metabolic abnormality, including but not limited to hypoglycemia, acidemia, and hyperbilirubenemia in excess of the usual exchange transfusion level
- Neonatal seizures or nonfebrile seizures during the first three years of life
- Central nervous system lesion or abnormality
- Central nervous system infection
- Biomedical insult including but not limited to injury, accident, or illness that might seriously or permanently affect developmental outcome
- Multiple congenital anomalies or genetic disorders that might affect developmental outcome
- Prenatal exposure to known teratogens
- Prenatal substance exposure, positive infant neonatal toxicology screen, or symptomatic neonatal toxicity or withdrawal
- Clinically significant failure to thrive including but not limited to weight persistently below the third percentile or age on standard growth charts or less than 85 percent of the ideal weight for age or acute weight loss or failure to gain weight with the loss of two or more major percentiles on the growth chart
- Persistent hypotonia or hypertonia beyond that otherwise associated with a known diagnostic condition

High risk for a developmental disability also exists when a multidisciplinary team determines that the parent of the infant or toddler is a person with a developmental disability and the infant or toddler requires early intervention services based on evaluation and assessment.

Resources

C

This appendix suggests Web sites that might be useful to refer to when providing physical activity opportunities for individuals with differences in ability. The list is intended to provide a foundation for information and is in no way meant to be comprehensive or indicative of all the resources that currently exist or that could be accessed to support physical activity practitioners.

Legal Information

Americans with Disabilities Act
www.usdoj.gov/crt/ada/adahom1.htm

Job Accommodation Network
http://janweb.icdi.wvu.edu

Individuals with Disabilities Education Act
www.ideapractices.org/lawandregs.htm

Education Law
http://edlaw.net

National Dissemination Center for Children with Disabilities
www.nichcy.org

Disability Sports and Physical Activity

American Association of Disability Sports Programs
www.aaasp.org/about/overview.html

International Paralympics Committee
www.paralympic.org

Wheelchair Sports USA
www.wsusa.org

States Association of Blind Athletes
www.usaba.org

Disability Sports USA
www.dsusa.org

United States Quad Rugby Association
www.quadrugby.com/toc.htm

National Sport Center for the Disabled
www.nscd.org

International Blind Sport Federation
www.ibsa.es/eng

Special Olympics
www.specialolympics.org

International Tennis Foundation
www.itfwheelchairtennis.com

National Wheelchair Basketball Association
www.nwba.org

National Disability Sports Alliance
www.ndsaonline.org

World Organization of Volleyball for the Disabled
www.usavolleyball.org/disabled

USA Deaf Sports Federation
www.usadsf.org

United States Racquetball Association
www.usra.org

Canadian Wheelchair Basketball Federation
www.cwba.ca

Wilderness Inquiry Outdoor Adventures
www.wildernessinquiry.org

United States Handcycling Federation
www.ushf.org

National Center on Physical Activity and Disability
www.ncpad.org

Special Populations Learning Outdoor Recreation and Education (S'PLORE)
www.splore.org

Cooperative Wilderness Handicapped Outdoor Group (C.W. HOG)
www.isu.edu/cwhog

Success Oriented Achievement Realized (SOAR)
www.soarnc.org

Adapted Physical Education

PE Central
www.pecentral.org

PALAESTRA: Forum for Sport, Physical Education, Recreation for those with Disabilities
www.palaestra.com

Texas Woman's University Project INSPIRE
http://venus.twu.edu/~fheuttig

Legislation and Individuals With Disabilities

The inclusion of individuals with ability differences into society has been strongly influenced by legislation focused on equalizing access and opportunity for all citizens. This appendix chronicles significant disability legislation that has helped shape practices and policies within our schools, workplaces, communities, and physical activity programs.

1961   P.L. 87-276 Special Education Act

This act was designed to train professionals to prepare teachers of deaf children.

1965   P.L. 89-10 Elementary and Secondary Education Act

This act enabled states and local school districts through provision of monies from the federal government to develop programs for economically disadvantaged children.

1966   P.L. 89-750 Amendments to Elementary and Secondary Education Act

This act created the Bureau of Education for the Handicapped (now the Office of Special Education) focused on professional preparation of personnel to serve individuals with disabilities.

1973   P.L. 93-112 Section 504 of the Rehabilitation Act

This act adopted and affirmed that people with disabilities cannot be excluded from any program or activity receiving federal funds solely on the basis of having a disability.

1974   P.L. 93-247 Child Abuse and Prevention Act

This act created systems to protect children from abuse and mandated that a person who suspects child abuse must report it.

1975   P.L. 94-142 Education for All Handicapped Children Act

This act mandated a free appropriate education for all handicapped children between the ages of 3 and 21 years. It required that students with disabilities must be educated to the maximum extent possible with their peers without disabilities in the least restrictive environment and that all qualifying children have an Individualized Education Program (IEP) developed and written by a team of individuals and reviewed annually. This act identified physical education as a direct instructional service. The act states that students must be evaluated for services every three years.

1978   Amateur Sports Act

This act mandated that the U.S. Olympic Committee ensure competitive opportunities and programming for persons with disabilities. The U.S. Olympic Committee formed the Committee on Sports for the Disabled. Eight organizations governing disabled sports were formed.

1983   P.L. 98-199 Amendments to the Education for All Handicapped Children Act

States were required to collect data to determine the anticipated service needs for children with disabilities. It provided incentives to states to provide services to handicapped infants and preschool children.

1986   P.L. 99-372 Handicapped Children's Protection Act

Attorney's fees were reimbursed to parents who were forced to go to court to secure an appropriate education for their child. Parents who prevailed in a hearing or court case could recover the cost incurred for lawyers to represent them.

1986   P.L. 99-457 Education for All Handicapped Children Amendments of 1986

This law expanded services for preschool children ages three to five. States were also required to develop comprehensive interdisciplinary early intervention services for infants and toddlers with disabilities, birth through three years of age.

1987   Reauthorization of the Child Abuse Prevention and Treatment Act

The National Center on Child Abuse and Neglect was directed to study the incidence of abuse of children with disabilities and the incidence of disabilities that result from abuse.

1988   The Technology-Related Assistance for Individuals with Disabilities Act

This act made amendments to the Education of the Handicapped Act P.L. 100-407 to develop and extend technology-related assistance for individuals with disabilities and their families.

1990   P.L. 101-476 Individuals with Disabilities Education Act (IDEA)

This act replaced the term "handicapped" with "disability" and expanded the types of services offered and conditions covered. The act also required that transition plans and services be provided for students transitioning from high school to the community.

1990   P.L. 101-336 Americans with Disabilities Act

This act expanded civil rights protections for persons with disabilities to all public accommodations and addressed private discrimination. It specifically included nondiscrimination in areas of employment, transportation, public accommodations, state and local government, and telecommunications.

1997   Individuals with Disabilities Education Act Amendment

This act amended and reauthorized discretionary programs, strengthening services to at-risk children. It increased focus on parents' participation in assessment, placement, and IEP development and required reporting periods to match those of the general education curriculum. It increased the emphasis on placement of students with disabilities in the general education environment.

1998   Workforce Investment Act of 1998

One provision of this act is to develop research and demonstration projects to evaluate how adapted physical education programs can develop health and related skills that improve work performance.

1998   Reauthorization of the Technology-Related Assistance for Individuals with Disabilities Act

This act made technical amendments to the 1998 Technology-Related Act

2001   *Physical Education for Progress Act*

The act is designed to improve physical education for all children, including children with disabilities, in public schools by providing competitive grants.

2003   *Reauthorization of the Amateur Sports Act*

The act reinforces the rightful place of "elite athletes" with disabilities in the community of "elite athletes" who participate in amateur athletics, particularly the Olympics and Paralympics.

Adapted, by permission, from D. Auxler, J. Pyfer, and C. Huettig, 2001, Principles and methods of adapted physical education and recreation, 9th edition (New York: McGraw-Hill Companies). © McGraw-Hill Companies.

Assessment Instruments

The following list of assessment instruments comes from the Adapted Physical Education Guidelines in California Schools (August 2001, appendix C). Additional information regarding guidelines for adapted physical education can be obtained on the California State Council for Adapted Physical Education Web Site: http://sc-ape.org/.

Assessment Instruments

Test name	Type of test	Description	Age	Time	Score	Available
AAHPERD Motor Fitness Testing for the Mentally Retarded	Physical fitness	Includes: arm strength, abdominal strength and endurance, power, agility, speed and endurance	6-21 yrs. Moderately retarded	Indiv. 20 min. Group 60 min.	Percentile	AAHPERD, 1900 Association Dr., Reston, VA 20091
Adapted Physical Education Assessment Scale (APEAS)	Motor performance	Test includes: motor development perceptual motor function, motor achievement, posture, fitness	5-18 yrs.	Indiv. 20 min. Group 30 min.	Percentile	Los Angeles USD, 450 N. Grand Ave., Los Angeles, CA 90010
Alberta Infant Motor Scale	Motor abilities, early movement milestones	58 items performed in 4 positions: prone, supine, sitting, and standing	Birth-18 mo.	20-30 min.	Criterion referenced	W.B. Saunders, 6277 Sea Harbor Dr., Orlando, FL 32821
Analysis of Sensory Behavior Inventory (Morton/Wolford)	Interview and/or clinical observation	Hypo- or hyper-responsivity to sensory input	3 yrs.-adult	15-30 min.	Quantitative observation	Skills with OT, 733 W. Naomi, Unit 1, Suite 108, Arcadia, CA 91007
Assessment, Evaluation, & Programming System for Infants & Children From Birth to Three Years (AEPS)	Early movement milestones, fundamental movement skills, functional movement skills	164 objectives hierarchically organized into 6 curricular domains: fine motor, gross motor, adaptive, cognitive, social-communication	Birth-3 yrs.	15-30 min.	Criterion referenced	Paul H. Brookes Publ., P.O. Box 10624, Baltimore, MD 21285-0624
Basic Motor Ability Test	Motor performance	Nine test items: small and large muscle control, balance, eye-hand coordination, and flexibility	4-12 yrs.	Indiv. 15 min. Group 25 min.	Percentile	*The Clumsy Child*, Arnneim, Daniel C.Y. Mosby, St. Louis

Instrument	Focus	Skills/Description	Age range	Time	Type	Source
Battelle Developmental Inventory (BDI)	Motor abilities, early movement milestones, fundamental movement skills	Identify developmental strengths and weaknesses of children with and without disabilities in infant, preschool, and primary programs. Training needed	Birth-8 yrs.	Entire test 1-2 hrs.	Norm referenced	DLM, 1 DLM Park, Allen, TX 75002
Bayley Scales of Infant Development II	Standardized	Mental: cognitive, language, and social Motor: fine and gross	Birth-3.5 yrs.	1-1.5 hrs.	Standard mental, developmental, and motor index	Psychological Corp., P.O. Box 839954, San Antonio, TX 78283
Brigance Inventory of Early Development	Motor development	Psychomotor skills: locomotor, balance, strength, ball skills, rhythm, and fine motor	Birth-7 yrs.	Varies	Criterion referenced, age norms available	Curriculum Association, Wobum, MA 01801
Brockport	Physical fitness	Variety of fitness items, include alternative items for individuals with disabilities	10-17 yrs.	Varies	Criterion referenced	Human Kinetics, P.O. Box 5076, Champaign, IL 61825-5076
Bruininks-Oseretsky Test of Motor Proficiency	Motor ability	Gross and fine motor skills: speed, agility, balance, coordination, strength, dexterity, visual-motor, bilateral coordination	4.5-14.5 yrs.	Complete: 45-60 min. Short: 15-20 min.	Age-based standard score	American Guidance Service, Publisher's Building, Circle Planes, MN 55014
Cajon Valley Motor Assessment Instrument	Motor development, motor ability	Gross and fine motor skills measured while student is in various positions. Ability: transferring, maneuvering wheelchair	3 yrs. and up	Indiv. 30-40 min.	Criterion referenced, curriculum related	Cajon Valley School District, 189 Roanoke Rd, El Cajon, CA 92020

(continued)

Assessment Instruments (continued)

Test name	Type of test	Description	Age	Time	Score	Available
California Curriculum for Infants & Toddlers with Special Needs	Norm referenced	Cognitive, language, social, fine motor, and gross motor	Birth-2 yrs.	Varies	Age equivalencies	Kaplan School Supply, 1310 Lewisville-Clemmons, P.O. Box 609, Lewisville, NC 27023
California Physical Performance Test	Physical fitness	Tests include: body composition, flexibility, endurance, cardiorespiratory endurance, strength	10-18 yrs.	Indiv. 30 min.	Percentile, T-scores	California State Department of Education, P.O. Box 944272, Sacramento, CA 94244
Callier Asuza Scale	No standardization	Assessment for blind and multidisabled children in sensorimotor, cognitive, psychosocial, work, play, and self care	Birth-7 yrs.	Not reported	Not reported	Robert Stillman, Univ. of Texas, 1966 Inwood Rd., Dallas, TX 75235
CARE-R Curriculum, Assessment, Resources, Evaluation	Motor development, early movement milestones, fundamental movement skills, and motor ability	Curriculum based assessment: gross motor, object control, health and physical fitness, perceptual motor, and fine motor	Birth-17 yrs. Varies for each area	Varies	Age equivalencies (age ranges)	Adapted Physical Education Office/Lincoln Annex, 600 E. Grand Ave., San Gabriel, CA 91778 or L.A. C.O.E., 9300 E. Imperial Hwy., Downey, CA 90242
Carolina Curriculum for Preschool & Special Needs	Norm referenced	Cognitive, language, social, fine and gross motor	2.5-5 yrs.	Varies	Age equivalencies	Kaplan School Supply, 1310 Lewisville-Clemmons, P.O. Box 609, Lewisville, NC 27023
Cratty Six Category Gross Motor Test	Motor ability, perceptual motor	Perceptual-motor functioning involving body perception, agility, balance, throwing, and tracking skills	4-11 yrs.	Indiv. 30 min.	Decile, ranking converted to percentile	*Perceptual Motor Behavior & Ed. Process*, Cratty, Bryant J., Thomas, Springfield, IL

Test	Type	Domain/Description	Age range	Time	Reference	Source
Crawford Small Parts Dexterity Test	Standardized performance test	Fine eye-hand coordination for vocational testing	Adolescent-Adult	15 min.	Not reported	Psychological Corp., 304 E. 45th St., New York, NY 10017
DeGangi-Berk Test of Sensory Integration	Movement skill foundations	36 items organized into 3 subdomains: postural control, bilateral integration, reflex integration. Scores can be summed by subdomain or for all items	3-5 yrs.	30 min.	Criterion referenced	Western psychological Services, 12031 Wilshire Blvd., Los Angeles, CA 90025
Denver Developmental Screening Test II	Standardized and normalized	Personal-social, language, gross motor, and fine motor	Birth-6 yrs.	15-30 min.	Not reported	Denver Developmental Medicine, Inc., P.O. Box 20037, Denver, CO 80220
Developmental Handwriting & Hand Skills Observation (Benboe)	Informal observation, structured observation	Neurodevelopmental sensory and motor function affecting hand skills and handwriting	5 yrs. and up	30-45 min.	Criterion referenced	Mary S. Benbow, AOTA Publications
Developmental Test of Visual Motor Integration Beery (VMI)	Norm referenced	Visual motor	2-15 yrs.	15-30 min.	Age equivalencies, standard scores, percentiles	Modem Curriculum Press, 13900 Prospect Rd., Cleveland, OH 44136
Erhardt Developmental Comprehension Assessment	Criterion referenced informal observation, structured observation	Praxis, reflexes, fine motor, visual motor and visual perception				Erhardt Developmental Hand Dysfunction, Laurel, MD
Erhardt Developmental Visual Assessment	Referenced and informal observation	Sensorimotor visual perceptual	Not reported	Not reported	Not reported	Erhardt Developmental Assessment, Laurel, MD
Evaluation of Motor Development of Infants	Motor abilities, early movement milestones	34 skills from 4 spheres of movement: head and trunk, sitting, standing, and locomotion	1 month-onset of walking	Not reported	Criterion and norm referenced	Wolanski & Zdanska-Brincken (1973)

(continued)

Assessment Instruments (continued)

Test name	Type of test	Description	Age	Time	Score	Available
Frostig Developmental	Sensory motor	Areas measured: eye-motor, coordinations, figure-ground, constancy of shape, body perception, spatial relations	4-8 yrs.	Indiv. 30-45 min. Group 50 min.	Perceptual quotient, perceptual age	Consulting Psychologist Press, Inc., 577 College Ave., Palo Alto, CA 94306
Frostig Movement Skills Test Battery	Gross and fine motor	Sensory motor, language, perception, higher cognitive, social and emotional development	K-6th grade	Not reported	Mean and scaled score, standard deviation	Consulting Psychologist Press, Inc., 577 College Ave., Palo Alto, CA 94306
Revised Gesell Developmental Schedules	Not reported	Adaptive, language, social, fine motor, and gross motor	4 wks.-36 mo.	30 min.-1 hr.	Age equivalencies	Developmental Test Materials, 389 Myrtle Ave., Albany, NY 12208
Gross Motor Function Measure (GMFM)	Early movement milestones, fundamental movement skills	88 items 5 dimensions: lying and rolling, crawling and kneeling, sitting, standing, walking, running and jumping	Persons with C.P. under 20 yrs.	<1 hr.	Criterion referenced	Dept. of Pediatrics, Chedoke-McMaster Hosp., McMaster Univ., P.O. Box 2000, Station A, Hamilton, ON Canada L8N 3Z5
Gross Motor Performance Measure (GMPM)	Early movement milestones, fundamental movement skills	20 items from GMFM, each matched with 5 attributes of performance: alignment, stability, coordination, weight shift, or dissociation	Persons with C.P. under 20 yrs.	<1 hr.	Criterion referenced	Dept. of Pediatrics, Chedoke-McMaster Hosp., McMaster Univ., P.O. Box 2000, Station A, Hamilton, ON Canada L8N 3Z5

Test	Assessment	Skills	Age	Time	Scoring	Source
Harris Infant Neuromotor Test (HINT) Developmental Edition	Movement foundation, early movement milestones	Identifying early motor deficits and cognitive delays in infants with known risk factors	3-12 mo.	<30 min.	Criterion referenced	School of Rehabilitation Sciences, Univ. of British Columbia, c/o 325-2211 Westbrook Mall, Vancouver, BC Canada V6T 2B5
Hawaii Early Learning Profile (HELP)	Structured observation and checklist	Cognitive, language, fine motor, gross motor, social-emotional, and self-help	Birth-3yrs.	30 min.-1 hr.	Age equivalencies	VORT Corp., P.O. Box 60132, Palo Alto, CA 94306
Hughes Basic Gross Motor Assessment	Motor ability	Gross motor ability, static and dynamic balance, motor coordination, locomotor, eye-hand coordination	5.6-12.5 yrs.	Indiv. 15 min.	Mean scores	Office of Special Education, Denver, CO 80203
I CAN Instructional Management System	Early movement milestones, fundamental movement skills, specialized movement skills	A large set of criterion referenced checklists for many skills	Not specified	Specific to checklist	Criterion referenced	PRO-ED, 8700 Shoal Creek Blvd., Austin, TX 78757-6897
Jacobs Prevocational Skills Assessment	Not reported	Sensorimotor cognitive psychosocial work skills	Preadolescent and adolescent learning disabled	Not reported	Not reported	Jacobs Occupational Therapy Works Related Programs & Assessments, Boston: Little Brown
Jebsen Taylor Function Test	Not reported	Self help work and fine motor skills	Child-Adolescent	Not reported	Not standardized	Sand, Taylor Hill, Korsky & Rawlings (1974). "Hand Function in Children With Myelomeningocele," AJOT, 28(2) 87-90.

(continued)

Assessment Instruments (continued)

Test name	Type of test	Description	Age	Time	Score	Available
Koontz Child Developmental Program	Motor development	Includes performances of skills which lead up primarily to ambulation	Birth–48 mo.	Varies	Functional level, training activities	Western Psychological Services, 12031 Wilshire Blvd, Los Angeles, CA 90025
Learning Accomplishments Profile (LAP)	Motor development	Gross motor areas: large muscle coordination, strength, stamina, ambulation, and balance	Birth–72 mo.	Varies	Criterion referenced	Chapel Hill-Outreach Prog., U.S. Office of Education, Bureau of Ed. For Handicapped, Washington, D.C.
Michigan Developmental Programming for Infants and Young Children	Criterion referenced	Personal-social communication, cognitive, self-help, gross motor, fine motor, visual motor, and integration	Birth–6 yrs.	30 min.	Age equivalencies	Univ. of Michigan, Ann Arbor, MI
Milani-Comparetti Motor Development Screening Test	Motor skill foundations	27 items in 6 categories of spontaneous motor behaviors and evoked responses	Birth–2 yrs.	4–8 min.	Criterion referenced	Meyer Children's Rehabilitation Inst., 444 S. 44th St., Univ. of Nebraska Medical Center, Omaha, NE 68131
Miller Assessment for Preschoolers (MAP)	Movement skill foundations, motor abilities, early movement milestones, fundamental movement skills	27 core indexes scored for 5 scales: neuromaturational, gross/fine/orgal motor, language, memory, problem solving, visual perception, and combined abilities	2.9–5.8 yrs.	30 min.	Norm referenced	Therapy Skill Builders, 555 Academic Court, San Antonio, TX 78204-2498
Minnesota Rate of Manipulation Test	Standardized performance test	Manual dexterity for vocational evaluation	13–15 yrs. and up	Not reported	Not reported	American Guidance Services, Inc., Publ. Bldg., Circle Pines, MN 55014

Test	Areas assessed	Description	Age range	Time	Type	Source/Publisher
Motor Control Assessment (MCA)	Motor abilities, early movement milestones, fundamental movement skills	Assessment of motor control of children with physical disabilities. Uses 5 performance areas: supine, prone, sitting, kneeling, standing and standing up, walking and general coordination.	2 yrs. and up	30-60 min.	Criterion referenced	Steel, Glover, & Spasoff (1991)
Motor Development Checklist (MDC)	Early movement milestones	Record spontaneous motor behavior in persons with severe developmental disabilities	Not reported	Minimum of 10 min.	Criterion referenced	Central Wisconsin Center for the Developmentally Disabled, 317 Knutson Dr., Madison, WI 53704
Motor-Free Visual Perceptual Test	Sensory motor	Spatial relationships, visual discrimination, closure, memory figure-ground	4-8 yrs.	Indiv. 10 min.	Perceptual age perceptual quotient	Academic Therapy Publications, Novato, CA
Motor Skills Inventory (MSI)	Movement skill foundations	30 items organized into 5 skill areas: body management, locomotor, body fitness, object movement, and fine motor. Also a curriculum	3-16 yrs.	Not reported	Criterion referenced	American Guidance Service, 44201 Woodland Rd., P.O. Box 99, Circle Pines, MN 55014-1796
Movement Assessment Battery for Children Checklist (MABC)	Motor abilities, fundamental movement skills, specialized movement skills	Used to screen children for possible movement problems, identify children for special services, and research	5-11 yrs.	1-2 wks.	Criterion referenced	Therapy Skill Builders, 555 Academic Court, San Antonio, TX 78204-2498

(continued)

Assessment Instruments (continued)

Test name	Type of test	Description	Age	Time	Score	Available
Movement Assessment Battery for Children Test (MABC Test)	Motor abilities, fundamental movement skills, specialized movement skills	32 items organized into a 4 (age level) × 8 (performance category) matrix	4-12 yrs.	20-40 min.	Percentiles	Psychological Corp., Order Service Center, P.O. Box 839954, San Antonio, TX 78283-3954
Movement Patterns Achievement Profile	Motor development	Observation and evaluation: locomotor, jumping, climbing, throwing, catching, balance, and body image	2-6 yrs.	Indiv. 30 min.	Motor age	*They Need to be Carefully Taught,* Evans, Jane R., AAHPERD, 1980
Ordinal Scales	Motor development	Tests through various substages: strength, mobility, coordination, balance	Birth-11 yrs.	Varies	Age norm	FOREWORKS, Box 9747, North Hollywood, CA 91609
Ohio State Univ. Scale of Intra-Gross Motor Assessment (SIGMA)	Fundamental movement skills	Skills tested: walking, stair climbing, running, jumping, hopping, skipping, ladder climbing, throwing, catching, striking, kicking	2-14 yrs.	Not reported	Criterion referenced	Tichenor Publ., P.O. Box 669, Bloomington, IN 47402-0696
Peabody Developmental Motor Scales	Standardized	Gross and fine motor	Birth-6.5 yrs.	30 min.-1hr.	Age equivalencies	DLM Teaching, One DLM Park, Allen, TX 75002
Pediatric Evaluation of Disability Inventory (PEDI)	Self-administered questionnaire	Functional skills, self-care, mobility, and social function	3-18 yrs.	30 min.-1 hr.	Scaled score age norms	PEDI, New England Center Publ., Boston (1992)
Physical Best	Physical fitness	Includes tasks for fitness testing and prudential fitness gram	5-17 yrs.	30-60 min.	Percentiles	AAHPERD, 1900 Association Dr., Reston, VA 22091
Project Unique	Physical fitness	Skills modified for orthopedic and sensory impaired	5-17 yrs.	30-60 min.	Percentiles	Human Kinetics, P.O. Box 5076, Champaign, IL 61825-5076

Test	Domain	Description	Age range	Time	Scoring	Publisher
Purdue Perceptual Motor Survey	Sensory motor	Areas tested: balance, posture, body image, motor match, ocular control, form perception	6-10 yrs.	Indiv. 45 min.	Means, standard deviations	Charles E. Merrill Publ. Co., 1300 Alum Creek Dr., Columbus, OH 43216
Quick Neruological Screening Test	Sensory motor	Indicates need for further testing in motor development, muscular control, motor planning, perceptual motor skills	5 yrs. and up	Indiv. 25 min.	Number score to use on chart	Jastak Associates, Inc., 1526 Gilpin Ave., Wilmington, DE 19806
Stanford Functional Developmental Assessment	Motor development	Gross motor development: coordination/ strength, balance, locomotion, visual motor	Birth-12 yrs.	Varies	Age norm	Physically Handicapped Children, Bleck, Eugene, M.D. Grune & Stratten, FL
Test of Visual Perceptual Skills (n-m) Revised (TVPS-R)	Visual perception using non-motor response	Standardized and normed test, dev. for professionals to determine a subject's visual perceptual strengths and weaknesses based on non-motor visual perceptual testing	4.1-13 yrs.	9-25 min.	Visual-perceptual, standard score T-Score	Psychological & Educ. Publ., Inc., P.O. Box 520, Hydesville, CA 95547-0520
Test of Visual Perceptual Skills (non-motor) Upper Level (TVPS-UL)	Visual perception using non-motor response	A standardized and normed test, developed for professionals to determine a subject's visual perceptual strengths and weaknesses based on non-motor visual perceptual testing	12-18 yrs.	Varies	Stand. scores scaled score, T-Score, percentile rank, stanine	Psychological & Educ. Publ., Inc., P.O. Box 520, Hydesville, CA 95547-0520

(continued)

Assessment Instruments (continued)

Test name	Type of test	Description	Age	Time	Score	Available
Top-Down Motor Milestone Test (TDMMT)	Early movement milestones, fundamental movement skills	74 skills organized into 16 sitting, standing, and walking skill heading	Infant-young adult	15 min.	Criterion referenced	MOVE International, 1300 17th St., City Centre, Bakersfield, CA 93301
Transdisciplinary Play Based Assessment	Early movement milestones, fundamental movement skills	6 phases: unstructured facilitation, structured facilitation, child-child interaction, parent-child interaction, motor play, and snack	Birth-72 mo.	Varies by phase	Criterion referenced	Paul H. Brooks Publishing, P.O. Box 10624, Baltimore, MD 21285-0624
Ulrich Test of Gross Motor Development	Motor development	Provides performance criteria for different locomotor skills and object control skills	3-10 yrs.	Indiv. 15 min.	Percentile, standard score	ProEd, 5341 Industrial Oaks Blvd., Austin, TX 78735
Visual Motor Integration	Sensory motor	Measures the ability to copy different shapes: horizontal and vertical lines, circles, crosses, squares, and so on	2-15 yrs.	Group: 15-20 min.	Age norm	Follett Educational Corp., 1018 W. Washington Blvd., Chicago, IL 60607
Vulpe Assessment Battery (VAB)	Movement skill foundations, early movement milestones, fundamental movement skills	Designed for children with disabilities, 8 subtests: basic senses and functions, gross motor, fine motor, language behaviors, cognitive processes, organization of behavior, activities of daily living, and the environment	Birth-6 yrs.	1 hr.	Criterion referenced	National Inst. On Mental Retardation, Kinsmen/NIRNR Bldg., 4700 Keele St., North Yorke, ON Canada M3J 1P3

Sample Medical History and Referral Form

This appendix serves as a sample medical history and referral form. It is designed for practitioners to use in community-based programs when working with individuals with diverse abilities and skills. Before starting any physical activity program, individuals should consult with their physicians. A physician referral form is also important and should be completed by a physician before (or along with) the medical history form. All forms and records should be kept in the individual's program file along with emergency contacts.

Health and Medical History

General reference information:

Name: _____ Age: _____ DOB: _____ Sex: _____

Address: _____ (City/State) _____ Zip _____

Day phone: _____ Evening phone: _____

Emergency contact: _____ Relationship: _____

Career/Education/Hobbies:

Occupations: _____ Education: _____

_____

_____

_____

_____

Hobbies: _____

_____

History of physical activity:

Favorite physical exercises and activities to participate in: _____

_____

_____

Favorite sports and activities to be a spectator at: _____

_____

_____

Major exercise/fitness goals and objectives: _____

_____

_____

_____

Information regarding physical disability:

List and describe disabilities: _____

Associated physical concerns: _____

_____

_____

_____

_____

Associated health information:

YES NO   Briefly describe

❏   ❏   Cardiac disorder _____
        _____

❏   ❏   Angina _____
        _____

❏   ❏   Chest pain _____
        _____

❏   ❏   Irregular HR/murmur _____
        _____

❏   ❏   Hypertension _____
        _____

❏   ❏   Stroke _____
        _____

❏   ❏   High cholesterol _____
        _____

❏   ❏   Atherosclerosis _____
        _____

❏   ❏   Arteriosclerosis _____
        _____

❏   ❏   Embolism _____
        _____

❏   ❏   Shortness of breath _____
        _____

❏   ❏   Asthma _____
        _____

❏   ❏   History of pneumonia and infections _____
        _____

❏   ❏   Pulmonary disorders _____
        _____

❏   ❏   Phlebitis _____
        _____

❏   ❏   Diabetes _____
        _____

❏   ❏   Heat or cold sensitivity _____
        _____

YES NO   Briefly describe

❏   ❏   Bleeding disorder _____

_____

❏   ❏   Recent illness _____

_____

❏   ❏   Thyroid disorder _____

_____

❏   ❏   History of smoking _____

_____

Motor condition:

YES NO   Briefly describe

❏   ❏   Spasticity (tightness) _____

_____

❏   ❏   Reflexes _____

_____

❏   ❏   Tactile loss _____

_____

❏   ❏   Kinesthetic loss _____

_____

❏   ❏   Static balance _____

_____

❏   ❏   Dynamic balance _____

_____

❏   ❏   Equilibrium _____

_____

❏   ❏   Grip strength _____

_____

❏   ❏   Fine motor _____

_____

❏   ❏   Postural concerns _____

_____

❏   ❏   Numbness/tingling in extremities _____

_____

❏   ❏   Epilepsy _____

_____

YES NO   Briefly describe

❏ ❏ Fainting _____

_____

❏ ❏ Urinary tract infections _____

_____

❏ ❏ Kidney disorders _____

_____

❏ ❏ Arthritis _____

_____

❏ ❏ Gout _____

_____

❏ ❏ Hernia _____

_____

❏ ❏ Incontinence _____

_____

❏ ❏ Obesity _____

_____

❏ ❏ Corrective lenses _____

_____

❏ ❏ Hearing loss/aids _____

_____

❏ ❏ Anemia _____

_____

❏ ❏ Cancer _____

_____

❏ ❏ Skin disorders _____

_____

❏ ❏ Chronic pain _____

_____

❏ ❏ Speech disorder _____

_____

❏ ❏ Ambulatory skills _____

_____

❏ ❏ Gait _____

_____

YES NO Briefly describe

❏ ❏ Orthotics _____

_____

❏ ❏ Prosthetics _____

_____

❏ ❏ Assistive devices _____

_____

Pulse rate: _____

Blood pressure: (Systolic) _____ (Diastolic) _____ (Opposite arm) _____

Family History:

Are your parents living: Mother: ❏ yes ❏ no   Father: ❏ yes ❏ no

If not, list their age and cause of death: _____

_____

Have your parents, grandparents, or siblings suffered any of the following:

❏ Heart attack _____

❏ Stroke _____

❏ Obesity _____

❏ Arthritis _____

❏ Hypertension _____

❏ Diabetes _____

❏ Cancer _____

❏ Other _____

_____

Medical treatments:

Physicians' names: _____

_____

Phone numbers: _____

_____

Addresses: _____

_____

When did you last see a physician? _____

Most recent hospitalization: _____

History of surgeries: _____

_____

_____

_____

Medications / Dosage / Purpose / Side effects

_____

_____

_____

_____

_____

_____

_____

_____

_____

Are you currently receiving physical or occupational therapy: _____

_____

Reason(s) for therapy: _____

_____

Name of therapist: _____

Phone number: _____

Location: _____

Exercise contraindications: _____

_____

_____

_____

_____

_____

_____

Personal general information: _____

_____

_____

_____

Other relevant information: _____

_____

_____

_____

_____

Personal impression of level of health and wellness: _____

_____

_____

_____

_____

_____

_____

What are your greatest concerns in participation in regular exercise: _____

_____

_____

_____

Potential individual risk factors associated with exercise participation: _____

_____

_____

_____

Recommendations for additional assessment: _____

_____

_____

_____

_____

_____

_____

_____

_____

_____

_____

_____

_____

_____

_____

Medical Referral Form

_____ is interested in participating in the BE:WEL Program.
(Participant)
This program is an individually based exercise and wellness class that provides activities for individuals with disabilities.

The following types of activities are available to participants. Please indicate any activities that the individual **SHOULD NOT** participate in and list any special considerations for programming.

SHOULD NOT

- ❑   Water jogging _____
- ❑   Lap swimming _____
- ❑   Water walking _____
- ❑   Stretching _____
- ❑   Range of motion _____
- ❑   Diving _____
- ❑   Weight training _____
- ❑   Treadmill _____
- ❑   Stationary cycling _____
- ❑   Recumbent bicycle _____

Please list any special considerations that we should be aware of: _____

_____

_____

_____

Please list any contraindications: _____

_____

_____

Physician's signature: _____   Recommend participation: ❑ yes ❑ no

Print name: _____   Phone number: _____

Thank you for your time and consideration in reviewing this patient's program.

Sincerely,

Rebecca K. Lytle, PhD
Adapted Physical Education Program Coordinator
Department of Physical Education and Exercise Science
CSU, Chico 95929-0330

References

Almond, L. (1986). Reflecting on themes: A games classification. In Thorpe, R., Bunker, D., & Almond, L. (Eds.). *Rethinking Games Teaching*. London: Exmonde Publications.

Asch, A. (1984). The experience of disability: A challenge for psychology. *American Psychologist*, 39, 529-536.

Asch, A., & Fine, M. (1988). Introduction: Beyond pedestals. In *Women with disabilities: Essays in psychology, culture, and politics*, M. Fine & A. Asch (Eds.), (pp. 1-37). Philadelphia, PA: Temple University Press.

Atkinson, D.R., & Hackett, G. (1995). *Counseling diverse populations*. Dubuque, IA: Wm. C. Brown & Benchmark.

Balan, C., & Davis, W. (1993). Ecological task analysis: An approach to teaching physical education. *Journal of Physical Education, Recreation and Dance*, 64(9), 54-61.

Bandura, A. (1977). Self-efficacy: Toward a unifying theory of behavioral change. *Psychology Review*, 84(2), 191-215.

Baumgartner, T.A., & Jackson, A.S. (1995). *Measurement for evaluation in physical education and exercise science* (6th ed.). Boston: McGraw-Hill.

Behler, G.T. (1993). Disability simulations as a teaching tool: Some ethical issues and implications. *Journal of Postsecondary Education and Disability*, 10(2), 3-8.

Best-Martini, E., & Botenhagen-DiGenova, K. (2003). *Exercise for frail elders*. Champaign, IL: Human Kinetics.

Bishop, K.K., Woll, J., & Arango, P. (1993). Family professional collaboration for children with special health needs and their families. Family/Professional Collaboration Project: U.S. Department of Health and Human Services.

Bisson, C. (1999). Sequencing the adventure experience. In *Adventure programming*, J. Miles and S. Priest (Eds.). State College, PA: Venture.

Block, M., Lieberman, L., & Connor-Kuntz, F. (1998). Authentic assessment in adapted physical education. *Journal of Health, Physical Education, Recreation and Dance*, 69(3), 48-55.

Block, M., & Rizzo, T. (1995). Attitudes and attributes of physical educators associated with teaching individuals with severe and profound disabilities. *Journal of Association of Persons with Severe Handicaps*, 20(1), 80-87.

Block, M.E. (2000). *A teacher's guide to including students with disabilities in general physical education*. Baltimore, MD: Paul H. Brookes.

Block, M.E., & Krebs, P.L. (1992). An alternative to least restrictive environments: A continuum of support to regular physical education. *Adapted Physical Activity Quarterly*, 9, 97-113.

Block, M.E., Provis, S., & Nelson, E. (1994). Accommodating students with severe disabilities in regular physical education: Extending traditional skill stations. *Palaestra*, 10(1), 32-38.

Block, M.E., & Zeman, R. (1996). Including students with disabilities into regular physical education: Effects on nondisabled children. *Adapted Physical Activity Quarterly*, 13, 38-49.

Bradley, D.F. (1994). A framework for the acquisition of collaborative consultation skills. *Journal of Educational and Psychological Consultation*, 5 (1), 51-68.

Brehm, S.S., & Kassin S.M. (1996). *Social psychology* (3rd ed). Geneva, IL: Houghton Mifflin Company.

Burton, A., & Miller, D. (1998). *Movement Skill Assessment*. Champaign, IL: Human Kinetics.

California Department of Education (1998). Challenge standards for student success: Physical education, Sacramento, CA.

Cardinal, B.J., Kosma, M., & McCubbin, J.A. (2004). Factors influencing the exercise behavior of adults with physical disabilities. *Medicine & Science in Sports and Exercise*, 36(5), 868-875.

Choate, J., & Evans, S. (1992). Authentic assessment of special learners: Problem or promise? *Preventing School Failure*, 37(1), 6-9.

Coben, S.S., Thomas, C.C., Sattler, R.O., & Morsink, C. V. (1997). Meeting the challenge of consultation and collaboration: Developing interactive teams. *Journal of Learning Disabilities*, 30, 427-432.

Conoley, J.C., & Conoley C.W. (1988). Useful theories in school-based consultation. *Remedial and Special Education*, 9(6), 14-20.

Conn, V.S. (1998). Older women's beliefs about physical activity. *Public Health Nursing*, 15(5), 370-378.

Covey, S.R. (1990). *The seven habits of highly effective people: Powerful lessons in personal change*. New York: A Fireside Book, Simon & Schuster.

Cowden, J., & Eason, B. (1991). Pediatric adapted physical education for infants, toddlers, and preschoolers: Meeting IDEA-H and IDEA-B challenges. *Adapted Physical Activity Quarterly*, 8, 263-279.

Cowden, J., Sayers, K., & Torrey, C. (1998). *Pediatric Adapted Motor Development and Exercise*. Springfield, IL: Charles C. Thomas.

Danforth, S., & Navarro, V. (1998). Speech acts: Sampling the social construction of mental retardation in everyday life. *Mental Retardation*, 36(1), 31-43.

Davis, L.J. (1997). Constructing normalcy. In *The disability studies reader*, L.J. Davis (Ed.). New York, NY: Routledge, 9-28.

DePauw, K.P., & Doll-Tepper, G. (2000). Toward progressive inclusion and acceptance: Myth or reality? The inclusion debate and bandwagon discourse. *Adapted Physical Activity Quarterly*, 17(2), 135-143.

Dettmer, P., Dyck, N. & Thurston, L. (1999). *Consultation, collaboration and teamwork* (3rd ed.). Needham Heights, MA: Allen & Bacon.

Dickens-Smith, M. (1995). *The effect of inclusion training on teacher attitudes toward inclusion*. (ERIC Document Reproduction Service No. ED381486).

Dishman, R.K. (1994). Motivating older adults to exercise. *Southern Medical Association Journal*, 87(5), 579-582.

Doyle, M.B. (1997). *The paraprofessional's guide to the inclusive classroom*. Baltimore: Brookes Publishing.

Dustin, D., & Ehly, S. (1984). Skills for effective consultation. *School Counselor*, 32(1), 23-29.

Ellery, P.J., & Rauschenbach, J. (2000). Impact of disability awareness activities on nondisabled student attitudes toward integrated physical education with students who use wheelchairs. *Research Quarterly for Exercise and Sport*, 71, pA-106.

Ellmo, W., & Graser, J. (1995). *Adapted adventure activities: A rehabilitation model for adventure programming and group initiatives*. Dubuque, IA: Kendall/Hunt.

Elward, K., & Larson, E.B. (1992). Benefits of exercise for older adults: A review of existing evidence and current recommendations for the general population. *Clinics in Geriatric Medicine*, 8(1), 35-50.

Emes, C., Longmuir, P., & Downs, P. (2002). An abilities-based approach to service delivery and professional preparation in adapted physical education. *Adapted Physical Activity Quarterly*, 19, 403-419.

Friend, M. (1988). Putting consultation into context: Historical and contemporary perspectives. *Remedial and Special Education*, 9(6), 7-13.

Friend, M., & Cook, L. (1996). *Interactions: Collaboration skills for school professionals* (2nd ed.). White Plains, NY: Longman Publishers.

Friend, M., & Cook, L. (2000). *Interactions: Collaboration skills for school professionals* (4th ed.). White Plains, New York: Longman Publishers.

Gentile, A.M. (2000). Skill acquisition: Action, movement, and neuromotor processes. In J.M. Carr, R.B. Shepherd, J. Gordon, A.M. Gentile, & J. M. Hinds (Eds.). *Movement science: Foundations for physical therapy* (2nd ed., pp. 111-187). Rockville, MD: Aspen.

Graham, G., Holt-Hale, S., & Parker, M. (2001). *Children moving: A reflective approach to teaching physical education* (5th ed). Columbus, OH: McGraw-Hill.

Grimes, P.S., & French, L. (1987). Barriers to disabled women's participation in sports. *Journal of Physical Education, Recreation and Dance*, 58(3), 24-27.

Gutkin, T.B. (1996). Patterns of consultant and consultee verbalizations: Examining communication leadership during initial consultation interviews. *Journal of School Psychology*, 34 (3), 199-219.

Gutkin, T.B., & Curtis, M.J. (1982). School based consultation: Theory and techniques. In T.B. Gutkin & C.R. Reynolds (Eds.), *The handbook of school psychology* (pp. 796-828). New York, NY: Wiley.

Hahn, H. (1988). The politics of physical difference: Disability and discrimination. *Journal of Social Issues*, 44, 39-47.

Hahn, H. (1991). Theories and values: Ethics and contrasting perspectives on disability. In R.P. Marinelli & A.E. Dell Orto (Eds.), *The psychological and social impact of disability* (3rd ed.) (pp. 18-22). New York: Springer.

Hamel, R. (1992). Getting into the game: New opportunities for athletes with disabilities. *Physician and Sports Medicine*, 20(11), 121-122, 124, 126-129.

Haywood, K., & Getchell, N. (2001). *Life span motor development* (3rd ed.). Champaign, IL: Human Kinetics.

Heward, W.L. (2000). *Exceptional children: An introduction to special education* (6th ed.). Upper Saddle River, NJ: Merrill Publishing Co.

Holt, K.G. (1993). Toward general principles for research and rehabilitation of disabled populations. *Physical Therapy Practice*, 2(4), 1-18.

Hopple, C., & Graham, G. (1995). What children think, feel, and know about physical fitness testing. *Journal of Teaching in Physical Education*, 14(4), 408-17.

Horner, R.H., Dunlap, G., & Koegel, R.L. (1988). *Generalization and maintenance: Lifestyle changes in applied settings*. Baltimore: Brookes.

Horton, G.E., & Brown D. (1990). The importance of interpersonal skills in consultee-centered consultation: A review. *Journal of Counseling and Development*, 68(4), 423-426.

Horvat, M., & Kalakian, L. (1996). *Assessment in adapted physical education and therapeutic recreation*. Dubuque, IA: Brown & Benchmark Publishers.

Huizinga, J. (1955). *Homo ludens: The play element in culture*. Boston: Beacon.

Idol, L. (1988). A rationale and guidelines for establishing special education consultation programs. *Remedial and Special Education*, 9(6), 48-58.

Idol, L., Nevin, A., & Paolucci-Whitcomb, P. (1994). *Collaborative consultation* (2nd ed.). Austin, TX: Pro-ed.

Idol, L., Paolucci-Whitcomb, P., Nevin, A. (1995). The collaborative consultation model. *Journal of Educational and Psychological Consultation*, 6(4), 329-346.

Johnson, L., Kasser, S., & Nichols, B. (2002). Including all children in standards-based physical education. *Journal of Physical Education, Recreation and Dance*, 73(4), 42-46.

Jones, S.R. (1996). Toward inclusive theory: Disability as social construction. *NASPA Journal*, 33(4), 347-354.

Joyner, A.B., & McManis, B.G. (1997). Quality control in alternative assessment. *Journal of Physical Education, Recreation and Dance*, 68(7), 38-40.

Kampwirth, T.J. (2003). *Collaborative consultation in the schools*. Upper Saddle River, NJ: Merrill Prentice Hall.

Karge, B.D., McClure, M., & Patton, P.L. (1995). The success of collaboration resource programs for students with disabilities in grades 6 through 8. *Remedial and Special Education*, 16 (2), 79-89.

Kauffman, J.M. (1998). Commentary: Today's special education and its messages for tomorrow. *Journal of Special Education*, 32(3), 127-137.

Kaye, H.S. (1998). *Is the status of people with disabilities improving?* National Institute in Disability and Rehabilitation Research, Washington, D.C.

Kaye, H.S., & Longmore, P. (1997). *Disability watch: The status of people with disabilities in the U.S.* Disability Rights Advocates, Inc. Volcano, CA: Volcano Press.

Kelly, L., & Gansneder, B. (1998). Preparation and job demographics of adapted physical educators in the United States. *Adapted Physical Activity Quarterly*, 15, 141-154.

Kinne, S., Patrick, D.L., & Maher, E.J. (1999). Correlates of exercise maintenance among people with mobility impairments. *Disability and Rehabilitation*, 21(1), 15-22.

Knoff, H.M., McKenna, A.F., & Riser, K. (1991). Toward a consultant effectiveness scale: Investigating the characteristics of effective consultants. *School Psychology Review*, 20(1), 81-96.

Knudson, D., & Morrison, C. (1996). An integrated qualitative analysis of overarm throwing. *Journal of Physical Education, Recreation and Dance*, 67(6), 31-36.

Knudson, D., & Morrison, C. (2002). *Qualitative analysis of human movement* (2nd ed.). Champaign, IL: Human Kinetics.

Kowalski, E.M., & Rizzo, T.L. (1996). Factors influencing preservice student attitudes toward individuals with disabilities. *Adapted Physical Activity Quarterly*, 13(2), 180-196.

Kugler, P.N., Kelso, J.A.S., & Turvey, M.T. (1980). On the concept of coordinative structures as dissipative structures: I. Theoretical lines of convergence. In G.E. Stelmach & J. Requin (Eds.), *Tutorials in motor behavior*. New York: North-Holland.

Laplante, M.P., Kennedy, J., Kaye, H.S., & Wenger, B.L. (1996). Disability and employment. Disability Statistics Abstract Number 11. National Institute on Disability and Rehabilitation Research, Washington, D.C.

Lieberman, L.J. (1996). The effects of trained hearing peer tutors on the physical activity levels of deaf students in inclusive elementary physical education classes. *Dissertation Abstracts International*, 57-03A, 1074.

Lieberman, L., & Houston-Wilson, C. (1999). Overcoming the barriers to including students with visual impairments and deaf-blindness in physical education. *Source Review* (Washington). 31(3), 129-138.

Lieberman, L.J., & Houston-Wilson, C. (2002). *Strategies for inclusion: A handbook for physical educators.* Champaign, IL: Human Kinetics.

Linder, T. (1996). *Transdisciplinary play-based assessment: A functional approach to working with young children.* Baltimore, MD: Paul H. Brookes.

Liu, J., & Pearson, D. (1999). *Teachers' attitude toward inclusion and perceived professional needs for an inclusive classroom.* Washington: Resources in Education. (ED438274).

Lockette, K.F., & Keyes, A.M. (1994). *Conditioning with physical disabilities.* Champaign, IL: Human Kinetics.

Longmuir, P.E., & Bar-Or, O. (2000). Factors influencing the physical activity levels of youths with physical and sensory disabilities. *Adapted Physical Activity Quarterly*, 17(1), 40-53.

Lund, J. (1997). Authentic assessment: It's development and applications. *Journal of Physical Education, Recreation and Dance*, 68(4), 25-33.

Lytle, D. (1989). The crucial elements in cognition: Embodiment and playful action. California Folklore Society and the Association for the Study of Play Conference. Berkeley, CA.

Lytle, D.E. (1999). Defining play: Problems, paradoxes and provocation. In the *Encyclopedia of Sports Medicine and Exercise Physiology*, T. Fahey (Ed.). www.sportsci.org/encyc/encyc.html.

Lytle, R., & Bordin, J. (2001). Enhancing the IEP team: Strategies for parents and professionals. *Teaching Exceptional Children*, 33(5), 40-44.

Lytle, R., & Collier, D. (2002). The consultation process: Adapted physical education specialists' perceptions. *Adapted Physical Activity Quarterly*, 19, 261-279.

Lytle, R., & Johnson, J. (2000). Adapted physical education survey. *California Association of Health, Physical Education, Recreation and Dance Journal/Times*, 62(4), 12-13.

Lytle, R.K. (1999). Adapted physical education specialists' perceptions and role in the consultation process (Doctoral dissertation, Oregon State University, 1999). *Dissertation Abstracts International*, 60, 992646Z.

Lytle, R.K., & Hutchinson, G.E. (2004). Adapted physical educators: The multiple roles of consultants. *Adapted Physical Activity Quarterly*, 21, 34-49.

Magill, R.A. (2001). *Motor learning concepts and applications* (6th ed.). Boston: McGraw-Hill.

Martin, J.N., & Nakayama, T.K. (2000). *Intercultural communication in contexts* (2nd ed.). Mountain View, CA: Mayfield Publishing Company.

McCollum J.A., & Hemmeter, M.L. (1997). Parent-child interaction intervention when children have disabilities. In M.J. Guralnick (Ed.), *The effectiveness of early intervention* (pp. 249-268). Baltimore: Paul H. Brookes.

Melograno, V. (1994). Portfolio assessment: Documenting authentic student learning. *Journal of Physical Education, Recreation and Dance*, 65(8), 50-55, 58-61.

Miller, P.D. (1995). *Fitness programming and physical disability.* Champaign, IL: Human Kinetics.

Morris, D., & Stiehl, J. (1999). *Changing kid's games.* Champaign, IL: Human Kinetics.

Mosston, M., & Ashworth S. (2002). *Teaching physical education* (5th ed). San Fransisco, CA: Benjamin Cummings.

Murata, N.M. (1995). *The effects of physical educators, teacher assistants, and peer tutors on the academic learning time of students with and without disabilities in regular physical education.* Unpublished doctoral dissertation, The Ohio State University, Columbus.

National Dissemination Center for Children with Disabilities, Public Law 105-17 (1998, June). The IDEA amendments of 1997. *NICHCY News Digest*, 26, (Revised Ed.). Available [Online]. www.nichcy.org/pubs/newsdig/nd26txt.htm.

Nies, M.A., Vollman, M., & Cook, T. (1998). Facilitators, barriers, and strategies for exercise in European American women in the community. *Public Health Nursing*, 15(4), 263-272.

O'Brien-Cousins, S. (2000). My heart couldn't take it: Older women's beliefs about exercise benefits and risks. *Journal of Gerontology*, 55B(5), 283-294.

Pike K., & Salend, S. (1995). Authentic assessment strategies: Alternatives to norm-referenced testing. *Teaching Exceptional Children*, 28(1), 15-20.

Pratt, P., & Allen, A. (1989). *Occupational therapy for children* (2nd ed.). St. Louis, MO: C.V. Mosby.

Priest, S., & Gass, M. (1997). *Effective leadership in adventure programming*. Champaign, IL: Human Kinetics.

Proudly, D. (1999). A brief history in adventure programming. In *Adventure programming*, J. Miles and S. Priest (Eds.). State College, PA: Venture.

Public Law 105-17 (1998, June). The IDEA amendments of 1997. *NICHCY News Digest*, 26, (Revised Ed.). Available [Online]. www.nichcy.org/pubs/newsdig/nd26txt.htm.

Pugach, M.C., & Johnson, L.J. (1995). *Collaborative practitioners, collaborative schools*. Denver, CO: Love Publishing.

Resnick, B. (1998). Health promotion practices of the old-old. *Journal of the American Academy of Nurse Practitioners*, 10(4), 147-152.

Rhodes, R.E., Martin, A.D., Taunton, J.E., Rhodes, E.C., Donnelly, M., & Elliot, J. (1999). Factors associated with exercise adherence among older adults: An individual perspective. *Sports Medicine*, 28(6), 397-411.

Rimmer, J., Rubin, S., & Braddock, D. (2000). Barriers to exercise in African American women with physical disabilities. *Archives of Physical Medicine & Rehabilitation*, 81(2), 182-188.

Rink, J.E. (1998). *Teaching physical education for learning* (3rd ed.). Boston: McGraw-Hill.

Rizzo, T., & Vispoel, W.P. (1991). Physical educators' attributes and attitudes toward teaching students with handicaps. *Adapted Physical Activity Quarterly*, 8(1), 4-11.

Rizzo, T., & Vispoel, W.P. (1992). Changing attitudes about teaching students with handicaps. *Adapted Physical Activity Quarterly*, 9(1), 54-63.

Rohnke, K (1989). *Cowtails and Cobras II: A guide to games, initiatives, ropes courses & adventure curriculum*. Dubuque, IA: Kendall/Hunt.

Ryan, R.M., & Deci, E.L. (2000). Self-determination theory and the facilitation of intrinsic motivation, social development, and well-being. *American Psychologist*, 55(1), 68-78.

Sanders, S. (2002). *Active for life*. Champaign, IL: Human Kinetics.

Scheer, J. (1994). Culture and disability: An anthropological point of view. In E.J. Trickett, R.J. Watts, & D. Birman (Eds.), *Human diversity: Perspectives on people in context* (pp. 7-26). San Francisco: Jossey-Bass.

Sherrill, C. (1998). *Adapted physical activity, recreation, and sport: Crossdisciplinary and lifespan* (5th ed.). Boston: WCB/McGraw Hill.

Smith, J. (1997). MR as educational construct: Time for a new shared view. *Education & Training in MR & DD*, 32(3), 167-173.

Smith, R.W., Austin, D.R., & Kennedy, D.W. (1996). *Inclusive and special recreation: Opportunities for persons with disabilities* (3rd ed.). Madison, WI: Brown & Benchmark Publishers.

Smith, T. (1997). Authentic assessment: Using a portfolio card in physical education. *Journal of Physical Education, Recreation and Dance*, 68(7), 46-52.

Stainback, S., & Stainback, W. (Eds.). (1991). *Teaching in the inclusive classroom: Curriculum design, adaptation and delivery*. Baltimore: Brookes.

Stainback, S., Stainback, W., & Ayres, B. (1996). Schools as inclusive communities. In S. Stainback & W. Stainback (Eds.), *Controversial issues facing special education* (pp. 31-40). Needham Heights, MA: Allyn & Bacon.

Stainback, W., Stainback, S., & Bunch, G. (1989). A rationale for the merger of regular and special education. In W. Stainback, S. Stainback, & M. Forest (Eds.), *Education of all students in the mainstream of regular education* (pp. 15-28). Baltimore: Paul H. Brookes.

St. Clair, S.A. (1995). Differences in gross motor performance among multihandicapped deaf children using inclusion versus special day class models in adapted physical education (Masters Thesis, California State University, Fullerton). *Masters Abstracts International*, 33-06, 1662.

Sugarman, D. (2002). Inclusive outdoor education: Facilitating groups that include people with disabilities. *Journal of Experiential Education*, 24(3), 166-173.

Taylor, W.C., Baranowski, T., & Young, D.R. (1998). Physical activity interventions in low-income, ethnic minority, and populations with disability. *American Journal of Preventive Medicine*, 15(4), 334-343.

Thelen, E. (1985). Developmental origins of motor coordination: Leg movements in human infants. *Developmental Psychology*, 18, 1-22.

Thelen, E. (1995). Motor development: A new synthesis. *American Psychologist, 50*, 79-95.

Thomas, C.C., Correa, V.I. & Morsink, C.V. (2001). *Interactive teaming: Enhancing programs for students with special needs* (3rd ed). Upper Saddle River, NJ: Merrill Prentice Hall.

Ulrich, B., & Ulrich, D. (1995). Spontaneous leg movements of infants with Down syndrome and nondisabled infants. *Child Development, 66*(6), 1844-1855.

Ulrich, D. (2000). *Test of gross motor development.* Austin, TX: Pro-Ed.

U.S. Department of Health and Human Services. (1996). *Physical activity and health: A report of the surgeon general.* Washington, D.C.: U.S. Government Printing Office.

U.S. Department of Health and Human Services. (2000). *Healthy People 2010: With understanding and improving health and objectives for improving health* (2nd ed.). Washington, D.C.: U.S. Government Printing Office. [www.healthypeople.gov/publications].

Verderber, J.M., Rizzo, T.L., & Sherrill, C. (2003). Assessing student intention to participate in inclusive physical education. *Adapted Physical Activity Quarterly, 20*(1), 26-45.

Villa, R.A., Thousand J.S., Nevin, A.I., & Malgeri, C. (1996). Instilling collaboration for inclusion schooling as a way of doing business in public schools. *Remedial and Special Education, 17*(3), 169-181.

Vogler, E.W., Van der Mars, H., Cusimano, B., & Darst, P. (1990). Relationship of presage, context, and process variables to ALT-PE of elementary level mainstreamed students. *Adapted Physical Activity Quarterly, 7*, 298-313.

Weiner, R., & Koppelman, J. (1987). *From birth to five: Serving the youngest handicapped children.* Alexandria, VA: Capitol Publications, Inc.

Wessel, J., & Zittel, L. (1995). *Smart start.* Austin, TX: Pro-ed.

Wilson, S., & Lieberman, L. (2000). Disability awareness in physical education. *Strategies, 13*(6): 12, 29-33.

Winnick, J.P., & Short, F.X. (1999). *The Brockport physical fitness test manual.* Champaign, IL: Human Kinetics.

Wolfe, P.S, Ofiesh, N.S., & Boone, R.S. (1996). Self-advocacy preparation of consumers with disabilities: A national perspective of ADA training efforts. *Journal for Association for Persons with Severe Handicaps, 21*(2), 81-87.

Wood, J.W. (1998). *Adapting instruction to accommodate students in inclusive settings* (3rd ed.). Upper Saddle River, NJ: Merrill Publishing Company.

Wright, B.A. (1980). Developing constructive views of life with a disability. *Rehabilitation Literature, 41*(11-12), 274-279.

Yocom, D.J., & Cossairt, A. (1996). Consultation courses offered in special education teacher training programs: A national survey. *Journal of Educational Psychological Consultation, 7*(3), 251-258.

Young, E. (1992). *Seven blind mice.* New York: Philomel Books.

Zelazo, P.R., Zelazo, N.A. & Kolb, S. (1972a). 'Walking' in the newborn. *Science, 176*, 314-315.

Zelazo, P.R., Zelazo, N.A. & Kolb, S. (1972b). Newborn walking. *Science, 177*, 1058-1059.

Index

Note: The italicized *f* and *t* following page numbers refer to figures and tables, respectively.

About the Authors

Susan L. Kasser, PhD, is an associate professor in professional physical education at the University of Vermont. She has taught adapted physical education for more than 10 years to children ages 3 to 14 and has conducted adapted aquatic exercise programs for adults in community-based programs. She currently teaches professional teacher preparation coursework in adapted physical education and conducts adult exercise programs for people with movement differences.

Dr. Kasser is involved with numerous national and international groups that focus on physical education and various populations, including the American Alliance for Health, Physical Education, Recreation and Dance; the International Federation of Adapted Physical Activity; the National Consortium on Physical Education and Recreation for Individuals with Disabilities; and the North American Federation of Adapted Physical Activity. She has established adapted physical exercise programs for adults in three states and has presented numerous workshops at the international, national, state, and regional levels. Currently the director of the Individually Designed Exercise for Active Lifestyles (IDEAL) program at the University of Vermont, she received an Outstanding Educator Award from the Vermont Association for Health, Physical Education, Recreation and Dance in 2001, the Kroepsch-Maurice Excellence in Teaching Award from the University of Vermont in 2000, and the Outstanding Volunteer Award from the National Multiple Sclerosis Society–Vermont Division in 2004.

Rebecca K. Lytle, PhD, is an associate professor and adapted physical education program coordinator in the department of kinesiology at California State University at Chico. She taught adapted physical education for more than 10 years in the public schools to students in infancy through age 21. She conducts exercise programs for both children and adults with disabilities, and she has presented trainings regionally, nationally, and internationally. Dr. Lytle is the past chair of the California State Council for Adapted Physical Education and is a member of numerous other organizations related to adapted physical education, including the Council for Exceptional Children, the International Federation of Adapted Physical Activity, and the National Consortium on Physical Education and Recreation for Individuals with Disabilities. Dr. Lytle's work has been published in numerous journals, and she has contributed information to four books: *Making Connections: From Theory to Practice in Adapted Physical Activity* (2003), *Developmentally Appropriate Movement Concepts and Skill Themes for Children: Becoming a Master Teacher* (1993), *Strength Training in Children* (in press), and *Paraeducators Guide to Physical Education* (in press).